Grinnell College in the Nineteenth Century

Grinnell College
IN THE NINETEENTH CENTURY

———

From Salvation to Service

Joseph Frazier Wall

Iowa State University Press / Ames

Authorization to photocopy items for internal or personal use, or the internal or personal use of specific clients, is granted by Iowa State University Press, provided that the base fee of $.10 per copy is paid directly to the Copyright Clearance Center, 27 Congress Street, Salem, MA 01970. For those organizations that have been granted a photocopy license by CCC, a separate system of payments has been arranged. The fee code for users of the Transactional Reporting Service is 0-8138-2989-5/97 $.10.

♾ Printed on acid-free paper in the United States of America

First edition, 1997

Design by Robert A. Campbell

FRONTISPIECE: *Magoun Hall seen through the arches of Blair.*

Library of Congress Cataloging-in-Publication Data

Wall, Joseph Frazier.
    Grinnell College in the nineteenth century : from salvation to service / Joseph Frazier Wall.—1st ed.
        p.   cm.
    Includes bibliographical references (p.   ) and index.
    ISBN 0-8138-2989-5 (alk. paper)
    1. Grinnell College—History—19th century.   I. Title.
LD2055.G52W35   1997
378.777'596—dc20   96–44104

Last digit is the print number: 9 8 7 6 5 4 3 2 1

To Grinnell College

and to our children, Ane, Joel, and Julie,
Grinnellians by heritage and association

CONTENTS

FOREWORD

"She returned only once to Grinnell, in 1912, to give a eulogy at the memorial service for Gates in which she praised the former president's support for women's rights."[1]

With these words, Joseph Frazier Wall laid aside his pen for the last time. He died suddenly a few days later on October 9, 1995.

Joe Wall was in the midst of researching and writing the history of Grinnell College, and this volume contains the story that he had completed when he died. It begins with the Congregational missionaries who created the college and ends with the transforming presidency of George Augustus Gates (1887–1899). After reading this book, you will be acutely aware of how Joe's death has deprived us of a vivid account of twentieth-century Grinnell. What we do have is a masterful narrative of frontier missions and the creation of one of America's premier colleges, told against tableaux of American history in the eras of Manifest Destiny, the Civil War, and the late nineteenth century.

When in February 1990, as president of Grinnell, I commissioned Joe Wall to write a history of the college, I knew it would be exceptional. A valuable history exists from the hand of John S. Nollen, Grinnell's fifth president, published in 1953. However, with the college's sesquicentennial on the near horizon (now, in 1996, being celebrated), the time for a fresh treatment had arrived. Joe Wall was the perfect person to write it. He had just finished his biography of Alfred I. DuPont and his family, soon to be nominated for a Pulitzer Prize. As Grinnell's premier faculty member, an alumnus of the college, a Bancroft Prize winner, and the bicentennial historian of Iowa, he was in a unique position to write the college history as a segment of the history of American higher education and a fragment of the story of our Republic. The Grinnell story would not be parochial in the hands of Joe Wall.

I suppose that parochial interests alone justify institutions telling their stories. Yet the story of the independent liberal arts college is unique and so important by any standard of measure that it deserves more than a narrow frame. Those who travel the world perhaps have a better appreciation of U.S. higher education than do those who are accustomed to viewing it as the norm. Nowhere is private tertiary education nearly as common as in the United States. Even more unusual is the presence of hundreds of small free-standing colleges dedicated exclusively to undergraduate liberal learning. In fact, visitors to our country often are astounded by even one of these colleges, not to mention their thickness on the ground. In Iowa alone, for example, there are twenty-eight such colleges. Approximately thirty "National" colleges, Grinnell among them, have achieved prominence as institutions where undergraduate education at its finest occurs. None of this would be possible without our nation's unusual tradition of private philanthropy. Each of these institutions has depended from the beginning on a deep well of giving and almost all owe their foundation to the burning faith of Protestants and Catholics. This faith often led to collegiate foundations on the raw frontier, beginning with Harvard in 1636 and including Grinnell two hundred and ten years later.

Until the Morrill Act in 1862, which established the base for land-grant colleges and universities, private higher education was the norm in the United States. If no longer normative, nonetheless, independent colleges and universities remain unusually numerous and strong in those sections of the nation that were well settled before the Civil War (including Iowa). Having preceded public education by many years, it was the private colleges that determined the character of U.S. higher education until the "practical" curricula of the land-grant institutions challenged the reign of the liberal arts in the latter half of the nineteenth century.

It can be argued that the characteristically democratic flavor of U.S. primary and secondary education was enabled by the unusual spread and availability of higher education. With the possible exception of Canada, we educate a significantly higher proportion of our population at the post-secondary level than do other countries. One of the important consequences of this is that the curricula of our elementary, middle, and high schools are pitched toward the middle range of ability, with the addition of special education for students with unusual needs. The result is a reasonably well-educated general populace as well as solid underpinning for social democracy because, usually, all social classes attend the same public schools. This is not the case in many countries where intellectual and social elites are separated into special programs and institutions. When such separation does occur in our country, generally it is at the collegiate level.

We have enjoyed the "luxury" of undereducating the academically talented in the public schools because we rely on higher education to reel in the slack. In particular this is the task of highly selective institutions such as Grinnell. Following what is for most a fairly leisurely academic pace in high school, intense demands are made throughout the collegiate years and, for not a few, the postgraduate years. Very few collegiate institutions anywhere are as intense as are highly selective American undergraduate colleges and universities. These institutions form essential cogs in a remarkable educational environment that combines democratic public education with an unusually open but demanding postsecondary system.

Joe Wall's history of Grinnell College demonstrates how one institution has fulfilled the intentions of its founders to become one of those places where talented undergraduates are nurtured to realize their potential. Though not a universal story, it nonetheless is evocative of the history of many independent liberal arts colleges established on America's rolling frontier.

A student of one of America's great narrative historians, Allan Nevins, Joe Wall developed his art to a new standard. Such was his mastery, that he required only minor revisions of first drafts to produce a polished finished product. People come alive on his pages, animated by a few deftly crafted phrases and adjectives. It takes but little imagination to visualize his scenes, beginning with Andover Theological Seminary in March 1843, where twelve members of the graduating class were persuaded that God had called them to a mission on America's raw frontier. There, hazards frequently exceeded those of foreign missions, a condition underscored by the discouraging letter sent by the "father" of the Iowa mission, Asa Turner of Denmark, who had come to the Blackhawk Purchase in 1838. Turner hadn't expected to see the Andover graduates, so he rewarded them with the freedom to choose their locations when, after a long water and overland journey, they arrived on his threshold in late October 1843.

Turner, Reuben Gaylord, and Julius Reed, all Yale graduates, had preceded the Andover group and they share the credit for fulfilling the Iowa Band's intention to found a college along with individual churches. Really, the driving commitment for such a difficult venture animated only a minority of the Andover men: Ephraim Adams, Daniel Lane, Erastus Ripley, and Ebenezer Alden.

Joe Wall's vivid portrayal of the difficulties faced by the missionaries on a physically and socially hostile frontier etches the early pages of this volume. It was a place for "small things" in a time of national Manifest Destiny. In fact, Iowa College (Grinnell's name until 1909) doesn't enter the story until the middle of Chapter 2, after the Andover missionaries had settled throughout eastern Iowa.

In March 1844, Asa Turner invited a meeting of Congregational ministers to "remain awhile" to discuss the founding of a college. Proceeding from the June 1846 meeting at which a Board of Trustees was formed, with James Hill's famous silver dollar laid on the table to establish an endowment (now grown to almost $500,000,000), through the opening of a preparatory school in November 1848, to the actual opening of Iowa College in Davenport with six students in October 1850, the story unfolds. Erastus Ripley, the prize-winning scholar among the Iowa Band, was the first member of the faculty, presiding over a classical curriculum common to all liberal learning at the time: Greek, Latin, and Mathematics engrossing twenty-eight of thirty-six term courses required for graduation. John and William Windsor were the first to complete this demanding curriculum in 1854.

Amidst the story of souring relations between Iowa College and Davenport over abolitionism, temperance, and the penchant of the city to drive streets through the campus, the story shifts to J. B. Grinnell and the 1854 foundation of his "ideal community" on the highest ground between the Iowa and Des Moines rivers. Tipped off by Henry Farnam, the builder of the Rock Island Railway, that his line would pass over this landscape with the likelihood that it would intersect with a proposed north/south line, Grinnell chose the anticipated junction for his colony. Within nine months, fifty-eight people had settled and, ever the entrepreneur, J.B. began to woo Iowa College away from Davenport to fill the 160 acres set aside for a "University."

The move came in 1858 after the bitter opposition of the faculty failed to deter the majority of trustees who had become deeply alienated from Davenport. With only a wagonload of books and a name, Iowa College came to Grinnell quite literally to begin again; soon to be disrupted by the Civil War in which eleven of its students would die. Only the 1856 decision to admit women to a Ladies Course (less classical and yielding only a diploma) kept the college open. The surprise is how quickly Iowa College was resurrected. The faculty recruited to Grinnell proved to be excellent, and in 1864 the redoubtable George F. Magoun was chosen as the college's first president. Reputed to be the best orator in Iowa, Magoun's self-assured strength drove the college until he, in turn, was driven from the presidency in 1884. Joe Wall's depiction of the Magoun years and the personality that shaped them is one of the highlights of the book. Ironically, Magoun's finest hour came after he had worn out his welcome. In June 1882, the entire college and a significant portion of the town were destroyed by a tornado that still ranks as the second most devastating of human life (thirty-eight deaths, including two students) in Iowa history. Never had a U.S. college been so completely destroyed by a natural disaster, but the combination of Magoun's granite resolve and J. B. Grinnell's fundraising prowess once again resurrected Iowa College from the ashes; twice dead, twice revived, all within a quarter century.

The constant search for funds, especially following the tornado, gradually produced a change in the Board of Trustees from the exclusively clerical group of the Davenport years to a body dominated by businessmen. In turn, the community of interest and understanding that bound together the trustees and faculty despite occasional conflicts, began to dissolve. Once disrupted, the two have been bound tenuously in a mutually dependent but uneasy relationship.

George Magoun's resignation in 1884 began one of the most bizarre episodes in the college's history: a two-and-one-half-year search for a replacement. It was a comedy of errors and misapprehensions, involving J.B.'s son-in-law, David Mears, the money for Goodnow Hall, and a proposal to buy a name change for the Iowa College. Out of this soup, almost by accident, came George Augustus Gates; all the more startling because this thirty-six-year-old Congregational minister from Upper Montclair, New Jersey, was to become one of Grinnell's greatest presidents and the obvious hero of Wall's history.

While Magoun was a domineering Old Testament patriarch, Gates was a disciple of the Jesus of the Sermon on the Mount. Afire with educational ideals that emphasized body as well as mind, inquiry over dogmatism, learning as a prelude to public and personal service, and elevated admission standards, Gates gave an inaugural address that, in Joe Wall's words, "should be read today by trustees, administrators, faculty, and students for their own edification." Wall devotes more space to Gates's inaugural address than to any other event in the college's history. Gates's ideas and their embodiment during his thirteen years as president are worthy of such attention. The poignancy of Joe Wall's untimely death is underscored by the fact that it came before he could finish the story of the Gates years; years in which the college was transformed into a twentieth-century institution while becoming a national leader in the Social Gospel movement.

The remaining history of the Gates presidency had been fully researched by Joe. Using this material, his wife and fellow Grinnell alum, Bea Wall, has finished Chapter 8. She details the tempest created by Grinnell's professor of Applied Christianity, George Herron, which ultimately led to Herron's resignation in 1899, to be followed in five months by that of his protector, George Gates. Also included is a description of Iowa College athletics, so strongly supported by Gates and a distinguishing mark of the college at the end of the century. It features accomplishments, such as the defeat in 1889 of the University of Iowa by a score of 24-0 in the first collegiate football game played west of the Mississippi. In the big three sports, baseball, football, and track, Iowa College was a dominant force in the West.

The account of college athletics is emblematic of the comprehensive view of Iowa College to be found in these pages. Its life emerges in all dimensions: faculty, students, curriculum, governance, as well as extracurricular and social activities.

IN MEMORIUM

It is an indulgence for a student to write about a mentor like Joe Wall. To sit in one of Joe's classes was to be ignited by powerful lectures delivered with a grave demeanor, leavened by wit. Their spontaneity was such that we were impelled to question and comment, so no class passed without interesting and challenging exchanges. Above all, history was alive and important, partially through ever-present connections with current issues. The grand old man of the History Department, Frederick Bauman, who believed that the study of history was meant only for the intellectually and emotionally tough, once complained to me that Joe had made history *"popular."* And so he had, attracting many of the liveliest students to the major.

The Grinnell History Department during the Wall years

produced an unusually large number of professional historians, many of whom grace departments in such institutions
as the University of Chicago, Iowa State University, the University of Colorado, Temple, and Colorado College as well as
Grinnell. They testify that it was Joe's influence that drew
them to the profession both as teachers and writers. As one
wrote in a *Grinnell Magazine* tribute:

> I remember entering Professor Joseph Wall's class in
> modern European history as a first-semester freshman and
> immediately falling under his spell. As teacher and pupil,
> Joe Wall and I were a perfect match. Here was a person
> who was showing me that I could get academic credit for
> learning about things I had always been interested in and
> at the same time presenting that learning with consum-
> mate artistry and an admirable humanity. In subsequent
> years, I had many fine teachers, both at Grinnell and else-
> where, but Joe Wall was always in a class by himself. I can-
> not separate my affection for Grinnell from my affection for
> him. He was and will always remain my example of Grin-
> nell College at its best.[2]

Joseph Frazier Wall was born in Des Moines, Iowa, on
July 10, 1920. He spent most of his precollegiate years in
Fort Dodge, Iowa, first experiencing Grinnell College at a
summer church camp following high school graduation in
1937. In fact, he had plans to attend the University of
Chicago, but was persuaded by his summer experience to remain in Iowa. He graduated Phi Beta Kappa from Grinnell
in June 1941, moving on to Harvard where he earned a Master of Arts in history in 1942. From 1942 to 1946 he served in
the United States Navy, rising to the rank of Lieutenant.
Later, classes were sobered by his eyewitness account of the
takeoff from Tinian of the Enola Gay on its flight to Hiro-
shima.

Joe married Beatrice Mills (Grinnell, class of 1940) in
1944 and, in the course of their life in Grinnell, they nurtured three children, a son and two daughters.

Returning from the war, Joe entered Columbia University where he received his Ph.D. in 1951 as a student of the eminent American historian, Allan Nevins. Joe loved to tell of Nevins's demanding seminar on biography, which steeped its students in the narrative style. Nineteen forty-seven was the year when Joe Wall returned to Grinnell as an instructor in history. Promoted to assistant professor in 1951 when he finished his Ph.D., he rose through the ranks to become professor of history in 1957, followed by designation to the L. F. Parker Chair in 1961. He was chair of the faculty from 1966 to 1969, followed by appointment as dean of the college in 1969. He served with distinction through the difficult years of the late '60s and early '70s, capped by the closing of the college (which he had the duty of announcing to a packed Darby Gymnasium) two weeks before commencement, 1970. In 1973, he returned to full-time teaching and scholarship, which was interrupted from 1978 to 1980 when he moved to the State University of New York at Albany as chair of the history department. He returned to Grinnell in August 1980, as professor of history and director of the newly established Rosenfield Program in Public Affairs. His teaching was reduced to one course per semester, leaving him time to launch the Rosenfield Program on the trajectory that it has enjoyed since 1980. In addition, he had time vigorously to pursue his scholarship and writing. Joe retired from teaching and administration in 1985.

While at Grinnell, Joe Wall served three times as a Fulbright Professor: Edinburgh, Scotland, 1957–58; Gothenburg, Sweden, 1976–77; and Salzburg, Austria, 1987–88. Elected to the Society of American Historians in 1970, he also became a senator-at-large of Phi Beta Kappa in 1988.

Probably never in the history of Grinnell College has anyone combined excellence of teaching with superior scholarship as successfully as Joseph Frazier Wall. For countless Grinnellians he was *the* great teacher in their lives (this certainly was the case for me). But for many others, who never set foot on the Grinnell campus, he was a consummate writer of history. To anyone familiar with the huge demands of the classroom at an intense teaching institution, the pace and quality of Joe's scholarship is nothing less than miraculous: *Henry Watterson: Reconstructed Rebel,* Oxford University Press, 1956; *Andrew Carnegie,* Oxford University Press, 1970 (winner of the Bancroft Prize in American History, 1971); *Iowa: A History,* (U.S. Bicentennial Series), Norton, 1978; *Skibo,* Oxford University Press, 1984; *Alfred I. DuPont: The Man and His Family,* Oxford University Press, 1990 (finalist for the 1991 Pulitzer Prize); and *The Andrew Carnegie Reader,* Oxford University Press, 1992.

Joe Wall published a number of articles and was in demand as a contributor to a variety of publications, including the introduction to the *WPA Guide to the 1930s Iowa,* published by the Iowa State University Press in 1986.

Grinnell College in the Nineteenth Century is Joe's last publication. It ranks with his best, and we celebrate its completion while mourning the loss of the man and his vital presence for family, friends, colleagues and students. Would that he had lived to remain among us and to complete his history of Grinnell.

GEORGE DRAKE

ACKNOWLEDGMENTS

The author would have acknowledged with heartfelt appreciation the many suggestions and valuable assistance he received from Grinnell College alumnae and alumni, colleagues, and other friends. Regrettably it is impossible for me to mention them all by name.

Alan Jones and the author of this book spent hours of research together in the Grinnell archives, sharing information and the delight of discoveries. Rhonda Huber '92, Travis Pollack '92 and Brett Fechheimer '94 were conscientious and able assistants. Ann Kintner, archivist, was invaluable and generous with her expertise. Leslie Czechowski, newly appointed archivist, also contributed to the solution of historical mysteries. The help of the Burling Library staff, and the never-ending assistance given by Grinnell College Sesquicentennial Committee, Wayne Moyer, and Richard Ridgeway were much appreciated.

George Drake first suggested the writing of this history to the author whose final project it became, one particularly fascinating and enjoyable for him.

Iowa State University Press deserves great credit for bringing this work to fruition. I have especially appreciated the patience and kindness, as well as all the work, of Laura Moran, Jane Zaring and Linda Speth, and the graciousness and careful attention given in the interim by Gretchen Van Houten.

I would like to thank Ralph E. Luker, associate professor of history at Antioch College and associate editor of the

Martin Luther King Papers, for sharing his knowledge of the Social Gospel movement and its philosophical background. He kindly offered to read that part of the manuscript dealing with the Social Gospel era in Grinnell. Alan Jones and George Drake of the Grinnell College history department also read and gave helpful suggestions for the last part of Chapter 8.

B.M.W.

Grinnell College in the Nineteenth Century

1

Mission to the Prairie Land

A s is true of all good legends, the often repeated story of the genesis of Grinnell College has an appropriately dramatic opening scene: twelve senior men of the Andover Theological Seminary meeting secretly in early March 1843 in the school's library to discuss their future. The sun at this time of year, when visible at all, arrives late and leaves early in this northern Massachusetts town close to the New Hampshire border. Gloom was already deepening in this otherwise deserted room, but the men dared not light a candle to shed even feeble light on their deliberations, for the library was closed to students after three P.M. Fortunately, one of their group, Daniel Lane, had a key to the room, for he was earning his tuition by serving as assistant librarian.

This was not the first time these students had met either collectively or in smaller groups to discuss what they should do with their lives after graduation in early September when they must face "the real world." As was, and would ever be, the case with seniors, "what next?" had been a major topic of their thoughts and discussions throughout the year. These twelve men, to be sure, already knew what they were going to be engaged in following graduation. They all ardently desired only to give the most useful service to their God, and for them, this all consuming ambition pushed them in but one direction—missionary service. Their question, which they

3

had asked themselves repeatedly over the past eight months, was not "what shall we do?" but "where shall we do it?" It was not an easy question to answer, for only the clear, unmistakable voice of God could direct them to where there was the greatest need for their services. They had talked a lot, questioned a lot and, above all, prayed a lot for the right answer.

It was not that opportunities were limited for them to engage in the mission which their faith and their training had prepared them. Indeed, the whole world, they were convinced, cried out for their services. Many of their predecessors at Andover had selected fields far removed from that familiar and much loved little corner of the nation which the map labeled New England and they called home. Foreign missionary service would always be attractive to the romantically inclined—inscrutably exotic China, savagely dark Africa, and dangerously seductive South Sea islands. These descriptive terms were not trite clichés to Andover students, but intriguing realities which they could experience while serving God. The foreign missionary service, moreover, had a preferred status among the benevolent organizations which provided support to those going out into the field to spread the Gospel. These particular young evangelists knew they would be better paid, better housed, and better cared for (by native servants) in distant lands than they could ever expect to be in the home missionary service, for they had read the published letters of those serving in Shanshi province, the Fiji islands, and Madagascar. But these twelve idealists did not want pecuniary rewards or creature comforts. They sought the hair shirt which clothed personal atonement for past sins and the rude frontier cabin which housed the abnegation of self-pride and worldly ambitions. So they had rather quickly decided that it would be the American Home Missionary Society to which they would offer their sacrificial service. By Home Mission they didn't really mean home—not New England certainly, or not even Ohio, but some place farther west, as distant from what they called home in its geography and culture, they imagined, as anything labeled foreign.

Over the past year, many places had been considered: the western states of Illinois or Michigan, even Missouri (although the existence of slavery in that state put a damper on this suggestion)—or possibly the still largely unsettled territory of Wisconsin. Calls had come into the AHMS from all of these regions to send out more Congregational and Presbyterian ministers before the uneducated Methodist circuit riders had completely preempted the field. The most persistent calls of all had come from the Reverend Asa Turner who had in 1838 left his well-established base in Quincy, Illinois, to cross the mighty Mississippi River and enter the new territory of Iowa. This district had been opened to white settlers along its eastern border only in 1832 by ruthlessly driving the Meskwaki and Sauk Indian tribes farther west. Turner was a determined man. After establishing the first Congregational church in Iowa in July 1838 in the little village of Denmark, some fifteen miles southwest of Burlington, Turner had never ceased in his insistent demands that the AHMS send more home missionaries to augment the pitifully few evangelists of the true faith whom he had himself conscripted to join him in Iowa.

The Andover students knew of these requests and were sure of the warm reception they would be accorded, but was Asa Turner's strident voice truly the voice of God? Two of the twelve, Daniel Lane and Ephraim Adams thought so. In their frequent walks together around little Rabbit Pond on the campus and past the big granite boulder called Missionary Rock, where future foreign missionaries would gather each year on the eve of their graduation to pledge their service to Christ, Lane and Adams had finally made their commitment. No matter what the others might decide they themselves would go to Iowa.

Now on this evening in March, the twelve were meeting to make their final decision. They had met to decide if they should all go to the place where two of their members had already chosen. After much discussion, the decision was yes. It was at that moment the Iowa Band was born.[1] In exultation, Ephraim Adams cried out, "If each one of us can only plant one good permanent church, and all together build a college, what a work that would be."[2] The mission had been briefly and boldly stated, and would never be forgotten by this band, or by these who were to come after them.

All twelve were immediately taken aback by the awesome decision they had just made, and the more cautious ones suggested that it might be prudent before this commitment was made final and irrevocable for them to write the Reverend Mr. Turner to get answers to some very practical questions. Iowa sounded as alien to them as Timbuktu. One of the Band, Edwin Turner, although born in Massachusetts, had, to be sure, recently moved with his parents to Godfrey, Illinois, and had graduated from Illinois College prior to coming to Andover Seminary. But the Mississippi was a formidable barrier between Illinois and all the empty land that lay to the west, and he knew little more about Iowa than his eastern brethren. So collectively they composed a letter of interest and inquiry to that remote and legendary pastor. What was the climate like in that place called Iowa? Was it hostile to the health of white men? What kind of clothes would they need out there? Was it really safe to bring wives to that wild frontier? This last question was of pressing urgency to two of their members who had made plans to marry as soon as they had graduated. With some trepidation they posted their letter, and then there was nothing else to do but eagerly await a response.

As quickly as the postal service of that day allowed, a letter came back from Turner. It was for these young, aspiring missionaries their first introduction to the man into whose hands they would be entrusting their future. If they had expected a "dear, dear boys—Welcome to Iowa" greeting, they were to be painfully disappointed. In the decades that lay ahead, Turner's brusqueness and no-nonsense honesty would become familiar and greatly appreciated attributes to

all of them, but at the moment they must have been somewhat piqued by his blunt response to what in their minds
was their generous offer of service.

Turner wrote:

> I am happy to hear that a reinforcement from Andover
> is talked of. I hope it will not end in talk, but I fear ...
>
> Don't come here expecting paradise. Our climate will
> permit men to live long enough, if they do their duty. If
> they do not, no matter how soon they die. Chances for
> health if one is inclined to pulmonary complaints, I think
> are greater than in New England. I have known many per-
> sons improved by residence here. ... I never knew so much
> good health for so long a time. Office and station are but
> little regarded here. People will not speak of you or to you,
> as the Rev. Mr. So-and-So, but will call you simply by
> name, and your wife Peggy or Polly, or whatever her name
> may be. ...
>
> Come prepared to expect small things, rough things.
> Lay aside all your dandy whims boys learn in college, and
> take a few lessons of your grandmothers before you come.
> Get clothes firm, durable, something that will go through
> the hazel brush without tearing. Don't be afraid of a good,
> hard hand, or a tanned face. If you keep free from a hard
> heart, you will do well. Get wives of the old Puritan stamp,
> such as honored the distaff and the loom, those who can
> pail a cow, and churn the butter, and be proud of a jean
> dress or a checked apron. Tell those two or three who think
> of leading out a sister this fall, we will try to find homes as
> good as Keokuk, the high [Indian] chief and his lady live in,
> and my wife will have the kettle of mush and the johnny-
> cake ready by some cold night in November.
>
> But it is no use to answer any more questions, for I
> never expect to see one of you west of the Mississippi river
> as long as I live.[3]

Disappointingly cool as this letter may have seemed to
the recipients, Turner had nevertheless given exactly the
right response to their inquiry. He had answered their questions forthrightly, and in the concluding paragraph, written
either in bitter skepticism, or with canny deliberation, he

achieved the desired effect. He had challenged the strength of both their faith and their manhood. These Andover "college boys" had no choice but to accept the dare so tauntingly thrown at them by Turner.

It could hardly have escaped the notice of these Biblically imbued scholars that they were twelve in number even though it would have been for any of them an act of sinful pride to liken their Band to Christ's holy band of disciples. That analogy became even more painfully obvious, however, when shortly after another letter had been sent off to Turner announcing that in spite of his doubts he could expect the twelve of them in Iowa in the late autumn, one of the brethren defected. William Hammond had not been reassured by Turner's assertion that the climate of Iowa was salubrious, nor by the promise that a dwelling as good as that of an Indian chief would be provided to those who brought wives with them. If a savage's tepee was the best the country had to offer, what in Heaven's name could the unmarried missionaries expect? Pleading ill health, Hammond suddenly announced that he would not be going with the others after all. Iowa did not seem a suitable place for one with his delicate constitution.

So now they were the Iowa Band of eleven. Although there is no record of this event, it would have been fitting if these dedicated young home missionaries had emulated those going into foreign missionary service by gathering at Missionary Rock to pledge their loyalty to each other, and in the name of Christ, their undying faithfulness to their mission.

There was much in their backgrounds to bind this Band together. Ten of the eleven had been born and raised in New England: two from New Hampshire—Ephraim Adams of New Ipswich, and from Alstead, Harvey Adams, the oldest of the group; two from Maine—James J. Hill, son of a distinguished judge and later United States senator, and Daniel Lane; one from Connecticut—Erastus Ripley, the best classical scholar in their class; and the largest single state contingent, five from Massachusetts—Ebenezer Alden, proudly bearing the name of his remote progenitors, John and Priscilla Alden; Horace Hutchinson, who kept to himself his dark fear that he was afflicted with the dread disease of consumption; Alden B. Robbins; Benjamin Spaulding, the only Harvard graduate of the group; and Edwin B. Turner, born and raised in Great Barrington, but now an Illinois westerner. The only outsider of the group, and he was not very far outside New England, was William Salter of Brooklyn, the son of a wealthy merchant and at the age of twenty-one, the youngest of the Band. Except for Edwin Turner, probably none of them had even traveled more than a hundred miles west of the Connecticut river.

Before entering Andover, all of them had graduated from liberal arts colleges where they had been strongly disciplined in the Greek and Latin classics. Three were graduates of Amherst (Alden, Hutchinson and Robbins); two from Bowdoin (Hill and Lane); one from Harvard (Spaulding); one from Dartmouth (Ephraim Adams); one from Union College in New York (Ripley); one from the University of Vermont (Harvey Adams); one from New York University (Salter); and one from Illinois College (Turner). Diverse as their educational background might appear, they had all experienced virtually the same traditional curriculum with its emphasis upon Greek, Latin, mathematics, and Biblical studies. Even Turner had found at the newly established Illinois College the faithful duplication of the curriculum the college's founders had known at eastern colleges.

Above all other things they had in common, these eleven were bound together by a single faith, a faith inherited from their Calvinist forebears, strong enough to accept without question the often inscrutable will of God coming down from on high, no matter what that will decreed. Yet it was also a faith independent enough to resist any imposed dictates, either by political ruler or clerical prelate emanating from mere man below. Although a few of the Band had first learned their Calvinist tenets within the Presbyterian denomination of John Knox and Jonathan Edwards, it was the Congregational independence of William Bradford and Lyman Beecher to which they now all subscribed. No hierarchical superstructure of Synod or Vatican would impose conformity upon the individual churches they planned to form in Iowa or the college they were to build. Only the word of God and a faith in His wisdom would provide the guidelines which they must obey.

In spite of the homogeneity of their regional background, educational training, and abiding faith, it would be a mistake to regard this group as a single monolithic unit, propelled by God to move westward like a single granite boulder from the rocky New England soil. It was a united Band, but one consisting of very distinct individuals. They were not all immature college boys as Asa Turner had seemed to imply, for they ranged in age from Harvey Adams, who was thirty-four, to William Salter, who had only recently attained his majority, with the average age of the group being twenty-eight.

Most of them were the sons of farmers, who scrabbled for a mere subsistence for their large families from the thin New England soil. These were youths who had had to work hard for the finest education that their region offered, often obliged to teach in local grammar schools before they could attend the colleges of their choice. James Hill, whose father was a political power in Maine, and William Salter, whose wealthy merchant father could provide his only son with every advantage, were the only two who had been raised in homes of affluence and prestige.

All eleven were abolitionists who regarded slave holders as the Devil's own agents, defiling the pristine purity of the nation's republicanism, but they differed in their commitment to political activism. Ephraim Adams had angrily left Philips Andover Academy, giving up his coveted scholarship when the principal of that distinguished preparatory school had forbidden him to establish an Anti-Slavery Society on campus. Some of the others, including Salter, whose father's mercantile business profited from the cotton trade, were content to condemn slavery in principle, but sought only to contain it within the confines of the Southern states which were already forever damned.

Bound together as they were by the camaraderie they had enjoyed within the Andover Seminary and by the singleness of commitment to their mission, the twelve had been as zealous in persevering their individuality as persons as they were in respect to congregational independence in church polity. To use peer pressure to force a majority decision upon those who might be hesitant about accepting that decision was totally alien to their nature. There had been no remonstrance against Hammond's withdrawal, for every man must be fully convinced that he had individually and unmistakably heard the stern command of God to accept the mission, no matter how hard it might be personally to perform it. Nor in these long months of discussion, did any one of them emerge as a recognized leader of the group. Harvey Adams might have claimed such a role on the basis of seniority, or what was even more possible, the second oldest member. Edwin Turner, because of his knowledge of the western frontier, might have been chosen leader, but such was not the case. It was as equals they had banded together, and throughout their lives they would address each other as Brother. Only when they finally arrived in Iowa, would they find a leader, and without prompting bestow upon him a higher title. For all of them, it would thereafter be Father Asa Turner, their mentor and stalwart guide.

Within this communal equality of brotherly love, however, even closer ties had developed among individual members while still at Andover. When Lane first announced to his early-morning walking companions that he personally was going to Iowa no matter what the others might decide, Ephraim Adams, without a moments hesitation, announced he would join him. The two had been closely allied ever since Lane had counseled Adams on the necessity for exercise, too often neglected by Andover students intent on their assign-

11

ments, and the two had begun their early morning hikes together. A special bond of attachment had also been formed between Edwin Turner and young Salter. Salter had come as a transfer from Union Seminary to Andover only at the start of his senior year, and he felt somewhat lost in this new environment so different from the city streets of New York. Turner, the second oldest of the Band, who had himself come to Andover from a far more distant environment, at once took Salter under his wing. Salter had welcomed this entry into an already established group of friends, and if they did indeed decide upon going west, Turner was just the protector in an alien prairie land that Salter felt he desperately needed. Their close friendship earned for them the flattering designation of David and Jonathan from their classmates. The two agreed that when they got to Iowa they would ask for assignments close enough to each other so that they could communicate easily and frequently.

The months of doubt, of prayerful questioning, were over. The pledge of unity and commitment had been given, the future fixed. There remained only graduation, followed by less than a month for last visits with their families and all of the necessary preparations for travelling into the unknown. On Sunday evening, 3 September, those members of the senior class who had committed themselves to missionary service attended a special worship service in the meeting house of South Parish Church, Andover. There were prayers by the Rev. Dr. Woods of Andover and the Rev. Dr. Pierce, president of Western Reserve College in Ohio, followed by an address by the distinguished theological scholar from Yale, Dr. Leonard Bacon.

The future home missionaries on this occasion held center stage over the foreign bound missionaries, for never before had so large a group of graduating seniors not only designated home missions as their field of service, but had banded together to go as a group to the same field. The Rev. Mr. Milton Badger, secretary of the American Home Missionary Society, had himself come to Andover to present commissions from the Society to the eleven, and to give formal instruction as to the duties expected of them.

Graduation the next day came almost as an anticlimax to the previous evening's ceremony of induction into the home missionary service. Before bidding farewell to Andover and their other classmates, the eleven made hurried plans for their imminent reunion. They would meet at a central place on 3 October and head west together. The Delavan Hotel in Albany, New York, a well known temperance establishment which permitted no intoxicating beverages on the premises, was quickly decided upon as an appropriate gathering place for these strict teetotalers, who abhorred liquor as much as they did slavery.

The next four weeks passed all too quickly. Lane and Robbins went off to get married, and the others made hurried visits to tearful and fearful relatives and friends. Two of the Band regretfully informed the others that they would not be able to meet with them in Albany as planned. The sudden death of James Hill's father necessitated his staying behind for a few months to settle Senator Hill's complicated estate, and Erastus Ripley, the star pupil of their class, had been awarded the coveted Abbott Resident licentiate given each year to the outstanding senior for an additional year of studying and teaching at the Seminary. This was too great an honor to refuse. Both men, however, gave their solemn promise of joining their brethren in Iowa sometime in 1844.

The remaining nine joyously greeted each other at the Delavan on Tuesday, 3 October 1843, right on schedule and were joined by the newly wed Mrs. Lane and Mrs. Robbins. Harvey Adams had brought with him a letter from David Mitchell at whose home in Andover the men had had their meals. The letter was addressed to young Salter but was intended for all of them. Mitchell wrote:

> You and other dear Missionaries for the west are affectionately remembered by us all. We miss you exceed-

ingly & probably shall never have just *such a circle* as we had around our humble board last winter. But in another light, we do not regret your absence. We should much prefer to go where you go than to have you come back to us. We love to think of you as soldiers of the Cross, girding on the armor for the battlefield, determined never to lay it aside until you are "ready to be offered and to receive the victor's crown." We love to pray that you may be directed by Abraham's God to your field of labor, sustained under all discouragements, hardship, and problems to be expected by pioneers and act your part well as good soldiers of Jesus Christ. We shall love to think of you as an associated band, laying the foundation of many generations, raising a superstructure which will long survive the oldest of you, and stand as a monument of divine power through all coming time.[4]

With this as their rousing send-off, the "associated band" boldly set forth to their "field of labor." They left by train for Buffalo, where they took the obligatory side trip to view the fabled wonder of Niagara Falls. Not wishing to travel on the Sabbath, they booked passage on the Great Lakes steamer, the *Missouri,* leaving Buffalo the following Monday morning, 9 October, for the long circuitous route via Lakes Erie, Huron and Michigan to Chicago, due to arrive in that metropolis of the West (pop. 8,000) on Saturday evening, 14 October.

Several of the Band were invited to give sermons that Sunday evening, and then on Monday, the 16th, they were ready to face the most arduous leg of their long journey that would take them across the prairies of northern Illinois to the Mississippi, which seemed as distant and as mythical to these easterners as El Dorado. The last verse of a hymn that J. H. Bancroft had written for the graduation exercise at Andover to honor the Iowa Band's mission to the West kept running through Ephraim Adams's head:

> Where through the broad lands of green and gold
>   The Western rivers roll their waves,
> Before another year is told
>   We find our homes; perhaps our graves.[5]

While in Chicago, the Band encountered a young minister, Allen Hitchcock, and his wife who were also heading for Iowa. Hitchcock had gone to Iowa with his parents in 1837, even before Asa Turner had arrived. After graduating from Illinois College and the Yale Divinity School, he had returned to Iowa in September 1841 with his bride to join Asa Turner and to establish a church in Davenport. In the summer of 1843, he and his wife had gone back East to visit her parents in New Haven. They were eager to join the Iowa Band in travelling on to Iowa, and the Andover men were happy to team up with someone who knew Iowa well. Hitchcock advised their taking a shorter land route across Illinois to Davenport, some 175 miles away, rather than going south and west directly across the prairies to Burlington some 225 miles away. In Davenport they would then take a boat down to Burlington. This would be more expensive but far less tiring for the women, and while in Davenport they could all get a good rest before proceeding on to Burlington. This suggestion had great appeal, especially to the Lanes and the Robbinses. The seven bachelors were game for the longer but cheaper trek directly to the river opposite Burlington. So they decided to break up into two parties. Transportation was arranged for both groups and each departed Chicago on 16 October, hoping to rejoin forces within ten days at Father Turner's home in Denmark.

For the bachelor party, the start of the journey was a glorious lark. Except for Brother Turner, none of them had ever before had any real idea of what the word *prairie* meant, or how vast the western lands were. Ephraim Adams, the faithful chronicler of the Iowa Band's history, has left this account of their first days crossing Illinois:

> Now began Western life—and, for a while, it was well enjoyed. Now in a slough in the bottom-lands of some sluggish stream, and now high up on the rolling prairie; what a vast extent of land meets the eye,—land in every direction, with scarce a shrub or tree to be seen! How like a black ribbon upon a carpet of green stretches away in the

15

distance before them the road they are to travel! And occasionally some far-off cloth-covered wagon like their own is decried, like a vessel at sea, rightly named a "Prairie schooner." In the settled portions, what farms! What fences! how unlike their Eastern homes! No stores, no barns, children and pigs running together. Then what places in which to sleep! and what breakfasts! If after a morning ride, they made a lucky stop, such honey! such milk! such butter and eggs! and all so cheap—twelve and a half cents a meal! Day by day they traveled on, gazing, wondering, remarking and being remarked upon. Some thought them "land-sharks," some Mormons.

"But even this became at last wearisome and monotonous," Adams was forced to admit.[6] The track across the prairie stretched on ahead endlessly, and the rough plank seats became ever harder, but the oxen plodded on, seldom making more than thirty miles a day. The only advantage that this land travel in a prairie schooner had over their recent water travel in a steamer was that it did not induce the seasickness which most of the Band had endured on the Great Lakes.

Six days later, on Saturday evening, 21 October, they reached the village of Galesburg. Here the travelers observed the Sabbath day with more than their usual pious scrupulosity, for this was truly a day of much needed rest. This free day also gave them an opportunity to look over the college that the Presbyterians had opened only two years earlier. In the years ahead, they would hear a great deal more about Knox College, for it would be a strong competitor of their own college in soliciting the precious few dollars of support coming from the East.

They were now no more than forty miles from the river. On Monday morning they got an exceptionally early start in order to reach the ferry in late afternoon. These last miles seemed the longest of all, but there was no hurrying the stolidly deliberate beasts, who had already brought them the many miles from Chicago. It was nearly dark when the wagon reached the deserted landing across from Burlington, and ahead lay the mighty river, the Father of American Waters. The river was black and wide, impossible to ford, a barrier to further travel, as hostile in this flat prairie land as was any mountain ridge in New England.

They could see out in midstream the last ferry boat of the day heading for Burlington. They hallooed and waved, but ferries never turn back to retrieve tardy passengers. There was nothing to do but camp on the river bank for the night, for there was no town on this side of the river. While staring longingly at the still faintly visible opposite shore where the water-hugging trees formed a solid palisade, the seven weary passengers saw a canoe gliding down stream. They yelled at its lone occupant to pull into shore. Yes, he could transport passengers across the river if they were that determined to cross now. It would cost 25 cents a person, and he couldn't take all of them—only five at most, and no baggage. Salter, who much preferred a cold but dry and blessedly temporary bed on shore to a possible cold, wet and terribly permanent bed at the bottom of the river, quickly volunteered to stay behind with their baggage, and Turner agreed to remain with him. The other five, the two Adamses, Hutchinson, Ripley and Spaulding, having come this far, were determined to set foot on Iowa soil this very night. In an overloaded canoe which barely remained afloat, the first contingent reached the Promised Land on the night of 23 October 1843, three wearisome weeks after having gathered together in the Delavan Hotel, in what now seemed an incredibly distant time and world.

"Now in Iowa, at Burlington!" the exultant Adams would later write. "Kind friends, even here, were awaiting their arrival; and as the news spread, they were soon constrained to turn from tavern fare to Christian homes. The watchers by the stuff came over in the morning; and before another night they had travelled fifteen miles on Iowa soil to Denmark. They had seen the Western pastor in his home, and he scattered them for hospitality among the members of his flock.

The northern party (the Lanes and Robbinses) soon came in safety. All were to rest a while and then scatter."[7]

The Iowa Band remained in the small village of Denmark for nearly two weeks. There was much to learn, much to discuss, before heading out to whatever fields of labor might be designated. The most important issue to be settled was where they would go within this vast territory that stretched from Garnavillo, some fifty miles north of Dubuque to Lee County in the far southern part of the state, and west up the Des Moines River through the so-called New Purchase, obtained from the Indians only during the past year. It was a decision to be made that Father Turner approached with joy, and the new arrivals with no little concern. For years Turner had been writing such stridently pleading letters to the AHMS as the following:

> We want help and we want it immediately. Can you not send us some men who are full of faith in the Holy Ghost, who will be willing to labor among our log cabins for the purpose of saving souls.

And still again:

> There are more than thirty thousand souls in the whole territory, destitute of the means of Grace, a large portion of whom are under the withering blight of infidelity and all kinds of pernicious error. ... I have done all I could privately and publicly to enlist laborers for this field. ... The farmer, the merchant, the mechanic, the Doctor and the Sawyer, all find their way to the west, led on by interest. And are not the ministers of Christ led on by the love of souls? Burlington, a town of eighteen hundred inhabitants have [sic] twenty-six lawyers, and doctors in proportion, but no Presbyterian or Congregational ministers.[8]

But after five years of pleading, he had managed to recruit only thirteen men for Iowa. Many of these few came, saw, but were conquered by the immensity of the task and left—one after only a three-month trial. He currently had only seven Congregational ministers in the field. Now suddenly he had standing before him nine eager young missionaries with two more on the way. They looked as if they had the stuff in them to endure. Small wonder that he gave them a royal welcome. It was not difficult to read Turner's joy in the broad grin that lighted his countenance nor the thankfulness in the tears that filled the eyes of his faithful colleague Reuben Gaylord.

The new arrivals were quickly assigned to host families in the little village. "My first introduction to this pioneering in Iowa," Ephraim Adams would later write in his usual staccato style,

> We found ourselves guests among the families of Denmark. ... Those homes few and scattered ... quite small. ... None with any richness of furnishings. Pioneer said we ... Shall have to go without many things here. The first day was clear and sunny. Then came a heavy rain. Walking out with my host after the rain he saw me trying to pick my way around the mud. "Oh ho," said he laughingly. "You will get over that. We have to go through the mud here." Two impressions: That we had found a country with a soil fat as grease, and probably I should find myself in many a fix where one would have to go through things and no way around.[9]

Turner had arranged for the annual meeting of the Denmark Iowa Association of Congregational Ministers to be held in Denmark later in the year than was usual in order that his colleagues could be present to greet the Iowa Band. Of these, four were present: Julius Reed from Fairfield, Reuben Gaylord from nearby Danville (then called New Hartford), Charles Burnham at Brighton in Washington County, and Charles Granger, who had arrived in Iowa only four months earlier and had joined Burnham in Washington County. Granger was there to be ordained along with seven of the Band who had not yet been by this ritual formally admitted into the ministry. The three Iowa ministers who could not be present were John Holbrook, in far distant Dubuque; Allen Hitchcock, who had already met the Band and having just returned to his post in Davenport, was not ready to take another trip; and the most picturesque of all these first "patriarchs" of the church in Iowa, Oliver Emerson. He had come to Iowa as a Baptist but had been quickly converted to Congregationalism by Father Turner. He held on to his earlier Baptist creed in only one respect. He would always continue to baptize into the Christian faith only adults, never infants. Grotesquely deformed from birth with a club foot and a paralyzed left side of his body, Emerson had in spite of these handicaps become a truly itinerant minister with no established church, ministering, as he liked to say, to "the brethren of the dispersions." He could proudly boast that in a single year he would travel 4,570 miles, preach 141 sermons, hold 266 devotional meetings, often in the open air, and make 61 formal addresses in community centers.[10] Father Turner had no idea where Brother Emerson might be at this moment.

The Andover men were far more concerned as to where they might be in the coming month. To provide an answer to this crucial question Father Turner brought out a map of the Iowa territory. He and Brother Gaylord had made a long tour of the entire district late in the summer after they had received absolute assurance from Andover that the Iowa Band would soon be on its way. He pointed out to the nine where the need was the greatest, but he refused to assign them to their individual posts, as they had fully expected him to do. They must decide among themselves where each would go. His only advice was that Lane and Robbins should be allowed to choose those places of need that would offer the most congenial environment for their wives. He suggested two likely spots, Keosauqua, not too far up the Des Moines river from Keokuk, and Bloomington (later to be named Muscatine) on the Mississippi south of Davenport. Lane volunteered for the former, and Robbins for the latter place. The others knew that Hutchinson had been much taken with Burlington during their brief stop there, so he was by common consent allowed to have that choice spot. Harvey Adams opted for Farmington on the Des Moines river just over the Missouri border. In no particular order, the others made their choices. Edwin Turner and Salter, who wanted posts near each other and perhaps persuaded by Father Turner's inducement that the northern locations had fewer people but more from New England than did the southern area of Iowa, quickly selected the area southwest of Dubuque, with Turner going to Cascade and Salter to Maquoketa. It was up to the others to make selections for the two absent members of the Band. Ripley was given Bentonsport, close to Keosauqua, and Hill was picked for the most distant point of all—Garnavillo, far north of Dubuque on the very edge of land open to white settlers. That left Solon in Johnson County, not far from the newly established territorial capital in Iowa City; Mount Pleasant in Henry County, some thirty miles northwest of Burlington; and the most difficult assignment of all, someone to go into the recently acquired New Purchase land of 1842 to cover all of the territory along the Des Moines river from the small village of Ottumwa on up to the juncture of that river and the Raccoon river. Here was located the Indian Agency, which would be the site of the future city of Des Moines. Spaulding, who had always been something of a loner, immediately volunteered for that isolated region. It was now up to Ephraim Adams and Ebenezer Alden to choose between Mount Pleasant and Solon. As neither was willing to speak first, Father Turner intervened and gave Mount Pleasant to Adams and Solon to Alden. So the posts were filled. It had been done quickly and, according to Adams, "without an unpleasant word or a jealous thought; and everyone was satisfied."[11]

In the days that followed, there were frequent meetings, both formal and informal, among the Band and their experienced mentors. These meetings were generally held in the long, low building in the center of the village which served as both church and schoolhouse for the recently established Denmark Academy, the first high school in all of Iowa. Ephraim Adams, like his companions, had imagined that upon reaching Denmark, they would find that the first Congregational church in Iowa would be an impressive structure—if not of brick, then surely of neat white clapboard siding, comparable to the churches of New England. "But the meeting house," Adams wrote, "A little narrow elongated, broken-backed, unpainted building, serving very poorly the double purpose of schoolhouse and meeting house —and is it so elsewhere was the mental query. Very likely for this is the oldest largest church in the Territory."[12] To Adams and the others it looked more like a much neglected tool shed on their fathers' farms. They would soon discover, however, when they saw their own individual meeting places, that this was indeed the most impressive Congregational church in Iowa.

Father Turner, now that the Andover boys were really here, was ready to answer all their questions. They were told that there were now fifteen Congregational churches in Iowa already organized with a membership of about 425. A hundred of these, to be sure, belonged to the single church in Denmark. The fact that there were currently only seven ministers in the field but fifteen churches meant that each missionary would be responsible for establishing more than one church within the area which he had chosen. There would be a great deal of traveling by very primitive means—horseback, hitching rides on passing farm wagons, or simply walking. Few inns would be found. They must become inured to sleeping in a single room with farm families, often in the same bed with others. Such would be the accommodations for those fortunate enough not to have to sleep with the livestock.

He warned them that although the winters were harsh, the cold should not bother them as New Englanders, and winter was certainly preferable to spring when they might expect cholera brought up the river from New Orleans. In case of an epidemic, he advised them to tell their congregations to fear not. Turner, when residing in Quincy, Illinois, on the other side of the river, would always say to his people in times of sickness, that death did not matter that much. They should remain "calm and self-possessed. If Christians, death would be a gain, and if not Christian, it might not be so great a loss to have a sinful life cut short."[13] This advice may have seemed a solace to Turner, but as to how successful it was in allaying the fears of his congregation is less certain.

The Iowa Band was eager to discuss with Turner and his colleagues the second part of their mission which they intended to fulfill after each had established his permanent church. They were proud of having committed themselves to the founding of a college in Iowa, and they had been quite sure, back in Andover, that they were the first to have conceived of such an undertaking. They were, therefore, surprised and perhaps a little disappointed to learn in Denmark that such a proposed undertaking was not original with them. A college for Iowa had been a matter of serious discussion as early as 1837 among those Yale Divinity school students who were planning to come to Iowa in 1838. Led by Reuben Gaylord, they had founded the Iowa Educational Association to promote the establishment of such a college. When Gaylord arrived in Denmark in 1838, he found a receptive supporter in Asa Turner. Julius Reed arrived in 1840, and he too was equally enthusiastic. The plan was to establish a preparatory academy in Denmark, and when that institution had produced a sufficient number of students qualified to college work, they would open a college adjacent to the academy. They had even decided upon a name for this school—Philandrian College. Such were their plans, but in the harsh reality of frontier missionary life, these plans had remained illusory. As Mrs. Gaylord would write many years later, "Mr. Gaylord and Father Turner ... were nearly overwhelmed with the magnitude of the work to be done. If each could have multiplied himself 5 or 10, he would have felt better. ... It is not strange that he [Gaylord] did not think it best to make any movement toward founding a College in those days."[14] Now Gaylord and Reed could inform the Iowa Band that they still held to their earlier dream and would do everything they could to make the second part of the Band's mission a reality, which they now hoped might be accomplished in the near future. The Andover men were thus informed that the Yale men, like them, were as committed to the same goal as had been the men who had founded Harvard College two hundred years earlier when they had written, "One of the next things we longed for [after establishing churches in New England] and looked after was to advance Learning and perpetuate it to Posterity, dreading to leave an illiterate ministry to the Churches when our present Ministers shall lie in dust."[15] Church and college—this was the old Puritan mission first realized by Cambridge University–trained men coming to Massachusetts, now to be reenacted by Yale and Andover men working together on the prairies of Iowa.

Sunday, 5 November, was the biggest day in Denmark's short history. People came from miles around to crowd into the rude building bearing the proud titles of Denmark Academy and First Congregational Church of Iowa. They were there to witness the ordination of eight young men who had come to establish many more new churches. There would be no question as to the denomination of those churches, for when one of the Band had raised the question with Father Turner as to whether it made any great difference if their churches were Congregational or New School Presbyterian, should it be found that a majority in their communities wanted Presbyterian church polity, Turner had roared back, "Congregationalism—the world over!"[16]

It was an impressive ceremony of ordination and thanksgiving. Father Turner gave the opening prayer; Julius Reed the sermon based on a text from Acts 20:28; "Take heed therefore unto yourselves, and to all thy flock over which the Holy Ghost hath made you overseers, to feed the church of God, which He hath purchased with His own blood;" and Reuben Gaylord offered the hand of friendship to the in-

24

ductees. This ancient ritual of ordination, worn familiar with use, had now on this evening in a primitive frontier setting regained the freshness and purity that the Pilgrims at Plymouth Plantation had known two centuries earlier.

The following two days were feverishly active ones— packing, asking and answering last thought-of questions, arranging transportation among those heading out in the same directions. A farewell gathering was held on Tuesday evening at which Father Turner, giving way to his emotions, cried out, "For three weeks past, I have felt like weeping all the time. My heart has overflowed. O what a week we have had! The Lord be praised!"[17]

On Wednesday morning, 8 November 1843, these latter-day Pilgrims made their farewells to their generous hosts, to Father Turner and his little church and then, as Adams wrote, "they scattered," north, south and west, never realizing that this was the last time that they would ever again be all together in one place. They must by their own efforts now fulfill their mission.[18]

2

The Day of Small Things:

Churches and a College for Iowa

1843–1850

I n the weeks after receiving Asa Turner's response to
their inquiry about coming to Iowa, the twelve interested Andover students had read and re-read his memorable letter so many times that they all had committed
its contents to memory. One sentence in particular had stuck
in all their minds, "Come prepared to expect small things."
The significance of that phrase, "small things," had been
given an added emphasis by the learned Dr. Leonard Bacon,
who had preached the sermon at South Church, Andover, on
the eve of their graduation and had solemnly warned these
eager, young soon-to-be missionaries, "Despise not small
things," for that is what they would find on the frontier.

Yet it must have been difficult for any of them, especially
in this decade of the 1840s, to accept "small things." All
America was now thinking "big." This was the age labeled
"Manifest Destiny." It was the nation's destiny decreed by
God for his Chosen Peoples, to become ever bigger, to push its
continental boundaries beyond the Great Plains west to the
Pacific Coast. "Our manifest destiny," shouted the expan-
sionist editor of the *Democratic Review*, John O'Sullivan, "to
overspread the continent allotted by Providence for the free
development of our yearly multiplying millions," and a popular toast of the day was "To the United States, bounded on
the north by the aurora borealis, on the south by the Isthmus

of Panama, on the east by the Atlantic Ocean, and on the west by the mind of God." It was a time for building railroads westward to span this vast continental empire and for flinging bridges across the land's mighty rivers; a time to welcome the "yearly multiplying millions" of European immigrants, Germans fleeing military conscription and Irish fleeing the potato blight. The eastern port towns were becoming cities, the trans-Mississippi prairie rapidly filling up. The whole country was expecting "big things," including this band of missionaries who would bring the civilizing forces of Congregational Christianity and New England culture to the pioneer settlers who must surely be eagerly awaiting their arrival.

How clear their mission was in the individual fantasies they spun out to each other. "I am going to Iowa," William Salter joyously told his companions, "and, when I get there, I am going to have my study and library. Then I am going to write two sermons a week, and, when the Sabbath comes, I am going to preach them, and the people, if they want the gospel, must come to hear."[1] And of course they would come for surely they were parched with thirst for want of Christ and college.

So the Band came to Denmark, Iowa, and then "scattered out" to their self-assigned posts, expecting big things and big results. In spite of the adjurations of their elders, there was no way in which they could have prepared themselves for that which challenged and overwhelmed them— paradoxically enough, both in its bigness and its smallness, the bigness of the territory and the tasks expected of them, and the smallness of their means and their accomplishments. Their first need when they reached their individual posts, as Ephraim Adams would state, "of course was a shelter, a place to lodge and study. These were of the rudest kind—one in a lean-to of a hotel in a chamber with its sloping roof over the kitchen while its occupant boarded round like a schoolmaster. Another in a lean-to of the village store separated only by a thin partition from the gossip of the store, with horses kicking flies outside and pigs running in if the door was left open. ... Then the preaching places. Court-houses, schoolhouses, halls—sometimes in the open air—anywhere and everywhere but in churches for such there were not."[2] Brother Alden even had to be content with a meeting place in the county jail. And how naive had been Salter's dream of a cozy little study where he could peacefully write his two sermons each week. Salter, who had found the accommodations at Andover Seminary a bit too spartan for his taste when compared to his home in Brooklyn, was now lodged with a family "in which the one room must answer all the needs of the family, with the needs of the new minister superadded. The familiar quilt of those days partitioned off one corner for his bedroom and study; and his study-chair was a saddle."[3]

As for the expected multitudes waiting to hear the gospel, that too had been a fantasy. It wasn't the people who "must come to hear," but the missionary who must go out and try to find them. "I preached a Thanksgiving sermon this week to a very small congregation," Salter in Maquoketa wrote to his fiancée, Mary Ann Mackintire, back in Charlestown, Massachusetts. "Most of the people were in their fields husking corn. ... Oh, if we had such settlers as New England first had, we might hope that this wilderness would bud and blossom. But alas, the wicked and the worldly and the backsliders are the main settlers of this country, and what can be expected unless God remarkably interposes, but moral desolation."[4]

Salter's parish extended from Maquoketa northeast through the village of Andrew to Bellevue on the Mississippi some twenty-five miles away. These additional communities provided no more pious congregations than did his home base. In fact, Salter wrote Mary Ann, "Bellevue is one of the most abandoned places I was ever in—a most dreadful population. The only evidence I have that I have preached the truth among them is that they hate me. I can assure you that it is very trying to know how to get along with wicked men

29

here. I treat them kindly and take trouble to gain their confidence, that if by any means I may save them until I feel that necessity is laid upon me to repair their vices when a torrent of abuse is the only reward of my faithfulness. I have had much of this experience. The leading physician of this county [Jackson County] is of this character. Once he was polite and affable, but reproof has wounded him and now he never passes me without curling his lip in scorn."[5]

No matter how discouraging the task might be, there could be no letting up in the effort to save souls. It is difficult for twentieth-century secularists to appreciate the sense of urgency that goaded nineteenth-century missionaries into action. The Iowa Band's Andover friend David Mitchell had called the eleven, "soldiers of the cross, girding on the armor for the battlefield," but perhaps a more appropriate analogy would have been that of firefighters rushing fearlessly into a burning building to rescue its imperilled occupants. They had come not to kill but to save, and not for temporal but eternal salvation. Life was short, uncertain, and in God's great order of priorities unimportant except as a prologue to death. Heaven's bliss with Christ and Hell's fires with Satan were the realities that mattered, not earthly pleasures and woes. The annual reports that each missionary dutifully sent back to the American Home Missionary Society in Boston are replete with accounts of wrestling with the Devil for the soul of some poor sinner.

The Congregationalists had generally abandoned the stern, irrevocable predestination doctrine of John Calvin. Salvation was attainable for all, but not as the Roman Catholics preached through Good Works (although they were a blessing) and Faith; nor by Faith alone as Martin Luther had insisted (although faith in Christ's mercy was essential); but by a true conversion, which the individual alone must experience within his or her own soul and only God could accept as being true. There was so much to be done out on this frontier, where it was estimated only four percent of the population subscribed to the true religion, and so little time in which to do it that an air of frenzied urgency pervaded the entire mission. As Horace Hutchinson in 1846 lay dying after having for so long been slowly consumed by the sickness that ate at his lungs, he wept tears of frustration, not for his own death at a young age but for all the souls he had not helped to find salvation because he had not been granted time.[6]

Death was a constant companion to all of them. It came in many forms—by accident on the roads and farms, by cholera epidemics that swept up the river in warmer months, by measles and whooping cough, and in childbirth. Death struck at their pitifully small congregations. One minister reported that ten percent of his town had died in one cholera outbreak. It struck within their own families. Of the six children born to Benjamin Spaulding, only one survived infancy. Ephraim Adams was to lose three of his five children, an eight-year-old daughter, and another daughter and son before they reached thirty. "We live in a dying world," Father Turner wrote to Adams. "It is remarkable that the two men who carried on [in] my place both in the vigor of life should be cut down and my life spared ... but such has been the will of God."[7] Death was always attributable to God's will, but that will could be interpreted in two quite different ways. Either the person was "better prepared to join Christ in Heaven" than were those who lived on, or the sinner had been struck down by a wrathful God to stop further sinning. In either case, it was often hard to accept God's will. Edwin Turner wrote to Salter following the death of Turner's little son, "It seemed hard to explain the providence & make it harmonize with God's general character. ... But we have been graciously sustained."[8] Theirs was not to question why—it had to be "Thy Will, not my Will, O Lord."

Death was kindest when it gave ample warning, providing time to deal with such mundane affairs as making a will, giving final instructions and affectionate farewells to those left behind, and most important, time for professing that true conversion which assured salvation. Nineteenth-century Christians called such leisurely encounters "a beautiful dying."

Death was not usually so accommodating. It could come

31

without warning, without time to prepare for a "beautiful dying." Few could have the self-assurance attributed to Henry David Thoreau, who when asked on his deathbed by his aunt, "David, have you made your peace with God?" could reply, "I didn't know we had quarreled."

If death was the enemy, it was also the minister's greatest ally in promoting conversion. "Be prepared" was the selling argument for the evangelist long before it was the motto adopted by the Boy Scouts of America. Better to seek salvation while still in good health, but should one be foolhardy enough to procrastinate, then death-bed conversions were certainly acceptable if time allowed.

To prepare the sinner for a blessed conclusion to his or her life, the frontier missionary gladly slogged over mud roads, forded rivers, ate ill-prepared meals, slept with snoring strangers in a single straw bed, in order to preach the gospel to the unconverted and to pray with the dying for salvation before it was too late. Such conversions were the rewards which all of the Iowa Band shared in common.

In addition to their labors in the fields of the ministry, the primitive living conditions, their frequent tragedies, disappointments and only occasional rewards, the Iowa brethren shared other problems in common. They all encountered difficulties with the New School Presbyterians. In spite of the fact that the Congregationalists and the New School Presbyterians were almost identical in their theological doctrines, differing from each other only over church governance, there was a constant rivalry between the two for control of the territory. Efforts at cooperation and even fusion, which the AHMS encouraged through its Plan of Union, always came to naught. The Congregationalists were much more friendly with the Episcopalians than with the N. S. Presbyterians, for here the differences in both theology and polity were so great as to allay any suspicion that either was attempting to take over the other.

In the early days on the frontier, it was usually the Congregationalists, led by the indomitable Father Turner, who prevailed, but not always. Brother Alden, who had initially planned to establish his base at Solon in Johnson County, was forced to yield to the N. S. Presbyterians soon after arriving, and moved his church to Tipton in Cedar County. Ephraim Adams found within his Congregational church in Mount Pleasant two powerful, recalcitrant Presbyterian deacons, who made his life miserable and his service quite ineffective. Fortunately for him, the departure of Allen Hitchcock from Davenport in 1844 created a vacancy which Adams gratefully filled.

Many of the problems the various members of the Band encountered were, to be sure, unique to their particular situations. Brother Hill at Garnavillo in the far north on the very fringe of white settlement had to contend with the last two towns within the territory open to white settlement. His neighbors were corrupt Indian traders whose illegal business was to sell liquor to the nearby Indians, turning their communities into brawling dens of iniquity. The proper New England Puritans of Garnavillo gave to the neighboring towns to their north the unflattering Biblical names of Sodom and Gomorrah. Ephraim Adams recorded in his diary his visit in 1844 to Brother Hill: "The next place, north, they say, is Sodom, and then the Indians, so I guess I'll turn back." Beyond the fringe of Christian civilization, most of the Band did not care to go.[9]

At the other extreme limit of white settlement was Benjamin Spaulding's territory, stretching northwestward from Ottumwa into the New Purchase where the Indians were still making their slow and reluctant departure out of Iowa territory. Brother Spaulding had been the right man to volunteer for this assignment. Of all of the Band, he was the one most predisposed to empathize with the plight of these unfortunate displaced first inhabitants of the North American continent. Most of the other members were typical of most white Americans in their attitudes toward other races. As abolitionists, to be sure, they hated slavery as an institution, but this did not mean they had any great love or respect for

33

blacks as individuals. Like other Christians, the Congregationalists prayed to a white God and simply assumed that He
had meant only whites to be His Chosen People to have do-
minion over the earth. The idea of equality of races was as
alien to them as was the concept of religious equality among
Christians, Muslims, Buddhists and Pagans. They could
sympathize with the pain the Africans had suffered in being
forced into an exodus from their homeland; as abolitionists
they were willing to Christianize and even educate these unfortunate slaves, but they were also sincerely convinced that
the only ultimate resolution of this particular racial problem
was to return the African Americans to their original home.

The Indians presented a quite different problem. This
land was their homeland, there was no place overseas to ship
them, and so for the foreseeable future, the only solution was
to keep pushing them farther west, as white settlers continued to extend the frontier line. Unfortunately, the Indians
were far more reluctant to be assimilated into white culture
than were the blacks. This could only mean to white su-
premacists that in the God-ordained scale of racial rankings,
the Indians were inferior to the Africans. Look at Dartmouth,
as the Iowa Band was always prone to do. It started out as a
college to Christianize and educate the Indians, but had
quickly abandoned that mission as being a hopeless cause.
Few of the Iowa Congregationalists would have been as
unchristian as many of their white neighbors to say that "the
only good Indian is a dead Indian," but they might say that
the only good Indian is an Indian absent from their territory.

Benjamin Spaulding did not subscribe to such a harsh
policy. From the moment Spaulding entered the New Purchase territory his letters and annual reports carried com-
passionate cries for understanding and racial justice. "Alas
for the heartlessness of my countrymen," he wrote in his first
annual report in 1844. "May God forgive them! It is not true
that the wandering, unlettered man whom we thoughtlessly
call savage cares not for his home. There are strings in his
bosom which have never been touched by the cold hand of

avarice, nor rent asunder in the hot pursuit of pleasure or fashion. They will vibrate most vigorously at any sound that resembles home. Says one, the wife of a chief, as she was hurried away, 'Oh! let me go back, and take one drink from the old spring.' And yet these sensitive, immortal beings are driven into the wilderness, by a Christian nation, and left to perish for lack of knowledge, or be slowly tortured to death by that avarice which will gladly sell a soul for a farthing. ... Must immortal man be carelessly thrown away, while an old sword, if it had drunk the blood of Tecumseh or Black Hawk, could be preserved in our public halls, as a glorious trophy for civilized men to behold? Surely angels must look with astonishment upon such perversion." And again, "What Christians can find sometimes to weep at is the mercenary cruelty of the conquerors, as well as the wickedness and hopelessness of the conquered."[10]

Spaulding traveled 2,500 miles a year, chiefly on horseback, to minister to his dispersed flock. Worn out by his labors and grief-stricken by the deaths of five of his children, he retired from the ministry in 1864 and became superintendent of schools in Wapello County. He died three years later. There were no Indians left in the Des Moines river valley when this brave spokesman for their plight was finally silenced.

Brother Hill had to contend with the Sodomites and Gomorrhians in his territory, and Brother Spaulding had to weep over the forlorn and rapidly disappearing people of his broad parish, but surely Brother Harvey Adams could lay claim to having the most eccentric and willfully perverse neighbors of all. It was at Salubria, only two miles from Adams's post at Farmington that Abner Kneeland had planted his colony in 1839 to serve as the mecca for America's nonbelievers. Here he planned to make atheism into the new and rational creed of the future.

Kneeland had had a fascinating career in Massachusetts prior to coming to Iowa. He had run the gamut of Protestant Christianity from strict Scottish Calvinism to being a born-again Baptist, a Congregationalist, and then a Universalist. He had served with considerable distinction as a Universalist pastor in Boston for several years until at the age of fifty-five, he came to the conclusion that Christianity was a false myth and the only real truth was that there was no religious truth. As editor of *The Investigator,* a weekly promoting Robert Dale Owens's cooperative movement, free love, and atheism, Kneeland was tried and convicted of blasphemy. After serving six months in jail, he decided that liberty was dead in Massachusetts, and he had brought a small colony of like-minded free thinkers to Iowa four years before the Iowa Band arrived.[11]

Harvey Adams, and those other members of the Band who settled close by, for the next year after their arrival carried on a ceaseless attack against this infidel who they were convinced was the Anti-Christ Incarnate. They shocked and titillated each other with the latest Kneeland outrage: his contempt for the marriage relationship, for instance—"tie the tails of two dogs together, and they will fight; allow them to go free and they will be good friends;"[12] or for what passed as Kneeland's catechism:

> *Q.* What is religion?
> *A.* A superstition in fashion.
> *Q.* What is superstition?
> *A.* A religion out of fashion.[13]

In the spring of 1844, Kneeland captured control of the Van Buren County Democratic party and received that party's nomination for a seat in the territorial legislature. This unexpected and shocking occurrence prompted the Iowa Band to make its first entry into Iowa politics. Led by Harvey Adams, the three members of the Band in Van Buren County, successfully brought about a fusion of the local church-going Democrats with the Whig party and Kneeland was soundly defeated. Shortly thereafter, Kneeland died, and his death was followed by that of several of his followers, apparently all of natural causes. But the Iowa Band agreed with a local physician in Farmington who said, "It seemed as though God had killed off the Kneeland colony."[14] God's will, they could now see, was not always inscrutable after all.

It was to be expected that the three Van Buren County ministers, the two Adamses and Daniel Lane, would be in close contact with each other in these early years to deal with such threats as Abner Kneeland. What is more surprising was the continuing contact all eleven kept with each other—and not only by letters but by visits to each others' parishes. The eleven may never again after leaving Andover have all been together in one place at one time, but they all saw each other individually throughout these years of getting the mission underway, discussing mutual problems, sympathizing with the peculiar difficulties each faced within his own district. When spirits seemed particularly low due to a scarcity of converts, the inadequacy of facilities, and always the paucity of money, they would console each other with what had become their standard bywords: "Ah well, this is the day of small things!"

Nor were their travels restricted to the settled districts of Iowa Territory. Within three years of their arrival all eleven had made at least one trip back to their old homes in the East. Considering how long and arduous their first trip to Iowa had seemed to all of them, the frequency of their return trips to New England seems particularly remarkable. Before the decade of the 1840s had ended, however, it was possible to make the trip from the Mississippi to Boston by rail, and Ephraim Adams could now marvel that Boston in 1850 was closer to Davenport in terms of time spent in travel than Boston had been to Dartmouth College when he had been a student there in 1838.

No matter how pressing their parish problems might be, no matter how frequent their travels, none of the eleven had forgotten the second part of their mission—to found a college. With the eager cooperation of the earlier Yale pioneers, Asa Turner, Julius Reed, and especially Reuben Gaylord, it appeared within the first six months of the Iowa Band's arrival that they would indeed get their college underway very shortly. Throughout their first winter in Iowa, the new arrivals had received letters from Reed and Gaylord telling them of ideas for promoting a college.[15]

On 12 March 1844, Turner presided over a meeting of the Congregational ministers of Iowa which several of the Band attended. Ephraim Adams would recall that following a long day of discussing church affairs, Turner "invited those interested in a college to tarry a few moments and listen to plans for funding our college."[16] The proposal which Turner and Gaylord presented was both exciting and, to these avid college promoters, quite feasible. Briefly stated, those interested in establishing a college for Iowa would buy up land somewhere on the as-yet-unsettled open prairies at $1.25 an acre, with borrowed money. For $30,000 they could obtain 24,000 acres of Iowa land. At the rate that Iowa Territory was filling up, this land would in a few years be worth $200,000, and their college in Iowa would have an endowment to rival that of any college in the East.

Caught up in this dream of wealth, those present enthusiastically endorsed the proposal. A committee of exploration was quickly formed with Julius Reed, who was considered to have the soundest grasp of high finances, to serve as chairman and was requested to report back at another meeting to be held in Denmark on the third Tuesday in April to which all Congregational and Presbyterian ministers in the Iowa Territory would be invited.

Daniel Lane, who had been the first of the Iowa Band to decide upon going to Iowa, once again took the lead in promoting this all-important gathering on 16 April 1844. In great excitement, he wrote to William Salter, who had not been present at the March meeting, urging him to come:

> The principal object of all this college movement to secure a sufficient quantity of the public land ... which, when sold at a reasonable price, will raise for us a fund for the support of such an Institution. ... We feel it necessary to

take immediate action on the subject, because by delay the land we have in view ... may be entered by other individuals than the friends of the college. ... Come, won't you? We want all the wisdom we can get together at that time."[17]

A large gathering met on the appointed date to hear Brother Reed's report. His committee confirmed the findings of an earlier exploratory mission in December 1843 that the ideal spot to buy land was in northeast Iowa along the Wapsipinicon river in what would soon become Buchanan County. Here could be obtained twenty-four thousand acres conveniently adjacent to the falls on that river which could provide power for a mill. No town as yet existed in that unsettled region, but it contained some of the very best land in Iowa. With a college and a mill owned by the college located there, a town would soon appear, and so would hundreds of would-be settlers, eager to buy the college's land. (The town of Independence did develop on this spot within the next decade even without a college.)

It took only a brief discussion for the assembly to give a hearty endorsement to the proposal. Reuben Gaylord's motion "Resolved, that we deem it expedient without delay to adopt measures preparatory to laying the foundations of an institution of learning in this territory" was unanimously passed. The Iowa College Association was then formally organized. The 16th of April 1844 might well be considered as the memorable date of the formation of Iowa College.

The most pressing "preparatory measure" to consider was, of course, that of obtaining the necessary $30,000. It was essential to secure the backing of the American Home Missionary Society. Asa Turner was promptly appointed as an agent for the Iowa College Association to go to Boston to request that backing and each of the home missionaries generously offered to have $12 deducted from his account with the AHMS to cover Turner's travel expenses.[18]

Turner arrived in Boston in ample time to meet with the newly organized Society for the Promotion of Collegiate and Theological Education at the West, created as a subsidiary agency of the AHMS to consider all educational requests previously made to the AHMS. Its Board of Trustees included some of the most distinguished theologians in the New England area, among them being Edward Beecher, Calvin Stowe (Harriet Beecher Stowe's husband), John Ellis, Milton Badger, David Noyes and Theron Baldwin, secretary of the AHMS. If Turner expected the same enthusiastic reception to his proposal that he had received from the Iowa ministers, he was to be quickly disillusioned. This august assemblage listened in stony silence to Turner's enthusiastically impassioned presentation of the kind for which he was renowned. After some sharp questioning, these stern evaluators adopted a motion to appoint a committee of four, consisting of Noyce, Beecher, Baldwin and George Pierce to consider three questions: "1) Is it expedient at this time to begin an effort for the establishment of a college in Iowa; 2) Is the plan proposed by Mr. Turner best adapted to secure the end in view; and 3) If not, what plan is to be preferred to it." The committee was to report back the following afternoon at 3 P.M. Turner could hardly have been optimistic as to what that report would be.

The committee's report, prepared by Edward Beecher, confirmed Turner's fears. In response to the first question, the committee, to be sure, did answer in a carefully hedged affirmative. It was expedient at this time to begin "to put things in train for the foundation of a college in Iowa, in order ... to be in a condition to take advantage of all available means for securing the end." But in answer to question two, the committee gave a resounding "no." Turner's proposal was not an acceptable "available means" to the desired end. The reasons for rejecting the purchase idea were many: "the risking the success of the whole enterprise on the chances of making a wise purchase, sure to increase in value; the difficulty of securing land just where the great interests of collegiate education for ages to come would demand a college; the risking of the success of the enterprise on the financial skill of an association of benevolent men, whose main ends are intellectual and moral and not financial." The committee also felt that Turner's proposal raised serious moral issues that must be considered: "The primary steps [of purchasing and selling the land] would take the college out of the bosoms of the churches and throw it into the cold regions of speculation; the character and reputation of the ministry of Iowa would be exposed to great abuse, [for] there is a strong prejudice at the East against all plans of this sort from the failure of other plans based on securing endowments by the rise of land." In short, Turner's proposal smacked of shady land speculation only practiced by loan sharks, not Christian benevolent societies.

So if not Turner's proposal, what were "the available means" which would earn the AHMS's seal of approval? First, pick a location suitable for a college, not for its soil fertility or its access to water power; second, collect donations from the people interested in having a college; don't start building until you have the money in hand for "to avoid the contraction of debts" should be the founders' "first principle." Get every church in your territory to make an annual pledge and then "secure the immediate payment of all donations. Do not despise the day of small things [there was that phrase again] and trust in God to unite all hearts. Regard an elevated reputation, and the affections and confidence of the community as your best endowment. As early as may be safely done, begin instruction on a moderate scale and enlarge your plans with your means. ... Meantime, patience, perseverance, enlarged views and hope in God are essential to begin and to execute such a plan."[19] No one could fault the committee's report for lacking in fiscal conservatism or in proper piety, but unhappily for Turner, it did not put one penny in his pocket. He and his Iowa supporters had no alternative but to start anew in planning a college for Iowa. The dream of what might have been continued to haunt those who so enthusiastically endorsed the Turner-Gaylord-Reed proposal. In 1865, at the time of his inauguration as the first president of Iowa College, George Magoun wrote a brief history of the college in which he ruefully commented upon Turner's failure:

> The agent abandoned the original plan and returned without further effort. Had it been carried through, in all probability it would have been highly successful, and the College long since had a large endowment,—the site proposed, which had been secured by a friend of the College, embracing a superior water power "in a section of country mostly subject to entry," and being now occupied by one of our largest and most prosperous interior towns. The sympathies also of its friends in the State would have been enlisted and fostered as they could not be by years of weakness, suspense, and disheartenment.[20]

Turner's proposal might be dead, but his failure, as the Boston Committee stuffily put it, "to secure the confidence of the Eastern mind," did not shake the determination of the Western mind to push ahead in building a college for Iowa. It should be noted that from the start it had been the Yale men, Asa Turner, Gaylord, and Reed, who had been the most active in promoting the college. They would always feel that they never received the credit they deserved for the establishment of Iowa College, and they would be amused, if not a little irritated, in later years when they were erroneously reported as having been members of the Iowa Band, on whom popular accounts bestowed all the honors. Among the Band itself, it was only Ephraim Adams, Lane, Ripley and Alden who were truly vigorous in carrying forward the plans for a college to which they all had pledged at Andover. William Salter, for instance, had from the first been cool to taking any precipitous action in building a college, and in this sentiment he had a strong ally in John Holbrook of Dubuque.

Adams could not understand Salter's recalcitrance, and after Turner's failure in the East, Adams wrote Salter, "You seem to think that our college must be given up for the present. I hope not. Dr. Woods is making great efforts for Columbus City. Theron Baldwin you recollect mentioned Davenport. It takes well among the brethren here. If we must give up the idea of creating a fund by the purchase and sale of land, Davenport in my opinion is decidedly the place. If there is a spot on the whole Territory made on purpose for an institution of learning, that is the spot."[21] And at the same time, Ebenezer Alden wrote to his parents, "There has recently been an offer made to Mr. Woods of land in and about Columbus City for a College. Some money has been raised in the neighborhood for the College. The matter will be brought up at the Association. We may perhaps have an Institution after all."[22]

The Dr. Woods mentioned in the two letters was William Woods of Iowa City, a New School Presbyterian minister and a strong supporter of a college. He had offered to trade his land in Iowa City for land in Columbus City, a small village near the Iowa river in Louisa County. Nothing came of this possibility, but the Iowa College Association continued to push ahead with Davenport as the most likely spot, largely because of Theron Baldwin's strong support, and Ephraim Adams's active, on-the-spot promotion of the town to which he had that summer moved.

It wasn't until the early summer of 1846, however, that enough support had been expressed by the citizens of Davenport to ensure that the mission could become a reality. A majority of the Iowa College Association by then did agree with Adams that this rapidly growing community, if not an ideal spot, was certainly the most likely site for their college. It had great scenic charm (it had been the view from the bluffs overlooking the Mississippi that had sold Davenport to Baldwin when he visited Iowa in 1845). Of greater practical consideration was the fact that it was situated in the center of Iowa's population which then largely extended along the river valley from Dubuque to Burlington. There was already under construction a railroad from Chicago to Moline, Illinois, just across the river from Davenport, and it was quite clear that Davenport ultimately would be the eastern terminal of a railroad across Iowa westward to Council Bluffs on the Missouri river.

The major objection to Davenport, which carried a great

deal of weight with many members of the Society for the Promotion of Collegiate and Theological Education at the West, was that a college in Davenport would be too close to the existing institutions of Illinois and Knox Colleges across the river. Illinois College in Jacksonville was far enough away and too well established to cause it to object to a college in Davenport. Indeed, perhaps due to pressure from its alumnus, Asa Turner, Illinois from the first offered all the support and encouragement it could provide. Knox College, however, was a different matter. Only five years old and less than fifty miles away, it saw a college in Davenport as a potential threat both in the recruiting of students and in the soliciting of funds. Led by its aggressive and outspoken president, Jonathan Blanchard, Knox College voiced its opposition both to the AHMS and among the New School Presbyterian churches in Illinois and Iowa. In that opposition it found a few strong supporters among the Congregationalists, especially Salter and Holbrook in Iowa.

The momentum was with Asa Turner and Ephraim Adams, however. At the next Association meeting on 6 October 1845, a committee was appointed to recommend a location for the college and it reported back that Davenport clearly promised to be the best site, "a point which ... for ease of access and beauty of situation, stood forth without a rival."[23]

The next Association meeting, strategically arranged for by Father Turner and Ephraim Adams was to be held in Davenport on 10 June 1846. Prior to this important meeting, Theron Baldwin in May had written a long letter to Julius Reed offering his views on establishing a college in Iowa. As Baldwin was the chief spokesman for the Society for the Promotion of Education at the West, his opinions had carried great weight. He clearly favored Davenport, even though he admitted that a college located there "will essentially narrow the field of Knox," but Baldwin added, "If you should place your college anywhere within 50 or 100 miles of Davenport it would not make very much difference. That Iowa should have one college nobody doubts & if the brethren there are united on some one point as a site, it would at the proper time constitute one of the strongest appeals that could come before our Society. ... I believe they think at Galesburg that I am so prejudiced in favor of Ill. College that my whole judgment is suspect in reference to their Institution. Perhaps it is so." Because Knox was New School Presbyterian and Illinois College was Congregationalist, Baldwin was particularly anxious that in Iowa "Congregationalists & New School Presbyterians will blend in perfect harmony. It would in the highest degree be disastrous to have a division."

He urged Reed and the others to study carefully the steps then being taken by the men at Beloit in founding their college. Baldwin predicted "that within five years from this time [Beloit will be] ahead of Knox College & shortly ahead of Ill. College." He then offered some practical words of advice: He thought the college ought to have twice the land that Davenport was offering. "I should be very cautious about building. I think we made a great mistake at Jacksonville in building too early & too largely & too poorly. ... I should think you might put up a temporary building not to 'tear down' but to use eventually for some other purpose. ... They are inquiring in Wisconsin whether it best to put up rooms for students at all." And as a final word of advice, "All past experience says *Keep out of debt.*"[24]

At the June Association meeting, the discussion was spirited, with the pro-Davenport forces, led by Reed and Adams, armed with Baldwin's letter, clearly in control. Exasperated by the continuing debate, James Hill suddenly arose and dramatically threw down on the table a silver dollar. "Now then!" he exclaimed. "Appoint your trustees to take care of that dollar for Iowa College."[25] Quickly the Association then voted to accept Davenport as the site for the college providing the people of Davenport would give $1,500 in cash and provide thirteen acres of land. The election of a board of twelve trustees followed: the three stalwart Yale pioneers— Asa Turner, Reuben Gaylord and Julius Reed; five of the

Iowa Band—Ephraim Adams, Harvey Adams, Ebenezer Alden, Daniel Lane and Alden B. Robbins; one other of the Iowa Congregational Patriarchs—John Holbrook, who was the least supportive of the enterprise; two New School Presbyterians (the AHMS had insisted upon this being a joint enterprise)—J. M. Boal and William Woods, and one interested layman, W. H. Starr. The long-hoped-for college had now a site, an endowment of one dollar, and a Board of Trustees to guard that endowment. Gaylord could take satisfaction in thinking that what he had first proposed in 1837 was at last launched.

The debate was far from over, however. William Salter that evening wrote to Mary Ann Mackintire, "At Davenport we have been spending the day in talking about locating a college in Iowa. If we can carry out our projects it will be an important day, full of great results, to Iowa. May God bless our efforts to serve Him. But we have many embarrassments. Beyond question we have one of the finest locations in the whole Mississippi. ... But society in Davenport is very uncongenial to a literary institution of the character we wish to establish."[26]

Even though Holbrook had agreed to serve on the Board of Trustees—perhaps in order that his views might be represented—he was not at all happy with the outcome of the Davenport meeting. He quickly followed up on the suggestion in Baldwin's letter and wrote to Stephen Peet, the president of Beloit College, to get his views on the founding of Iowa College. Peet obligingly sent back a copy of Beloit's charter as well as some thoughts on how a liberal arts college should be formed.

"Our 'designs' are to build a *College,* not an Academy or grammar school to grow into a College. ... We have looked the subject all over and are of the opinion that these half-way colleges that are hardly equal to an eastern Academy do great injustice to the early students of the Institution and injures the cause of education. Let academies be such and use them for general education for preparing men for college. ...

The Board are decided on making a good institution or nothing. ... We should 'make haste slowly.'"[27]

These were words that Holbrook welcomed, for he feared that at Davenport the Iowa College Association had "made haste foolishly." He promptly sent off to Julius Reed Beloit's charter and Peet's letter, as well as his own views on pushing the college forward. "I have said from the beginning that we were in too much haste. Ten years from now or five at least will be as soon as a college is needed here & I would rather delay two or three years & then start on a higher scale than we propose to begin now. We can however get our charter and be collecting funds & making preparations. But I have said & I still insist that any place where the institution is located ought to pay & can well afford to pay $5,000 at least for its advantages. The sum designated for Davenport is meager indeed & where is the balance of our funds for our buildings, our professorships &c to come from? A few years hence there will be vastly new wealth in the Terr. of Iowa & we shall get far higher bids for the location."[28]

Even Ebenezer Alden, who had been an early proponent of starting a college, began to have second thoughts. In his frequent letters to his father he has left a record of his growing doubts about the wisdom of moving too fast on the college. Clearly Holbrook had been in contact with him and had had some influence. Soon after the June meeting in Davenport, Alden wrote to his father, "A board of 12 Trustees was elected, myself among others. ... We wish to erect some kind of building and commence with an institution which shall grow into a college as soon as possible. ... I did not succeed in getting down to the Davenport meeting so that my newly acquired honors came rather unexpectedly upon me. However, there is more labor than honor to be borne by a Trustee of an unincorporated, non-built Western College without funds." A few weeks later, Alden reported, "As to the Davenport College, I have a good deal of doubt about acting in the matter at present, & so has Br. Holbrook."[29]

By November, he was even more despondent over the

47

projects: "College matters are becoming critical. The land can only be obtained upon condition of expending upon it & in buildings. $1,500 within 18 months. $400.00 are necessary to purchase a portion of the site. A part of this site has been donated. $1,500.00 has been raised in Davenport, but it is doubtful whether the Trustees will locate the college there unless the $400.00 is also raised. ... A meeting of the Trustees is to be held upon Dec. 30, which will decide the location and probably the feasibility of at present erecting the college."[30]

There is no report from him on the trustee meeting in December, but apparently the pro-Davenport forces were still in control in spite of Holbrook's impassioned letter to Reed on 25 December urging delay. Holbrook once again insisted that "a college will not be needed in this State for 10 or 15 years to come. ... Now we must remember that we ought to suppose we are locating the only college for our state of our order & we ought to put it where our successors would 50 years hence. ... Would you *then* fix on Davenport as *the* site?" Iowa just the previous week had finally gained statehood, and Holbrook was convinced that the state capital would soon be moved from Iowa City to the juncture of the Raccoon river with the Des Moines river, at Fort Des Moines. Holbrook suggested that in fifteen years, Des Moines would be the best location for the college. Or perhaps in northeast Iowa on the Turkey river, or northwest Iowa, where there was a beautiful lake (Okoboji). In short anywhere but in Davenport.[31]

At the same time that he received Holbrook's urgent request for delay, Reed received a quite different letter from young Charles Burnham at Brighton, who had arrived in Iowa only shortly before the Iowa Band. Burnham forcefully stated the case for action. "Too much time and money has already been expended in this enterprise to think for a moment of giving it up now. ... I am confirmed in the opinion we ought to push the matter forward as fast as it can be done. ... I wish the Trustees to regard it as a settled point, that they must go forward with this enterprise. ... To do and act otherwise would seem to be distrusting God and going against the manifest indications of his providence."[32]

A majority of the trustees at the December meeting agreed with Burnham and God (as Burnham had divined God's will). The plan for a college at Davenport was reaffirmed, and a meeting of the entire Iowa College Association was called to meet in Denmark in late January 1847, to write a charter for the college. Alden reported to his father that he had "just returned from Denmark. ... It has been determined to go on with the project of locating a college at Davenport. ... As a member of the Ex. Com. quite a responsibility rests upon my shoulders. We think of immediately putting up a building which for a few years can be used by the preparatory department, but eventually will be employed as a chapel. The expense of enclosing this is not to be more than $2,000.00. About $1,800.00 are subscribed in Davenport, and the greater portion of the land necessary donated—by Catholics. The site proposed is just below the court house— buildings to stand on the edge of the bluff. ... We shall soon endeavor to secure a charter for the college. This is already drafted and approved by the Association. I am aware that we are undertaking a great enterprise, but still it seems to be thought desirable here to go on with it. Three good colleges, Jacksonville, Galesburgh & Beloit are already in full or partial operation in and on the borders of Illinois. But many think there should be an institution with which we can sympathize on this side of the Mississippi and on its banks. I have always had some doubts as to the expedience of at present engaging in such an enterprise, but either the plan of founding Iowa College ought for many years to be suspended, or the present plan carried out."[33]

The long debate over a college at Davenport was seemingly over. "The present plan" would be carried out, and rather quickly. Brothers Holbrook, Salter and Alden could only sulk in their tents as the Iowa Congregationalists and a few New School Presbyterians made "foolish haste." It should have been somewhat reassuring that it had been the Roman Catholics of Davenport not the Congregationalists or Presbyterians who had come up with the greater portion of the land in a choice scenic spot on the bluffs of the city. The Catholics, after all, were old hands in this business of founding colleges.

On 17 January 1847, the "Articles of Association," were formally approved by the newly appointed and somewhat expanded fifteen-member Board of Trustees, which in addition to the original board now included one additional Presbyterian and two additional laymen. The charter stated that "The object of this institution shall be to promote the general interests of education and to qualify young men for the different professions and for the honorable discharge of the various duties of life."[34] Over the next century and a half, the college would restate more elaborately its mission many times, but never more succinctly or more meaningfully (except for its exclusion of young women) than it did in this first statement of purpose.

Iowa College Association had no problem in getting the newly established Iowa State Legislature to approve of its Articles of Incorporation. The college now had official status under the state Legislative Act of 24 February 1847 which had authorized "general incorporations for other purposes than those of pecuniary profit."

Besides official status and a noble purpose, what did Iowa College have in the way of assets? It had $1,500 in cash, which had been wheedled out of the Davenport business men, thirteen acres of land, and reputedly the most scenic view of the Mississippi river to be found anywhere between St. Anthony's Falls in Minnesota to the Vicksburg heights in Mississippi. The list of what the college needed was far more impressive in length. Within the next year it needed an additional $500 to complete its one building; it needed another $500 minimum to hire a teaching staff for one year; it needed books for a library; and it needed students to attend the institution.[35] It was quite evident that in order to balance the assets with the needs, there would have to be lots of begging of the hard-pressed churches; lots of sacrifice from the individual ministers; and many, many prayers for the continuance of God's favor upon the enterprise.

Within a year, Iowa College had its first building—"a small one-story brick edifice with a plain cupola" from which one could enjoy the magnificent view below.[36] It also had a faculty of one—Erastus Ripley, the star pupil of the Andover class of 1843, the holder of the distinguished Abbott Residence licentiate at Andover in the year following his graduation, and unquestionably the most learned classical scholar in the entire state of Iowa. So Brother Ripley, with no great difficulty, was persuaded to leave his parish at Bentonsport and take up his true calling, teaching, as principal of the Academy and instructor of all of the subjects the Academy had to offer.[37]

To find students was a more difficult task. Iowa's first academy at Denmark had only begun instruction two years earlier. It was now under the supervision of the Rev. George W. Drake, an Oberlin graduate. Although Denmark Academy would eventually be looked to as a feeder to Iowa College, Drake had no students then ready to meet Iowa College's stiff entrance requirements of three years of Latin, Greek grammar, a reading knowledge of Xenophon's Anabasis and Algebra "through simple equations," as well as basic grammar-school competence in English grammar, geography and arithmetic. Nor were there students anywhere in the state who could meet those requirements. It had been apparent from the start that Iowa College would have to grow its own.

On a cold, wintry first of November day in 1848, the doors of Iowa College's preparatory school opened for the first time to two students. It was not an auspicious beginning, but it was a beginning. The trustees of Iowa College had done exactly what President Peet of Beloit had warned against doing, as Brother Holbrook might be happy to point out. They had opened a "half-way college"—an academy in the hopes it would "grow into a college." Those trustees who were for action now might respond by saying that at least in Principal Ripley they had an instructor who was the equal of anyone at Beloit—or at any Eastern college for that matter.

By the end of this shortened first year of operation, there were six students, and when the Academy reopened in October 1849 enrollment had leaped to thirty-four students.[38] Principal Ripley was authorized to hire an assistant instructor, and one of the entering students that fall, John Windsor, was employed as a tutor of penmanship. So by stretching matters a bit the school's first catalogue, issued in the fall of 1849, could claim an instructional staff of three. It could also proudly boast that the Preparatory Department under the care of Prof. E. Ripley "has surpassed the expectation of its most sanguine friends ... a large number of the Pupils are pursuing Classical Studies—26 in Latin and 8 in Greek. The latter number will be prepared to enter upon College Studies by the first of October next, at which time a Regular College Class will be formed. The friends of the Institution will then, to some extent begin to realize the object which they have, from the first, had in view—the establishment of a college— an Institution where young men of Iowa could obtain a thorough Collegiate Education. With this object in view, it is the intention of its Trustees to furnish additional Professors and facilities ... hoping that, by the blessing of God, they will be enabled ever to render the Institution worthy of the confidence which they can but think it is beginning to secure. The institution will continue under the care of Prof. Ripley, whose best recommendation is the affections and progress of his pupils."[39]

Iowa College did open in October 1850 with six students who had successfully met the entrance requirements. Ripley was joined on the faculty by Henry L. Bullen, a graduate of Dartmouth, who prior to his coming to Iowa College had been a supply minister at Le Claire, Iowa. Bullen was appointed professor of Mathematics and Astronomy. The trustees had also attempted to hire Daniel Lane to relieve Ripley from being principal of the Preparatory School, but Lane's congregation at Keosauqua insisted upon his staying there, so F. A. Ball was appointed on a one-year trial basis.[40]

Iowa College was now an operating reality. Ephraim Adams would write in his annual report of 1850 to the AHMS, "Our infant College is now baptized with the Holy Ghost."[41] It was a small, fragile infant, to be sure, but after seven years in Iowa, the Band had learned the full meaning of "Despise not small things." They might also have recalled the memorable peroration of Daniel Webster, who in 1819 had closed his argument before the Supreme Court in defense of the Dartmouth College charter by exclaiming, with tears in his eye, "It is a small college, but there are those who love it."[42]

3

A Scenic View,

An Unpleasant Environment:

The College in Davenport

1851–1858

If Ephraim Adams saw a vision of the Holy Ghost at the baptism of Iowa College on October 1850, there were others among the trustees who continued to be the doubting Thomases. They saw quite a different vision— that of foolish men rushing headlong into a venture where angels might not as yet dare to tread. The long-standing argument as to when and where to establish a college for Iowa had by no means ended when six young men were granted official status as matriculated students for the first Bachelor of Arts degree that would be granted west of the Mississippi river. John Holbrook was the most vociferous of these doubters, but he was not alone. William Salter had also been highly skeptical of such precipitous action, and so was Daniel Lane. He wrote to Salter:

> I was not at the last meeting of the Trustees. ... I learn that they formed no Freshman Class for this [coming] year in the college. For one, *I was glad of it.* If the Trustees had done the same *negative* thing last year, they would have reacted more wisely according to my convictions of the matter. I hate a life of spasms. If we can't breathe freely as a college, & if the college is unable to give free breath to the students, then let the Institution live a *preparatory life.* It can live in a *preparatory state,* and students can be well fitted there to enter other colleges. It ought to remain in such

55

a state until means are secured for advanced instruction. This is the ground I took last year at our annual meeting of the Trustees & I have seen no reasons since for changing my opinion.[1]

To those beleaguered promoters of the College now, such as Ephraim Adams, Asa Turner, and A. B. Robbins, who had been elected the first president of the Board of Trustees when Iowa College was incorporated in 1847, such gratuitously offered words of caution were neither welcome nor useful in meeting problems that demanded immediate attention. It was easy for the doubters to say, "I told you so," to those who were trying to make the college work. It was infinitely more difficult for the latter to be able to throw those words back in triumph.

Even if there should not be a freshman class for the coming year, there would be six sophomores who had successfully completed their first year and were eager to push ahead to obtain that coveted Bachelor of Arts degree. The real foolishness was that of Lane's urging a retreat back to a preparatory school status. These six students had fulfilled their part of the contract with the college by having assiduously met all of the academic requirements of the freshman year after having paid the twenty-four dollar annual tuition. The trustees, as honorable men, could do no less than live up to their obligation by proceeding with the college program. There were also seventy students in the Academy. Many of them were expecting to have a college ready for them whenever they were ready for college. The college must and would go forward.

However divided the Board of Trustees might be over the question of continuing the college, there was unanimity as to what any college should offer as a proper course of instruction. Over the long years ahead the question of defining the liberal arts would be the most persistent and fruitful source of argument of all the topics which a college must consider. But in 1850, both trustees and faculty knew precisely the meaning of liberal arts as an educational concept. Like the

Trinity, the liberal arts had been and, these men were confident, always would be an eternal fixed verity, world without end. The firm foundation of a college education had been laid in medieval European universities and had then been faithfully transported across the Atlantic by the Puritans in 1630 to be reassembled intact at Harvard and in the eighteenth century further replicated at Yale, Amherst, Bowdoin and Dartmouth. The supports for any college edifice worthy of the name were the Three Greats of Learning: Greek, Latin and Mathematics. Upon these three pillars of strength vested all other human inquiry and civilized accomplishment—grammar, rhetoric, logic, arithmetic, geometry, astronomy, and music. Indeed, man's understanding of the Holy Scriptures was itself dependent upon a knowledge of Greek and Latin. Plato, Aristotle, Euclid and Virgil were the Big Four of secular learning as the four apostles, Matthew, Mark, Luke and John were of apostolic enlightenment. No matter what profession the college graduate might enter, be it the ministry, law, academia or even medicine, it could be assumed that he had been sternly tutored in the three great disciplines of the liberal arts college. In the mid-nineteenth century, a professor at Amherst or a student at Bowdoin would find Iowa College's first catalogue to be as familiar in content as that of his own college.

Iowa College had adopted a three-term calendar, fourteen weeks of instruction in the first term, and thirteen weeks each in the second and third terms. The curriculum consisted of six fields of study:

1. *The Great Three*—Greek; Latin; and Mathematics—28 term courses

2. *Other Languages and Literature*—German (the only modern foreign language to be offered, and that for just one term); Elocution; Philosophy of English Grammar; and Rhetoric—4 term courses

3. *Moral Science*—History; Political Economy; Moral Science; and American Law—4 term courses

4. *Philosophy and Mental Science*—Intellectual Philosophy; Philosophy; Logic; and The Will—6 term courses

5. *Religious Studies*—Evidences of Christianity; Analogy; and Natural Theology—3 term courses

6. *Sciences*—Geology; Physiology; Botany; Astronomy; and Chemistry—5 term courses[2]

Of the fifty courses to be taken during the four-year program leading to the B.A. degree, 56 percent belonged to the first field, The Great Three, of which eleven courses were in Greek, nine in Latin and eight in Mathematics. With twenty courses devoted to the study of the classics, every student in effect was a classics major. Obviously there was no place in this program for elective or optional courses. Every student was expected to take all of the courses listed in precisely the order designated in the catalogue, which also prescribed the text book to be used in each course. For the trustees, the products of the same regime in the New England colleges, a liberal arts education was indeed an immutable, eternal verity, not subject to deviation to meet the changing interests of the student or the competency of the available faculty.

In addition to the fifty required term courses, every student was obliged to take, without credit, one lesson every Monday morning in the Greek Testament and devote every Wednesday afternoon to "exercises in Rhetoric and to the writing of compositions during all four years of residency."[3] This latter requirement would culminate with each graduating senior writing and delivering an oration as part of the Commencement exercises.

Erastus Ripley may have felt that he had performed arduous tasks as a minister in the Bentonsport area, but compared to what was now expected of him at Iowa College, his previous four years must in retrospect have seemed like a paid vacation. During the two years of the Academy's operation prior to the opening of Iowa College in 1850, Ripley had been the sole member of the faculty and had had to be responsible for all the courses offered at the Academy, in Latin,

Greek, English grammar and arithmetic. Fortunately for Ripley, the trustees had found the Rev. Henry Bullen to be the instructor in mathematics for the opening of the college. The two men must handle all of the courses given in their respective fields at both the preparatory and college level. To call this assignment a Herculean labor is something of an understatement.

Only the method of instruction which then prevailed in most academies and small colleges made the task possible. In the academies, the more advanced students taught the beginning students so that the faculty could devote their attention to the third- and fourth-year students. At the college level, the professor was not expected to present a prepared lecture. His task was to hear each student recite the assignment for that day and correct the errors. Learning came through reading the text, followed by a rote recitation of what had been read, except in the mathematics courses where the student had to go to the blackboard and write out his solution to the problem previously assigned. There was no general class discussion and precious little opportunity to ask questions. The text book was the infallible Bible, and the memorization of its contents was the sine qua non of learning. At the end of the term, each student was subjected to an oral examination to which the public was invited. In addition to the instructor, anyone in the audience, which always included a few trustees and an occasional visiting minister, might ask questions of the student, who could but pray that his reading during the past months had stuck in his memory. The academic guardians of the liberal arts might revere the Greek philosophers, but they were as remote from Socrates and Plato in their teaching methods as they were from them in time.

Ripley and Bullen were well aware in the winter of 1850–51 that the question of continuing the college without an assured entering freshman class was under serious consideration by the trustees. Both men were in complete agreement with Ephraim Adams and Robbins that the college had a moral obligation to do so. To force the trustees' hand, Ripley and Bullen issued a public statement announcing that the sophomore program as stated in the current catalogue would be fully implemented the following academic year, 1851–52, with Professor Ripley as instructor of Ancient Languages and Literature, and Professor Bullen of Mathematics and Moral Science. The announcement also expressed the hope and expectation that when the present students reached junior year status in the fall of 1852, there would be on hand another professor to teach the natural sciences—geology, botany, chemistry and physiology.

It was a bold move on the part of the faculty, and Daniel Lane, for one, was outraged. He wrote Ephraim Adams soon after the announcement appeared.

> I fear the trustees were premature in forming a college class. I do hope that hereafter the action of the board will [not] be anticipated by foreign powers. If we are going to allow teachers six months beforehand to state to the public what will be the action of the trustees, in reference to the college, we may as well dissolve the corporation and let teachers or teacher have the whole control, and especially if such statements are made to the public, as have not only been unauthorized by the trustees, but are made also in reference to subjects that have never been properly discussed by them. The trustees were very good natured and tame ... or they would have passed a vote of censure in reference to proceedings above hinted at.[4]

This was the first but certainly not the last time in the history of the college that an individual trustee would express resentment against the faculty's attempt to usurp the prerogatives of the Board of Trustees, although only rarely again would the faculty be referred to as "foreign powers."

Ephraim Adams, as might be expected, had quite a different reaction from that of his close companion of Andover days to the faculty's premature announcement of the college's continuation and expansion. When the college catalogue of 1850–51 had first appeared, he had proudly sent off a copy to his father-in-law, Jabez Douglass, back in Hanover, New Hampshire, with the plea to "please make no comparisons unless you hunt up and place beside it one of the first catalogues of Dartmouth."[5] For Adams, the college was well begun and he welcomed any action from whatever "foreign power" designed to promote its continuing progress.

Continuing progress was dependent, however, upon finding the money to finance it. Money would always be, throughout the college's history, the basic concern for survival. That tuition did not cover the cost of educating a student, and that every student in effect received a silent scholarship, was as true in 1850 as it would still be in 1990. That difference between cost and receipt would have to be balanced by begging. No kinder euphemism like "financial agency" or "development" could ever disguise the cruel reality of the alms-bowl or tin-cup approach that must forever be made to possible donors.

In 1850, the list of possible donors was pitifully limited. There were no alumni to appeal to, only impoverished Congregational ministers, and equally poverty-stricken and largely indifferent church congregations to approach for a hand-out. There were no great philanthropic foundations to apply to, only the Society for the Promotion of Collegiate and Theological Education at the West, whose resources were as minuscule as the demands upon it were magnitudinous. There were men of wealth in the East to be sure, but they were not prompted by any tax advantage to give, and if moved by some charitable impulse their philanthropy would not likely be directed toward an as yet unproven educational venture in the far West. Harvey Adams on a trip East in the late summer of 1851 to make an appeal to the Congregational ministers of wealthy congregations as well as to get some publicity for the college in Eastern newspapers quickly discovered "how little [is known] even among intelligent people about Iowa. Some lady asked my wife if Iowa belonged to the U.S. Some do not know whether Chicago is in Ill., Iowa

or Kentucky!" Even the great and learned Henry Ward
Beecher, who was the pastor of a wealthy church in Brooklyn, and, of greater importance, on the board of directors of
the all-important Society for the Promotion of Collegiate Education, "knows the Mississippi is out west there somewhere
but whether there are any people there, or what they are, he
does not know."[6] Eastern provincialism would always be a severe obstacle to Iowa College's fund-raisers.

The one great advantage the college had in seeking support from the Society for the Promotion of Collegiate and
Theological Education at the West was that its powerful general secretary, Theron Baldwin, was an enthusiastic supporter of the college in Davenport. He regarded it as having
the most beautiful site of all of the colleges in which the Society was interested. He had dismissed as unimportant its
proximity to Knox and Beloit, and he invited the college to
make application to the Society for a sizeable grant.

Encouraged by Baldwin's continuing support, the
trustees at their annual meeting in June 1851, gave approval
to the continuation of the college in the fall, and they hired
F. A. Ball of Fort Madison to replace Ripley as principal of the
Academy.[7] A formal application was then prepared by the Executive Committee of the Board, stating the assets of the college in land, building, library and apparatus and secured
funds [endowment] to be $5,800. The college estimated its re-
ceipts for the coming year would be $1,046 less than the es-
timated expenses. To meet this deficit the trustees were asking the Society for a $1,000 grant.

The Executive Committee assured the Society that "We
have not been wasteful," and that "we have no dormitories
for students, and intend to erect none. ... We have now laid
before you our plans & our conditions without reserve. We
have hitherto studied economy and retrenchment and have
labored in a small unpretending way, but we have now
reached a point where we must enlarge our plans, & increase
our means of instruction in order to keep pace with our students & the wants of the community." Then after giving tes-

timony to the serious religious interests of their students and stating with pride that, rumors to the contrary, there would be "three pious students" in the entering freshman class, they humbly asked for a grant of $1,000. "We cannot employ persuasion for we ought not to do it," they concluded. "You understand the whole subject well and need in our particular case only to be informed of the facts. These we have laid before you."[8]

Julius Reed sent off a copy of this application to William Salter's father-in-law, E. P. Mackintire, an influential Congregational layman in the Boston area. Mackintire replied, "I like your modesty ... but sometimes a little brass will go as far as silver."[9] No one, certainly, could accuse the trustees of Iowa College of being too "brassy." Nor was Reed very confident that they would get much silver out of the Society for all of their humble supplication. He wrote Ephraim Adams: "I apprehend the College Society will hesitate to aid Iowa College. ... A delay of a year will be as bad as refusal."[10]

Sympathetic as Baldwin was to the needs of Iowa College, Reed knew full well that the secretary had to deal with a Board of Directors that included several New School Presbyterians who were still resentful over a Congregational school having been started so close to the Presbyterian college at Galesburg. President Jonathan Blanchard of Knox was persistent in his efforts to keep that resentment alive. Baldwin was obliged to write asking for more information as to why the college had been located in Davenport, and if there had indeed been cooperation between the Congregationalists and the N. S. Presbyterians in Iowa in establishing the college from the time the Articles of Incorporation were drawn up in 1847 to the present, even though Baldwin already knew the answers to his questions.[11]

Three months later Reed finally got official word from Baldwin that the Society's grants for the current year would be $1,500 to Wabash and Beloit; $1,000 to Illinois, Iowa and Wittenberg (a German Evangelical college in Ohio); and $500 to Marietta, Knox, and German College in Missouri.[12] Reed was elated. Not only had Iowa College received exactly what it asked for, it had received twice as large a grant as Knox and the same amount as Illinois College. It was the first sizeable gift that the college had yet received. It meant that the college would indeed continue, and the trustees could begin the search for additions to the staff.

Such a bonanza was a rare and memorable event. For the remaining years at Davenport, funds dribbled in from the churches of Iowa in amounts measured in single dollars, dimes and even pennies, all carefully entered into the books. Ephraim Adams had to inform Salter in 1852 that he still owed $2.93 on his pledge of $20, and Salter noted on the back of the letter that he had sent 22 cents two days later.[13] In 1849, the institution had received $142.65 in individual subscriptions; in 1850, $450; in 1852, only $153; and in 1853, $711.[14] Clearly, the college would have to seek donors from outside the state.

During the summer of 1851, Ephraim Adams was in the East, pleading the college's needs to Theron Baldwin and calling upon men of wealth who were on his list of potential donors. In Waterbury, Connecticut, Adams hit what the college would always regard as its first mother lode. He had been given the name of Deacon Preserved Wood Carter, a man of some substance who had a great love of education and was receptive to the idea of showing his dedication in a very material way, particularly in helping some new college in the West. Adams lost no time in calling upon Carter. He reported back to his wife that "I am now at Mr. Carter's, most kindly and hospitably entertained. He is very anxious that I should spend the Sabbath with him and I feel under some obligation to gratify him both for his kindness to me and his remembrance of the college. To the latter he proposes to give now $1,000 and he has just put into my hands $20 for pocket money."[15] Carter was willing to do more than that. A few months after Adams's visit to Deacon Carter, he was given assurance that "if the Lord should prosper him in time to come as He had in time past, he should give us ... perhaps

four or five thousand dollars."[16] Adams's second son was born
at this time, and was given the name Henry, after Adams's
brother, and the second name of Carter, undoubtedly out of
gratitude for the contributions of the college's Waterbury
benefactor. Over the next two years, Carter gave $5,180 to
Iowa College, a princely and, for many years, an unrivaled
donation to the institution.[17] Erastus Ripley now held the
proud title of Carter Professor of Ancient Languages and Literature, the first endowed chair in the college's history.

Among other contributions that Adams received on his
trip East was a $100 gift from J. C. Barstow of Providence,
Rhode Island, to establish a scholarship fund for the college.
Asa Turner had also gone East and had raised several hundred dollars. Indeed, both men had proved so successful as
fund-raisers that Theron Baldwin, on behalf of the Society,
warned Adams that he and Turner had obtained funds from
former contributors to the Society who had then refused to
make their expected annual contribution to the Society.
Baldwin scolded,

> Now here, as you will see, is a large amount raised in
> the field which the Society is all the while cultivating &
> from Churches which are in the habit of contributing to its
> funds & yet as the matter now stands the Society gets no
> credit, for it. That credit must however be kept up with the
> churches or the means cannot be realized to meet the reg-
> ular annual appropriations to the Institutions aided. ... I
> feel now quite disposed to propose to the Board ... to make
> it an absolute condition of aid that each Institution ac-
> knowledge every dollar received in any way from the Soci-
> ety's field & furnish such vouchers to the Treasurer of the
> Society. ... Now why cannot your College give the Society
> vouchers for all that you have received during the current
> year that it may go into the report of the Treasurer & ap-
> pear in our list of donations?[18]

Baldwin was here bluntly expressing the fear that would
continue to bedevil philanthropic agencies and institutional
development offices of the future—the fear that individual

freelance solicitors would promote their own pet projects at the expense of the superior fundraising organization who understandably felt its overall goals should be paramount.

Whether or not Iowa College scrupulously observed Baldwin's dictates of reporting to the Society every dollar it collected on its own is open to question. It is certain, however, that the college continued quite independently to beat the bushes for whatever funds it could collect apart from the annual contribution received from the Society. Over the next few years it sent out its own financial agents to hunt for the elusive dollar: first, John Holbrook, and then the Rev. James Mershon, whose promises far exceeded his collections.[19]

Before the opening of the college for the fall term of 1853, even the nay-sayers had accepted the fact that the institution in Davenport was a going concern. Not only was Holbrook, who had wanted to delay a college in Iowa for another fifteen years, now eager to raise money for the college, but William Salter, who had refused election to the Board of Trustees in 1847, agreed in 1851 to join the Board.[20] Salter's election was regarded as a major coup for the college, for although the youngest member of the Iowa Band, during the eight years the group had been in Iowa, he increasingly was the one to whom the others turned for advice and support. Never himself a generous financial contributor to the college, Salter, nevertheless, by 1853 was giving his blessing to Iowa College and to its remaining in Davenport.

Even Daniel Lane agreed in the spring of 1853 to give up his pastorate in Keosauqua and accept the position of principal of the Academy, which had first been offered to him in 1851. In the summer of 1853, he hurried back to Andover for refresher courses in Greek and Latin to prepare himself for his teaching duties at the Academy.[21]

With the annual appropriation of $1,000 from Baldwin's Society and Deacon Carter's benefactions, the trustees were encouraged to expand the faculty size in the summer of 1852 by appointing David Sheldon as Professor of Chemistry and Natural Sciences. Sheldon, a graduate of Middlebury College and Andover Seminary, had come to Iowa in 1850 as a teacher of science in the Burlington schools. Here he attracted the notice of Salter who recommended him to the other trustees. At Iowa College, Sheldon quickly proved himself to be one of the trustees' most felicitous appointments. He would be but the first in a long line of teachers who would give distinction to the college's natural science offerings.[22]

Two years later, Lane was promoted to the position of Professor of Mental and Moral Sciences in addition to his continuing duties as principal of the Academy. With a faculty of four men of some considerable distinction, Ephraim Adams could now believe that the college had graduated from the day of small things to a position of some promise.

Expansion, however, made the quest for additional funds even more urgent. In 1855, Julius Reed offered Ephraim Adams a full-time position as the college's financial agent both in Iowa and in the East to succeed the unsuccessful Mershon. Adams, who had run into the same difficulty in Davenport with unreconstructed Presbyterian deacons in his congregation as he had experienced at Mount Pleasant, was relieved to be able to resign his pastorate. Once again he was out on the road, alms bowl in hand. During the next two years, 1855–57, he visited every Congregational church in Iowa and made several trips to the more lucrative fields in the East. He managed to raise $11,100 for the college, a truly remarkable feat which did not come easily.[23] It necessitated his being separated from his family for long periods of time, and often in his loneliness and weariness, he grew despondent. In January 1857, he reported back from Massachusetts to his wife, "Today I shall creep about picking up a dollar here and there like poor folks bone-picking in a great city." He longed to have a home of his own, either in another established pastorate in Iowa or even by founding his own colony of true Congregationalists, as Father Turner had done, somewhere in the unsettled region of northwest Iowa.[24] In spite of his frequent bouts of frustration and despair, however, Ephraim Adams did more than any

67

other man to ensure that the college would survive during the first decade of its existence.[25]

In the spring of 1854, Iowa College faced another crisis which raised anew the question of the suitability of Davenport as the location for the college. The immediate event that precipitated this crisis was the decision of the town council to build a street through the college's campus in direct violation of the deed which had banned any public thoroughfare crossing its land.

The college's differences with the town of Davenport went far deeper, however, than the single issue of putting a street through the campus. The college from the beginning had not felt itself a part of the larger community in which it was located. The age-old problem of town-gown relations, which was certainly not unique to Iowa College and Davenport, had been greatly exacerbated in this instance by the rapid growth of the town during the six years of the institution's existence. This population explosion had not only necessitated the opening of streets to accommodate the needs of the new commercial and residential areas, which the college found so irksome, but it also brought an influx of people, particularly recent German immigrants and Southerners, who had no appreciation of the college, and whose views on the great political issues of the day—temperance and abolition—were antithetical to those of the college personnel. Both the trustees and faculty were generally regarded as elitist snobs who thought that only they had a direct pipeline to God. Reuben Gaylord's wife would later recall with some bitterness the comments she had heard from some of the local citizens: "I am thankful that I never bruised my head against College walls," and "They call us ignorant because we never went to College, but I glory in such ignorance."[26] Ephraim Adams had not only angered some of his Davenport congregation because of his views on church polity, but he had outraged an even greater number of the townspeople by his fiery sermons against slavery, and by his political activities in leading a drive to outlaw the sale of alcoholic beverages in the town.

It was only too easy to blame the recent arrivals in the town for all of the controversy over liquor and slavery. Even Elizabeth Adams would write to her sister, "I am far from being satisfied with the state of the town—so many foreigners come among us that I sometimes fear they will influence us more than we them."[27] But her husband was less xenophobic in fixing blame for the problems of Davenport. Ephraim wrote to Brother Salter, "It has been a time of wars and rumors of war in our city of late. The Friends of Temperance are ... maltreated unless protected by the police, outbreaks are threatened, revolvers are drawn, in fact we are getting to be quite a city. So much for our Germans you say, so much for a few recreant Yankees say I who take such a course as to encourage these Germans."[28]

Some of the trustees had never been reconciled to locating the college in Davenport, and with this intrusion of a street into the campus, they were eager to take drastic action. Daniel Lane wrote to Salter that he had discussed the question of moving the college farther west with the Rev. James Houghton, the minister at Farmington. Houghton was much in favor of the move—possibly to the new community of Grinnell in Poweshiek County. Lane said he had also talked "to three or four others & they are very much of Mr. H's opinion. ... I dread another agitation of the subject. Still if the churches are feeling, or will feel, an unwillingness to send their sons to Davenport on account of temptation, foreign populations &c—then perhaps we ought to do something of the kind suggested by Mr. Houghton."[29] Oliver Emerson, who had recently become a trustee, wanted the trustees to close the college and "wait till we can endow a college & in the meantime establish academies."[30] Here was the old argument all over again.

In spite of the friction existing between the town and college, there was a sizeable group of Davenport businessmen who did not wish to lose the college as an asset to the town's economy. They made an offer of ten acres of land farther north from the center of town, and suggested a prospective buyer for the college's existing land who would provide the funds needed to erect a larger and finer college building upon the proposed new site.

At their annual meeting to be held on 12 July 1854, the trustees would have to decide whether they would accept this offer, or instead make a really big move westward. Both Father Turner and Theron Baldwin, asked for their counsel, refused to commit themselves.[31] The trustees must make this difficult decision out of their collective wisdom.

The trustees met as scheduled in what should have been a moment of joyous celebration, for on the following day, 13 July 1854, two young men, the brothers John and William Windsor from Maquoketa, would graduate in the college's first Commencement, and would receive the first Bachelor of Arts degrees to be awarded in all of the vast territory west of the Mississippi. Instead, it was for the trustees of Iowa College a day of fearful uncertainty and intramural strife. Even that indomitable college supporter, Ephraim Adams, came to the meeting stricken with despair and a sense of failure. On 19 June, he had written Salter, "As for the question pending, I care but little which way it goes so far as I am concerned, but still I have a lingering affection for this college and I pray God that what is done is done for the best." All he wanted at this point, he said, was for the trustees to arrive at a firm and final decision and that "for once the honorable members thereof may feel free to take time enough to do their business like men. I am sick of this scratch and scramble way—and if ever there was a time when the trustees should come together ... that time is now." Three days later in an even more despondent mood, Adams again wrote Salter, "I feel with you that the present condition of the college demands much prayer. Indeed the work of carrying on the college is one that cannot be done without constant prayer and faith on the part of the Trustees and its friends and especially by the Faculty and those of us who necessarily have to work in connection with them. And to my mind that all have not been working in that way in harmony with the whole soul and mind in the work for the glory of God is the reason why the College has not prospered. And unless this thing changes it will never prosper—go where it will or stay where it may."[32] The college in 1854 had adopted its official seal bearing the motto "Christo Duce," but Adams was convinced that not even Christ could lead if there were no followers.

There are, unfortunately, no records of trustee meetings prior to 1883 extant, so we do not know how the trustees' vote was divided at that critical meeting of July 1854. We can only infer from letters written prior to the meeting as to how some individuals cast their ballots on either staying in or leaving Davenport. Clearly Salter, Reed, Gaylord and Ephraim Adams voted for remaining. Quite probably Asa Turner and Robbins did the same. Oliver Emerson, John Holbrook and possibly Harvey Adams favored moving. Lane, who had resigned from the Board when he joined the faculty in 1853, was not present to vote, but certainly he had done his best to influence the trustees to support a move, but Salter's opposing view had a greater impact. The pro-Davenport faction carried the day. The college would relocate on the crest of another bluff in Davenport, farther removed from the river. With the proceeds from the sale of its original property, it could now erect a much more impressive facility. Adams could fervently hope that as the trustees had done "their business like men," the constant "scratch and scramble way" over the location of the college had at last come to an end.

In time for the beginning of the fall term in 1855, there was a handsome structure ready to admit students at the college's new site between Brady and Harrison streets on the highest point of land within the city limits. The architect, W. L. Carroll, had created an imposing, three-story building of limestone in the simplified Italianate style so popular in that day, adorned with massive central balconies on its second- and third-floor facade, and proudly bearing on its flat roof a high cupola to house the college bell. On the first floor was a large multipurpose room to serve as both chapel and classroom for the Academy. On the second floor were the library, rooms for the students' literary societies, and the college recitation rooms. The third floor provided for twelve student bedrooms. It was a building to delight the faculty and to allow the town to boast of having "the finest structure in the State."[33]

Such magnificence, however, did not come cheap—$22,000, to be exact, somewhat exceeding the amount the college had realized by the sale of its earlier property. Then there were the desperate needs of the library, which possessed less than 1,500 books, and the newly opened laboratory, for which Bullen and Sheldon begged to have adequate "apparatus." And always there were the persistent demands of the faculty for more staff and more pay. In the 1853 Faculty Report to the Trustees, the first still extant, Ripley wrote a moving appeal for a least one more instructor:

> We don't think it desirable to attempt to graduate a class with so small a corps of instructors. The Principal could not possibly do all that would be necessary in the two lower Departments; so, that in reality, the *whole work* of the Collegiate department, & no small part of that in the academic would be devolved upon three Professors. We think that it would be unwise economy for the Trustees to require such an amount of labor from them. We recommend therefore, the employment of another Teacher. ... We would further recommend the application of 150 or 200 Dolls. for the purchase of apparatus for the department of Chemistry. This is deemed indispensable to a proper understanding of a difficult but highly important study. The increased expenditures involved in the several steps recommended would render it necessary perhaps to ask of the Coll. Society for the coming year, 1500 instead of 1000 Dolls. The request, if made, we think, would be granted.[34]

As he set out in 1855 for his two-year stint as financial agent for the college, Ephraim Adams could hope that the "scratch and scramble way" over the location of the college was over, but he was under no illusion that for more dollars it would ever end.

72

While Adams was out in the field doing his "bone-picking of a dollar here and a dollar there," the faculty decided to get into the act of fund-raising as well. Ripley, for one, felt the trustees had not used enough brass in asking for more from Baldwin than the previous year's grant. Ripley on his own wrote to Baldwin a separate letter of application: "Learning that the application from the Trustees of Iowa College for an appropriation of *Two Thousand Dollars* for the ensuing year was not accompanied with such statements relative to the conditions, prospects & wants of the Inst. as would enable the Society to judge the reasonableness of the request, the Faculty have ordered me to forward such information as will supply the deficiency." Ripley then proceeded forcefully to provide that information. He pointed out that the college now held property with an estimated value of $62,400 as of July 1856, but this asset was encumbered by $11,500 interest due on outstanding debts, and $1,500 still owed on the construction of the building. Estimated receipts for the coming year— $3,000, estimated expenses—$5,000, leaving an operating deficit of $2,000. "The building is a noble one—just what was needed—but its erection has brought a heavy debt upon us, & rendered aid the more imperatively necessary." He pointed out that during the past year "there have been in attendance in the different departments of study 115 students with 10 of this number in the Collegiate department proper. ... Young men of great promise, both with reference to their devoted piety & their talent. ... The professors are living upon the nominal salary of $600 per annum which in this place would be hard enough if it were paid fully and promptly & of course the difficulty is infinitely harder if even that pittance cannot be relied upon." Ripley concluded his application with the desperate cry, "Unless the Society aids us more than last year we see not how we are to get along at all."[35]

Ripley's blunt appeal may well have been more effective than the trustees' formal and proper application in getting the Society to increase its annual appropriation to Iowa College, but most assuredly this direct approach of the faculty to the Society was effective in arousing the ire of some of the trustees. For the eight years of the institution's existence, it had survived without a designated chief executive officer. When Ripley first agreed to come to Davenport as the Academy's sole faculty member in 1848, he was offered the position of President of Iowa College, but he turned it down, preferring what he considered the more honorable title of Senior Professor. So for all intents and purposes, Alden B. Robbins, as President of the Board of Trustees, was the first chief executive officer of this institution. But Robbins, as pastor in Muscatine, had his own obligations to meet and could be on campus only infrequently. It was becoming increasingly apparent to the Board that there needed to be an active and designated head official to oversee the daily operations of the college and to keep this willfully independent faculty in line. "We need a man of much financial skill and of great weight," Robbins wrote Salter in June 1856. "The Prof's at Davenport need a man for President who will make them respect him.— *They* are grand fellows; but don't think much of each other. Their united respect will be [necessary] ... to a President."[36] The first presidential search in the college's history had begun in earnest.

None of the trustees had had any experience in or much knowledge of proper procedures for conducting such a search. The only thing they were sure of was that the faculty need not be consulted even for suggestions of possible candidates. The faculty might think they could on their own seek financial assistance, but surely even the professors would have to agree that the hiring and firing of a president were the sole prerogatives of the trustees.

The trustees aimed high in their consideration of candidates. The name of Ray Palmer of Albany, New York, was suggested and, after a very brief discussion by the selection committee, he became the trustees' first choice. Nothing was known of Palmer's financial skills, but that he was a man of "great weight" in Biblical scholarship was beyond question. Here surely was a man who would have the respect of the faculty and by his mere presence could bring order within the college walls.

74

So naive were the trustees in the process of selecting a president that they chose Palmer without first even bothering to contact him. The first that the president-elect knew anything about the matter was when he received a letter in late August 1856 from the Selection Committee of the Trustees, Asa Turner, A. B. Robbins and George F. Magoun with the abrupt announcement, "Rev and Dear Sir, We are authorized and directed, as a Committee of the *Board of Trustees,* of Iowa College to inform you that ... you are elected *President of Iowa College,* by a unanimous vote of the Trustees. We communicate this action of the guardians of our beloved institution with great and unalloyed pleasures, and with the earnest desire and hope ... that you will see your way open to accept the appointment."

Since the trustees had to assume that Palmer knew nothing about Iowa College, Davenport, or even the state of Iowa, the surprising opening paragraph was followed by four pages of detailed information, glossed with glowing descriptions of the present state of affairs and such optimism for the future as would do credit to the best efforts of any later public relations office. After concluding with the hope that the new president could be at his post "as early as may be," the committee added a hurried "P.S. If you should deem it best to visit Davenport before deciding it would meet with the wishes of the Trustees and of the Faculty."[37]

Some six weeks later, the trustees had Palmer's response. In a very courteous manner, he declined the offer: "I have delayed, perhaps too long, to give a formal answer to the proposal made to me ... on account of the great importance of the question which it devolved upon me to decide. ... I determined to look at the subject carefully, & to endeavor to ascertain, clearly if possible, the will of the Great Head of the Church. I have accordingly considered the subject, so far as I could in all its bearings. I have asked the counsel of the most disinterested & judicious brethren. ... I need hardly say, also, that I have asked divine guidance, with entire readiness, I trust, to go anywhere at the Master's call." Palmer said that he had hoped "to see one of you ... at the Conference at

Brooklyn or at the late meeting of the A.M. Board, but in this I have been disappointed." Although Palmer was "deeply sensible of the honor done me," it seemed clear to him "that Christ has committed to me a work here," and of the "wise counsellors whom I have consulted, *not one* has thought I ought to go." Palmer's "earnest hope that some one may be indicated to you who will be inclined to accept the office," hardly assuaged the trustees' disappointment in being turned down.[38]

At the suggestion of Magoun, the trustees turned next to the Rev. J. M. Post, pastor of the Congregational church in St. Louis and a former professor of religion at Illinois College. Here, too, they received an even more emphatic no. Post wrote, "I am not the man for the place. The presidency of Iowa College in the present stage of its history requires eminently a financier—a fiscal manager, provider, originator—a gatherer and economiser of moneys. For this I have no practice, no taste, and certainly no developed and cultivated faculty, and it is late in life for me to become learner and experimenter in the matter, even if I were willing to. ... Illinois College is still in the same struggle for pecuniary subsistence as when I first knew it twenty-three years ago." Moreover, Post added, he had a large family, "now in the most expensive stage." He did not "see how with my present stage of family ... I could be sustained compatible with the scale of salary the college is able to sustain, and on which younger or older men perhaps could subsist."[39]

With this second refusal, the trustees began to realize that finding a president was no easy task, but at least Post's letter of refusal had pointed out some hard facts to which the Board had given little attention: first, they needed a president who would be at least as concerned over fiscal matters as he was over teaching and scholarship—Post had even suggested that they might consider someone who had no distinction as an academician but who was "fitted to manage a manufactory or mercantile establishment"; second, the trustees must be prepared to pay a salary large enough to enable a president to sustain a lifestyle somewhat higher than that which the overworked faculty presently enjoyed.

In their desperation, the trustees even gave serious consideration to offering the position to the man who had for the past ten years been Iowa College's most unrelenting foe, Jonathan Blanchard. As president of Knox College, Blanchard had been a successful administrator and fund-raiser. He was also, however, a highly controversial figure, a staunch Presbyterian Calvinist who antagonized most Congregationalists especially because of his attacks on locating a Congregational college in Davenport. Even within his own community, Blanchard's extreme abolitionist views had aroused the anger of many townspeople. When he accused the Masonic fraternal order of being in league with the Southern slavocracy, even those who were most appreciative of his accomplishments at Knox agreed he had gone too far. In the spring of 1857, he was forced to resign. He was now unemployed, and clearly available.[40]

Several of the trustees were quite amenable to the idea of bringing him to Davenport, even if he was a fiery New School Presbyterian. They liked his strong, antislavery views, and they admired the way in which he had forcefully controlled his faculty. This would also be a way, one trustee wryly commented, of "getting Blanchard out of our hair," by making him head of their college. Robbins wrote to Salter, "I have talked with some of the Trustees as to Pres. Blanchard. Those here [in Davenport] will I think favor it ... [as well as] Magoun & Turner. Reed thinks it due Galesburg that we say not a word at present. The Faculty I am afraid will be much afraid of Revd. J. B."[41]

The word, however, quickly did get out. The faculty were not so much afraid as they were outraged at the suggestion. They might not have a role in the selection of a president, but they certainly had a voice to raise in effective protest. This trial balloon was quickly shot down before it had gained any altitude. By the end of 1857, other problems had arisen of such magnitude as to distract the trustees from continuing the presidential search at that time. Blanchard happily accepted the presidency of Wheaton College in northern Illinois, where in that rigidly Calvinist school he would find a much more congenial environment than that which Davenport would have provided.

The decade of the 1850s proved to be a singularly unfortunate and difficult time for Iowa College to be born and to survive. Quite apart from the college's problems in locating and building a campus, in employing a competent faculty, in rounding up a student body, and above all, in financing the enterprise—difficulties that the college would have encountered at any time—this was a decade in which the country was moving inexorably toward disunion.

The decade had begun auspiciously enough for those seeking sectional harmony with the great Compromise of 1850, designed to appease both the North and the South and so save the Union. But neither the Northern abolitionists nor the Southern fire-eaters would let die the question of the continuing co-existence of free and slave lands. In 1852 Harriet Beecher Stowe published her novel, *Uncle Tom's Cabin*, which immediately became a best-seller and did more to promote the abolitionist cause than had all the Congregational sermons and all of William Lloyd Garrison's editorials over the past two decades. Two years later the shaky truce that had been effected by the Compromise of 1850 was shattered by the Kansas-Nebraska Act, which by repealing the Missouri Compromise of 1820 had in effect opened all of the territory west of the Missouri river except California to the possible extension of slavery. The two major political parties were now in disarray. The Democratic leaders in Congress attempted to sugarcoat their notorious Kansas-Nebraska organizational bill with the doctrine of Popular Sovereignty—"let the people decide." The Whigs were even more sharply divided between the so-called "Conscience" and "Cotton" factions. As the territory of Kansas quickly became a scene of bleeding civil war, even those Northerners who had previously insisted that slavery was a local not a national problem began to have second thoughts and now feared that the disintegration of the Union would be the inevitable result of sectionalism.

Such frightening developments nationally could not but affect the college. One of the most pervasive and fallacious myths held by the general public is that academicians and students inhabit an ivory tower, isolated from and indifferent to the mundane trials which afflict those living in "the real world." Most of the Iowa Band and the Congregational patriarchs who had preceded them in Iowa had been for the past twenty years professed abolitionists. Living in the first free state west of the Mississippi, they were close enough to the slave-holding state of Missouri to have seen first-hand the ugly reality of slavery. Frightened fugitive slaves had passed through their towns in a desperate effort to get northward to Canada and freedom. Ephraim Adams recorded in his diary of 23 June 1855, "Fugitive slave arrested in Burlington." And then, three days later, "The Negro was not the Negro in the case. Pursuers could not identify so with a 20 minute trial, he was set free North Starward. Great rejoicing."[42] Adams would write to a friend in Grinnell, "I am proud of Iowa. She stands a Star in the West."[43]

Even among these antislavery Congregationalists, however, there was a wide range as to their concern about slavery. Daniel Lane wrote to Ephraim Adams in 1846 "They are having an anti-slavery meeting today in Denmark. I cannot make up my mind to identify myself with some of their ultra-members. How do you feel about this thing? I am expecting the general association will yet be rent by this troublesome question of slavery. I wish from the bottom of my soul that some good Christians were half as much awake in exterminating the sin of their own hearts as they are in their efforts to abolish slavery in the South."[44]

By the "ultra-members," Lane clearly meant Father Turner and Oliver Emerson, who were quite willing to break up the American Home Missionary Society or any other Christian association which by its silence was in effect condoning the existence of slavery, the Devil's own institution. Asa Turner's letter to Adams in 1850 in which he expressed the fear that "Br. Lane is no more than half-converted," was much more in line with Adams's own views than had been Lane's willingness to "drop the matter" in the interest of church unity.

Turner was outraged that a Missouri Presbyterian slaveholder had been suggested by one of the college's Presbyterian trustees, Gamaliel Beaman, as a good candidate for principal of the academy at Davenport. "I told him [Beaman] I would as soon have the devil—and I meant just what I said. We should know what to do with the devil—cast him out by prayer and fasting—and I fear there are too many of our brothers that do not hate slavery bad enough to pray in faith for its exorcism much less to fast. Who may think of a Presbyterian slave holder. No, no, that will not do. By the way, if our institution [Iowa College] is going to be a milk and water thing, dough faced on such things as slavery, we had better all make our will and hand it over to the Catholics. They will have Christianity enough about them to have a wooden cross on the top of the building."[45]

Turner had been an early advocate of the doctrine of "immediatism"—the immediate emancipation of all slaves without compensation to their owners. By 1852, he was a recognized leader of the Free Soil party, a small group of dissident Democrats who put candidates on the ballot for election to state offices in that year. In the uproar following the passage of the Kansas-Nebraska Act in February 1854, Turner became receptive to the idea of abandoning the quixotic pursuit of third-party politics by joining either one of the two major parties who would nominate a gubernatorial candidate acceptable to the Free Soilers. There was little chance that the Democratic party which had dominated the Iowa political scene since 1838 would do so. Turner's only hope lay with the "Conscience" Whigs gaining control of their party.

That opportunity came in late February 1854, at a meeting held in Denmark which George Magoun arranged. Magoun had given up his pastorate in Wisconsin in 1851 and had come to Burlington, Iowa, to study law. There he met a young and politically ambitious lawyer, James W. Grimes, a Whig member of the Iowa legislature who was now aspiring to the highest office in the state. Magoun brought Grimes to Denmark to meet Father Turner, who would later have good reason to recall that meeting with pleasure:

> Mr. Grimes came over to Denmark and said that if the Free-Soilers would vote for him he would be a candidate for Governor, and assured us that he would be true to the principles we wished should triumph. I believed he would be and that he could make our principles triumph. The Free-Soilers ... voted to entrust in his hands the interests of our organization ... with fear and trembling by some, by others with the confidence of faith. He took the stump. ... He gave his whole soul to the work. Wherever he went he secured favor with the people, and he was elected.

Grimes, in turn, would say of Turner, "You call him Father Turner; and I look to him as my political godfather."[46]

Grimes's election marked the end of an era in Iowa politics. The Iowa Democrats over the next two years would lose the dominance they had enjoyed since territorial days at both the national and state levels. But, it was not the Whig party which was to benefit by this turnabout. Before his first term as governor had ended, Grimes had taken his conglomerate of "Conscience" Whigs and Free-Soilers intact over to the newly formed Republican party. For the next eighty years Iowa would be a one-party state, as solidly Republican as Alabama was solidly Democratic.

The political activism on the part of several of its trustees in the mid-1850s had its effect upon Iowa College as well as the state of Iowa. The college's relations with the town of Davenport became ever more strained. Many of the local merchants, dependent upon the city's lively river traffic, saw the victory of Grimes, Turner, Magoun and company as a victory for abolitionist radicalism which might well drive the South out of the Union. In that event, the great artery of trade that flowed by their doors would have its Southern terminal within an alien and hostile country. The city's large German population feared another element of Republican radicalism that threatened its culture, for many of the new party leaders, especially those college Congregationalists were as opposed to liquor as they were to slavery. Before the end of the decade the one thing shared in common by the town and the college was an intolerance for each other's social and political views.

The townspeople's disaffection for the college was largely directed against its trustees and faculty but not toward the students. Youthful pranks and rowdyism were seldom perpetrated by these young men. Indeed most of the students out of piety and academic pressure had neither the time nor the inclination to participate in the revelries and bawdiness which the town's riverfront offered in abundance. Their college life had the orderly regimentation and discipline of the monastery, and whether they had rooms on the third floor of the college building or found lodging in town, they lived under the same rules of no alcoholic beverages, no tobacco, no card playing and no swearing. The faculty monitored student deportment, a responsibility which the professors undertook as seriously as they did classroom instruction. The early college faculty minutes reveal that most of the business was devoted to discussions of the rare student who dared to step out of line by using a cussword, furtively lighting a pipe, or failing to get to prayer meeting on time.

We have no way of knowing how the students reacted to this strict regimen for there was no student newspaper in which to air their opinions and complaints. Only rarely do faculty records provide an insight into student views—an occasional student appeal against a penalty imposed for an infraction of a rule or student reaction to college policies as reported by a faculty member. All that we have of the students' own verbalization of their college experiences are the few accounts written by alumni many years later which with the passage of time are suffused with the soft remembrance of things past, making the good things better than they were and the bad things nonexistent.

The recollections of the college's first two graduates, John and William Windsor, class of '54, and that of a student in the last class to graduate from Iowa College in Davenport, H. H. Belfield, class of '58, are remarkably similar. All expressed a great respect for their teachers and an appreciation for the quality of instruction offered by Erastus Ripley and especially by David Sheldon, whom Belfield called "the idol of the students—a man of rare accomplishments and grace."

All three men were well aware that they were attending "a college in its infancy," as Belfield titled it, but they had found glory not hardship in being a part of "a day of small things in the college's history." Belfield took pride in the fact that "There was no glee club, not a mandolin, a guitar, a fiddle or bones in the college. There was no Greek letter fraternities, composed of men ignorant of the Greek alphabet, no co-eds, no rushes, no teams, no inter-collegiate games, no destruction of private or public property as an exhibition of manliness. Ignorance of these blessings was bliss. Knowing nothing of them we did not cry for them."[47]

They all remembered with great pleasure the Chrestomathian Literary Society, the one extracurricular social organization which the college permitted. This society met every two weeks to debate topics selected for them by the faculty. The faculty minutes of 1852–53 reveal that the first debate topic of the year would be "Is the portraiture of slavery in Uncle Tom's Cabin truthful?" As Stowe's novel had only been published in book form a few months earlier than September 1852, this notation indicates how quickly and widely her antislavery message had been disseminated even out on the western frontier. It must have been difficult for the Chrestomathians to have found a member willing to debate the negative side of the proposition.

On 6 October the topic given to the students was "Are

party organizations favorable to the perpetuity of our Government?" This debate "proving to be very earnest" was continued for the next two meetings. On 3 November the students were asked to consider "Does a liberal education tend to make men more eloquent?" The following spring the students debated a topic which would evoke an equally impassioned discussion today, "Ought capital punishment be abolished?"[48]

Although the literary society was considered to be extracurricular and participation in it activities—debates and the reading of nontext books—not required, it could hardly be regarded as a frivolous pursuit. Like the courses and the prayer meetings, the society was committed to the advancement of the students' intellectual and spiritual growth. For the classic Latin prescription of *"mens sana in corpore sano"* these nineteenth-century pedagogues had replaced the word *body* with the word *soul*. The college left the students to their own devices to procure a sound body. The necessity of providing physical education courses, a gymnasium, organized sports and coaches would never have occurred to them. The students, nevertheless, did have young bodies that demanded physical exercise, and the means devised to meet that need were vigorous and varied.

"The claims on physical exercise were so great in sawing wood and doing chores [for the college] that the gymnasium and outdoor recreation were rendered unnecessary," John Windsor would remember. "Still we had some first-class baseball games ... though the game as we knew it would doubtless astonish the professionals of today." And Belfield recalled "Healthy games were played. ... The Mississippi River furnished boating, fishing, swimming, skating. The neighboring woods on the island and on both sides of the river afforded game. The writer remembers many a weary tramp with an old double-barrelled, muzzle-loading shotgun, a family relic, which did good execution at both ends. ... The present vigorous health of the early graduates who are now over sixty years of age, testifies that the brutality of football as now played is not a necessary foundation of a healthy manhood. ... The college life was studious, but it was not dull. On the contrary, it was heartily enjoyed, and is remembered with satisfaction."[49] It is an idyllic picture of college life on the prairie that these first alumni have given to their successors.

Of the tensions within their own college, however, there is no evidence that the students knew anything—the disagreements among the professors, the mutual suspicion felt by faculty and trustees toward each other, and the continuing pressure within the Board of Trustees to change the college's location. The withdrawal of the Southern states and the outbreak of the Civil War in 1861 which brought a tragic conclusion to the strife of the 1850s did not come as nearly a great surprise to the students as did the sudden withdrawal of the college from Davenport in 1858, which brought an end to a similar stormy decade between town and gown. For the latter event neither students nor faculty had been forewarned or prepared to accept.

4

The Big Move:

From River City to Saints' Rest

1858–1861

The decision in 1858 to move Iowa College from Davenport to a raw, recently-founded village on the open prairie some one hundred and twenty miles to the west was not a sudden and impetuous response of the trustees to the city council's forcing once again a street through the campus, as legend has long asserted. Great events in the life of any institution or a nation are seldom the result of a single, easily definable cause.

Dissatisfaction with Davenport had been evident among some of the trustees from the very beginning, and that hostility toward the college's host city had not lessened with time. It was only after a divisive and acrimonious debate that the trustees had voted to remain in Davenport in 1854, and in spite of the delight that both the faculty and students expressed in their new facility at the top of Brady Street hill, this sentiment was not shared by a unanimous board. To all the old arguments used against Davenport from the time of the college's incorporation in 1847, there were now in the mid-1850s some compelling new reasons that the college should seek another location farther west. No one, not even John Holbrook, had anticipated how rapidly the central and western parts of the state would become populated by the continuing flow of immigrants into the state. In recognition of this demographic phenomenon, the new state constitution

87

adopted in 1857 had specified that the state capital must be moved from Iowa City where it had been located since territorial days to the rapidly growing community at the site of old Fort Des Moines at the junction of the Raccoon and Des Moines rivers. The new capital would obviously become within the next few years the state's major metropolitan center.

Moreover, within the eastern section of the state new colleges were being established which would be seeking students in an area in which Iowa College had previously had no rivals. James Harlan, a resident of Mount Pleasant in southeast Iowa and a political figure of some prominence in the Whig party, had written Julius Reed in 1853, to inform him that the small Methodist academy in his home town now had three teachers "and it is intended to be of collegiate grade. About one year since the [Methodist] Church also authorised the commencement of a college edifice at Mount Vernon."[1]

No longer could the Congregationalists scoff at the Methodists for having only "uneducated circuit riders" for ministers. When three years later the trustees invited Ray Palmer to become president of Iowa College, with some reluctance they had to inform him that "the Methodists have an institution at Mt. Pleasant, the Baptists at Burlington, the O. S. Presbyterians at Dubuque, and the N. S. Presbyterians a 'collegiate institute' at Kossuth, Des Moines Co." But they hastened to dismiss these new arrivals on the collegiate scene: "none of these have any considerable number of students, any [scientific] apparatus, libraries, or have made any proficiency in collegiate training," they assured Palmer. "We are not going too far in saying that no one of them has the same hold upon public opinion in the state as *Iowa College*."[2]

The trustees were not as confident of that hold as they professed, however. The Methodists greatly outnumbered the Congregationalists in Iowa, and if their churches gave active support to Iowa Wesleyan and Cornell, these colleges could over the next few years surpass Iowa College in facilities, staff and student body. Moreover, here were five new liberal arts colleges as well as a state university at Iowa City, all being established within a sixty-mile wide strip along the eastern border of the state. There were also the three well-established colleges across the river in Illinois and Wisconsin. Yet in all of the land west of Iowa City to the Missouri river, some 250 miles distant, there was not a single institution of higher education. The opportunity for a college located in the central part of the state to attract students and financial support could not be denied. Trustee John Holbrook's advice in 1847 to delay the decision on a location for Iowa College until the state was more fully settled seemed much more prescient in 1856.

Although Ephraim Adams may have hoped that the question of location had been finally and irrevocably settled by the trustees in 1854 when they voted to build a fine new building on the highest bluff in Davenport, the questioning of that decision had never ceased. Even before the building was completed, the word was being circulated among the Congregational churches of Iowa that there was a growing conviction among the trustees that a serious error had been made. Overtures over the next couple of years were made by several communities—Anamosa, Maquoketa, Des Moines, even towns as far north and west as Webster City and Fort Dodge, indicating they would welcome Iowa College in their midst and would show themselves to be generous hosts. The most attractive offer of all, however, came from one of the smallest and newest of the communities—the village of Grinnell in Poweshiek County, some sixty miles west of Iowa City and fifty miles east of Des Moines.

At the time that the trustees decided in July 1854 to remain in Davenport, the settlement at Grinnell was only four months old and consisted of a single communal dwelling and a country store. It was unusual among the early towns in Iowa in that it had not been established on any navigable river to provide either an avenue or easy water transportation or timber for building. Instead it had been platted upon the open, treeless prairie, a good ten miles from the nearest stream. From the moment that the first crude shelter had been hastily erected, this incipient community had attracted the attention of the Congregationalists of Iowa, thanks to the enterprise of its energetic founder in publicizing himself and his mission.

Josiah Bushnell Grinnell was born in New Haven, Vermont, on 22 December 1821, the second of four sons of Myron Grinnell, a hardscrabble farmer who also served as the town's schoolmaster. Ambitious to obtain an education beyond that offered by his father in the local grammar school, the boy himself taught in country schools during the winter months in order to attend an academy in nearby Vergennes and then to enroll at Oneida Institute located near Utica, New York. This institution, under the presidency of Beriah Green, one of the founders of the American Anti-Slavery Society, had earned the reputation of being the most radical college in the country both in its nonclassical curriculum and in its political views, even exceeding Oberlin in its abolitionist zeal. Here Grinnell was thoroughly indoctrinated in the politics of President Green and the college's chief patron, the wealthy philanthropist Gerrit Smith. Even William Lloyd Garrison's teachings were not radical enough for the fiery, young Grinnell, who would later state, "The non-resistant doctrines of Garrison ... were not welcome to me whose blood leaped in a warm, youthful challenge."[3]

Following his graduation in 1843 from Oneida without a recognized degree, for Oneida was not authorized by the State Regents of New York to confer college degrees because of its extreme radicalism, Grinnell took his first western trip to serve as colporteur for the American Tract Society in distributing Christian literature in Wisconsin. Always eager to get his views before the public, Grinnell sent biweekly articles to the New York *Tribune,* which its noted editor, Horace Greeley, found interesting enough to publish. It was while in Wisconsin, according to his biographer, that Grinnell first conceived of the idea of founding "a religious and educational community" somewhere in the prairie lands.[4]

90

Returning East in 1844, Grinnell entered the Theological Seminary at Auburn, New York. Upon being ordained in 1846, he accepted a Congregational pastorate near Albany, before going to Washington, D.C., to establish the first Congregational church in the nation's capital in 1850. There he found "the air was filled with the poisonous miasmatic breath of slavery."[5] His extreme antislavery sermons soon got him into difficulty. Threats upon his life forced him into a hasty retreat north.

In New York City he accepted another Congregational pastorate, organized a school for newsboys and homeless urchins, and conducted open-air meetings for any passerby who might be interested in hearing his religious and social views. He occasionally had Horace Greeley in attendance at these soapbox meetings, and out of this developing friendship was born the most firmly established legend of the man who was to give his name to an Iowa town and its college. Grinnell would ever after proudly boast that when, concerned about his health, he went to Horace Greeley to ask advice as to what he should do with his life, Greeley responded, "Go West, young man, go West. There is health in the country and room away from our crowds of idlers and imbeciles. Go West and grow up with the country." These words were to become immortal, to rank along with Greeley's impassioned "On to Richmond" at the outbreak of the Civil War as the editor's most memorable sayings. That it was J. B. Grinnell who was told by Greeley to "Go West" remains the one "fact" about Grinnell's life the general public still remembers today. As a legend it is as endearing as it is enduring.

Unfortunately, according to Greeley, there is no truth in it. Like Marie Antoinette's famous "Let them eat cake," it was denied by the person to whom it was attributed, even though it was appropriate to the person and the occasion and should have been said. Greeley would spend the rest of his life vigorously protesting that he had never given this advice to Grinnell or to anyone else, and patiently pointing out that the real source was an editorial by John Soule which appeared in the Terre Haute, Indiana, *Express*.[6] But legends never die, nor do they fade away, especially when effectively promoted by so accomplished a publicist as Grinnell.

Even had it been given, Greeley's advice would not have been necessary. Grinnell's eyes were already turned toward the West for he had not forgotten his dream of founding his ideal community. What Grinnell needed at the moment was not advice but the financial means to tour the West in search of a site, and this Greeley did provide by assigning him to cover the Illinois State Fair in August 1853. After fulfilling this assignment, Grinnell made an exploratory trip farther west through northern Missouri and then back across Iowa. On this long trip, he discovered that there was not only health but also wealth to be had in the country, and the latter interested him even more than health. Grinnell had always evinced so absorbing an interest in both pietism and profits as to make him somewhat suspect to both the capitalist and the preacher to whom he looked for support. Like Rockefeller, Grinnell could solemnly say, "The Good Lord gave me my money," but just as devoutly he accepted the scriptural maxim, "The Lord helps him who helps himself."

Grinnell would always have the good fortune of making advantageous contacts, often quite fortuitously, but it was his own ambition and ability to take full advantage of those contacts that he owed his success. On this ground tour of the West he was to meet two men who were to change both his own future and that of Iowa College. In Iowa, he came across Julius Reed, who was visiting the Congregational churches on behalf of the AHMS. For the first time, Grinnell learned of Iowa's Congregational college in Davenport, upon which Reed was happy to discourse at great length, and Grinnell was equally happy to listen, for a new college was an essential part of Grinnell's plan for his ideal community. Reed did more than sing the praises of Iowa College. He filled Grinnell's head with statistics about the state of Iowa—its rapid growth, increasing wealth, and the rosy projections that one could make of its unlimited advancement. Before Grinnell left the state, he knew it was here that he must settle—not Wisconsin, and certainly not the slave state of Missouri where he found the environment as poisonous as that of the nation's capital.

It was a second chance meeting that he had while crossing the state of Illinois on the Rock Island railroad that would determine the precise location in which he would establish his community. On the train, he happened to encounter a couple of slave hunters who were going into Illinois to return a fugitive slave. Grinnell, as always, could not resist expressing his own views on slavery which so antagonized his travelling companions that they threatened to throw him off the train at the next stop. At this point, an impressive elderly man intervened and called a conductor to put these threatening bullies in their place. Grinnell's newfound friend then invited Grinnell to share his private compartment and introduced himself as Henry Farnam, the railroad financier who had built the Rock Island line. In the long ride across Illinois, there was ample time for talk. Farnam had been impressed with Grinnell's standing up to his opponents, and soon he was confiding in Grinnell that he had plans for extending his line across Iowa to the Missouri river. He suggested that Grinnell might be interested in establishing his community somewhere along this projected route, preferably at that point where Farnam was confident that a north-south line from Minnesota to Missouri, which was also in the early planning stage, would cross his road. If Grinnell was interested, Farnam offered to get him in touch with Theodore Bacon, Farnam's engineer, who would inform him of the projected route, provided that Grinnell would keep "the facts from the public."[7] Here was "insider information" which a later generation would hold illegal, but to men of Grinnell's day was simply known as "getting ahead."

Farnam was not acting out of pure altruism in letting Grinnell get this inside tip of the railroad's westward expansion. It was always to the railroad's interest to promote settlement along its lines, and Farnam saw in this eager young idealist/capitalist exactly the kind of promoter who could carry through on the building up of the country. Grinnell, after meeting Farnam, saw no need to find a navigable river upon which to locate his colony. The West's future lay with railroads, not river traffic.

Upon arriving back in New York, Grinnell lost no time in getting in touch with Theodore Bacon, who had already been instructed by Farnam to provide the young man with full information regarding the projected route of the Mississippi-Missouri line. Bacon told Grinnell that this extension of the Rock Island line would cross Iowa from its eastern terminus in Davenport, through Iowa City to Des Moines and then on to its western terminal in Council Bluffs on the Missouri river. The road would then be in a position to become a part of the great transcontinental line extending to California and the Pacific Ocean.

Bacon advised Grinnell to look into the acquisition of land in the northeast section of Poweshiek County. This was the highest point of land lying between the Iowa and the Des Moines rivers. There was a suitable pass through the hills immediately to the west allowing for easier grading and the railroad's surveyors had already determined that this would be the route they would follow. Bacon was also confident from information he had regarding the proposed north-south line that this would indeed be the point where the two lines would meet. He even gave Grinnell the precise location as being Township 80 North, Range 16 West, and promised Grinnell that should he go out to see the land for himself he would find "a large flag pole as the controlling point in our survey," which Grenville Dodge, assistant engineer, had planted. This land was still unsettled and unclaimed, but Bacon advised Grinnell if he was interested, "Lose no time for there will be a rush for the land and the best will be taken—the boys mean to take it up."[8]

Grinnell needed no prodding to leap into action. He had already published notices in Greeley's *Tribune* and the Congregationalists' leading journal, *The Independent,* stating his intent to establish a Congregational colony in Iowa and inviting applications from those few men of "good character and high ideals and some means" who might be interested in joining him in this enterprise.

Of the several responses he received, Grinnell, with his usual hard-headed practicality, brought three men as associates into the enterprise—Homer Hamlin, a Congregational minister from Wellington, Ohio, to add to the proper ministerial tone of the undertaking; Henry Hamilton, a knowledgeable young surveyor who could provide the technical skills for platting the land acquired; and a little later, Dr. Thomas Holyoke of Searsport, Maine, as the new community would need a physician in its midst. Grinnell met with the first two men in Cleveland on 23 February 1854, and they then hurried on to Davenport to meet with Bacon. At Iowa City, they entered claims for 5,000 acres of land, sight unseen, at the point designated by Bacon.

Hamilton went back east to secure additional funds as Grinnell, Hamlin and Holyoke pushed on west to find the magic flagpole around which their land and their hopes were now centered. Within three weeks after Grinnell's meeting with his associates in Cleveland, the town site had been determined. With a frenzied flurry, this young man had gone West and was ready for the country to grow up to meet his own great expectations.[9]

In paying for the 5,000 acres for which they had hastily entered a claim, Grinnell and his associates invested the resources that were available to them. Grinnell and Hamilton put in the largest amounts. In 1852, while still in New York, Grinnell had married Julia Chapin, the daughter of a well-to-do family in Springfield, Massachusetts, and it was largely her money that enabled Grinnell to purchase the largest portion of land. Hamilton had some capital of his own and was able to borrow additional funds on his trip East. Dr. Holyoke purchased a smaller share, but Hamlin, a poor Congregational minister, had nothing to offer but God's blessing on the enterprise. Providentially at this moment, a fifth town founder, Amos Bixby, appeared on the scene. He was able to contribute enough to acquire the fourth and smallest share of the town land.

Bixby, arriving in the Grinnell area two months after the other four, came from Norridgewock, Maine. The entire Bixby family in the early 1850s were motivated to head west. Several of Amos's brothers caught the "gold rush" fever and headed for California, but Amos, with his wife and young son, perhaps influenced by the publicity given to Grinnell's proposed colony, came straight to Poweshiek County. With money borrowed from his father, he was able to acquire 160 acres of the colony claim. He confidently wrote his brother in California, "We are expecting a large town to be built up here. I suppose I could sell 40 acres of my land for $8 to $10 per acre. ... It is one vast garden spot with a fine climate ... better than Minnesota." Besides farming, Bixby, who had a license to practice law, planned to open the first law office in Grinnell.[10]

With Bixby's entry into the association, the proposed town was divided into four unequal quadrants, with Grinnell taking the largest portion in the northeast area, Hamilton getting the southeast quadrant, and Holyoke and Bixby acquiring the two small areas to the west. This initial four-part division roughly approximated what would later become the four wards of the city of Grinnell.

Almost from the first, tension existed between Grinnell and Hamilton for control of the town. Grinnell appreciated Hamilton's technical skills, but resented his young partner's attempt to direct the development of the community. The first quarrel erupted over the naming of the town. Hamilton wanted to call it "Stella," which he considered a nice classical allusion to the town's becoming the "Star of the West." After a heated discussion and an impassioned plea from Grinnell that this ideal community had been his idea and should bear his name, J.B. won out. The newly acquired U.S. post office would bear the name of Grinnell, Iowa. When the first commercial establishments—a store, a blacksmith shop and stage coach stop—made their appearance south of the proposed line of the railroad tracks, Grinnell brought an abrupt end to this development by giving some of his land to form a central square and persuading an old friend, Loyal Phelps, to establish a hotel near the square with the expectation that this would attract other commercial enterprises.

The final point of controversy came over a location for the collegiate institute which Grinnell was determined to establish as quickly as possible. The only site that could possibly be considered scenic on this otherwise uniformly flat prairie land was the slightly rolling elevation in the southwestern corner. Again Grinnell, determined to have the college on his land, set aside twenty acres to serve as a campus. The land Hamilton had thought appropriate became the town cemetery, and only the dead would occupy for all eternity the town's one claim to a distinctive spot of natural beauty. This local north-south sectionalism of rivalry and mutual distrust which the Grinnell-Hamilton feud had generated would be perpetuated by the residents of both sections long after the personal ambitions of the founders had been forgotten.

J. B. Grinnell would have laughed at the cautious fears some of the Iowa Band had had about making foolish haste in establishing a college after having talked about it for seven years. Haste for J.B. was never foolish, it was eminently practical. As soon as he had spotted the surveyor's flag pole, he fully intended to have his institution underway within two years. All that he had in the way of assets was the land he had laid claim to, but with the much discussed railroad line now inching its way west, the value of this land would give his college its needed endowment. In an interesting way, the old scheme of Asa Turner, Gaylord and Reed of building Iowa College in Buchanan County—a plan which the AHMS had so contemptuously dismissed as being based on risky and crass land speculation—had found new life by a far more determined promoter, who no more shunned speculation than he did haste. Grinnell, to be sure, had only 5,000 acres to put into the game as compared with the 20,000 acres Turner had envisioned, but this asset would be enough to provide a larger endowment fund than Iowa College had when it finally began operations in 1848.

To establish an initial fund for the institution, 160 acres, divided into 348 town lots were set aside for its benefit. Grinnell gave outright 20 acres for the campus and Hamilton, the most generous contributor of all, pledged a percentage of the profits he would realize from the sale of 1,200 acres of his land to the fund, a gift which he felt should have given him the privilege of choosing the college's location. Amos Bixby a little later contributed $400 in cash to the fund. In addition, each new head of the family coming into the settlement after 1855 had to make an additional contribution of twenty dollars to the college fund over and above the price paid for a town lot. This surcharge entitled the purchaser to be an "Elector" of trustees for the fund. Because the town-lot owners were to have a vote in selecting the management of the fund, Hamilton had wanted to call the proposed institution "The People's College," but he lost that battle as well. On 26 January 1855, the "Literary Fund of Grinnell University" was formally incorporated. The stated purpose of the Fund was "to promote the educational, social, moral and religious interests of this place, known as Grinnell, Iowa."[11]

Considering the remoteness of its location, the difficulty in obtaining building material, and its dependence upon deep wells for its only water supply, Grinnell's little community grew surprisingly fast. By the end of 1854, there were 58 people in the town where only nine months earlier there had been nothing but a flag pole and a gleam in J.B.'s eye. Two years later 246 people were in residence, and the "ideal community" had become a reality.[12]

Such a well-publicized venture on Iowa's frontier had not escaped the notice of the Congregational ministers throughout eastern Iowa. As readers of *The Independent*, they had seen Grinnell's initial notice of his intention to establish a colony, and there had been much discussion of its rapid development in Poweshiek County. Julius Reed had been in correspondence with Grinnell since their first meeting in the fall of 1853, and George Magoun's acquaintance predated that. He had first met Grinnell in Wisconsin when the young man had been distributing literature for the American Tract Society.[13] Both Reed and Magoun could assure their brethren that here was a young man in a hurry to get to the top—someone to keep a close eye on as he made the climb. In response to Reed's recommendation, the trustees of Iowa College at their annual meeting in July 1854 elected Grinnell to the Board, only four months after his arrival in the state.

Grinnell made sure that the Iowa College trustees kept an eye on him and his fledgling community. As soon as he arrived in Poweshiek County he had sent out strong feelers respecting a possible fusion of Iowa College with his "University," which at this point existed only in the imagination of Grinnell and his associates. Grinnell knew that at the July 1854 meeting of the trustees the question of Iowa College's remaining in Davenport would be voted upon, and he did his best to influence this vote. Harvey Adams reported to Salter on 20 June, one month before the meeting, that Grinnell had stopped in Davenport on his way East to bring his wife to Iowa:

> Bro. Lane conversed with him about the Coll. He offered to give as his part, $1000 cash, 200 acres of land, and 3/4 of the town plot, which is laid off into lots. The whole plot is 200 acres, so that 3/4 of it will be 150 acres, including streets. He advised by all means that I should go direct to see the Colony, and see the people individually and lay the matter before them, giving it as his opinion that they would pledge $10,000, in moneys or lands, or in both.[14]

This considerably exaggerated proposal of what would be offered Iowa College if it moved to Grinnell was an unabashed attempt upon Grinnell's part to buy the trustees' vote. It didn't succeed. Grinnell got his election to the Board, but he failed to get the decision he wanted as to the College's future location. Always optimistic, Grinnell was confident that the future lay with him, and he was determined to keep up the effort to make the anti-Davenport minority on the Board into a pro-Grinnell majority. If he couldn't lure them with money, he could perhaps frighten them into compliance with the prospect of having another and better-endowed Congregational college in Iowa located near the center of the state.

Grinnell's continuing pressure on the Iowa College trustees had its effect. Even that staunch supporter of keeping the college in Davenport, Ephraim Adams, began to squirm. Before work had even begun on the new building high up on the Brady Street hill, Adams wrote to Salter in December 1854, reporting on the progress being made on the new campus, "The boarding-house does work well, and I hope Burlington will send some [students] to try it. College grounds are not yet fenced because the article of posts is not to be had. Shall we press the college building along or halt now by reason of the Grinnell movement?"[15] Salter remained committed to Davenport, and the new building was "pressed along," but the uneasiness among the trustees did not abate.

In the spring of 1855, Ephraim Adams on his tour of northwest Iowa to find a suitable location for establishing a Congregational colony of his own, decided to go by way of Grinnell to take a brief look at J.B.'s ideal community. Adams was not impressed. Forced to stay over longer than he had intended due to the lameness of his horse, Adams recorded in his diary in his usual telegraphic style, "In a fix surely. Here in Grinnell the colony. The shrewd money-making Christians. Here in a fix. Horseless horseless. Buy some oxen and go ahead."[16] It was J. B. Grinnell, however, who was really going ahead in a colony that was already flourishing. The university must be in operation as quickly as possible before Iowa College became too firmly fixed in Davenport.

While at Oneida, along with the other radical ideals he

100

had acquired, Grinnell became an advocate of women's rights through his friendship with Elizabeth Cady Stanton, a pioneer in the women's movement, and her husband Henry Stanton. Grinnell's allegiance to this reform was further encouraged by his wife Julia. There would be no debate over the question of the proposed university's being coeducational. Indeed the first building planned was to be for the Female Department with a curriculum modelled after that of Mount Holyoke, which Julia had attended in Massachusetts. The Male Department, located at a decorous distance from the females, would come later when funds permitted. In the meantime a preparatory department would be opened for both sexes. Enough progress had been made for Grinnell to issue a circular on 1 January 1856, addressed to "the People of Central Iowa; Families emigrating to the west; and benevolent Friends throughout the Country." Grinnell was willing to use precious funds to give his circular the widest possible distribution, for he was a great believer in "It pays to advertise."

In this circular, great emphasis was given to the religious and moral character of the proposed university. "The carrying out of our original designs have seemed with Divine favor to be easy accomplishments," Grinnell proudly boasted. "The making of a Home, the forming of a Christian Church; and an Institution of Learning, were the first objects of concern, and having succeeded in the first two Enterprises, it remains for us to call attention to our third ... which is the Establishment of Grinnell University."

The circular then gave extravagant description to the town's location:

> Our elevation and the purity of the water have contributed to health in such degree that all of us ... have passed a second Autumn [and] have been exempt from both Ague and Chills, and from Fevers. ... A pre-occupancy here by persons of intelligence and religious character has secured a oneness in public sentiment and moral force, we think, seldom met with in older communities. ... We are so

far fortified against the vice and woes of Intemperance,
that the establishment of a grogery [sic] on our town property causes a reversion of the land to the former proprietor.

The community, in short, was what some of the less temper-
ate in the surrounding countryside sneeringly referred to as
"Saints' Rest."

Grinnell made clear that his proposed institution would
be more than the traditional classical liberal arts college. It
would be a true university, for in addition to the regular college department there would be "a Normal Branch especially
for Teachers," and an Agricultural Department to teach the
sons of farmers scientific agriculture: the analysis of soils in
the college's laboratories, seed testing in the experimental
fields, and the proper use of labor-saving machinery. Here
again Grinnell was drawing upon his Oneida background of
that institution's work-study program and with this proposed Agricultural Department, Grinnell was responding to
the same spirit that a few years later led to the establishment of a land-grant college at Ames.

This circular was designed not just to promote the cause
of higher education in Iowa but also as an inducement to get
more people to buy his land. A special pitch was made to
prospective immigrants: "a sum of money usually required to
purchase a house lot ... will now purchase here acres of rich
and most desirable prairie. ... It is not a safe presumption
that the present comparative low prices can long obtain, and
if you are moved by a sense of duty to early co-operation with
us ... we hope that you will make an early decision." In other
words, don't walk, run to your nearest railroad station and
get here to grab your bargain.

Grinnell confidently promised that the Preparatory Department would open within three months, and the Normal
Department would be open in the fall. He then listed the faculty—five in the Preparatory Department, including himself
as President of the University and Professor of History,
Rhetoric and Elocution, and five in the Female Department

(four women and one man as an instructor in vocal music) with an additional lady principal yet to be secured. Only a community insider would know that Grinnell had drafted into the university service almost all of the local talent who had a specialty to offer.[17]

As a piece of promotional literature, Grinnell's widely circulated circular was a masterpiece. Few, if any, future pieces of college literature would ever equal it in exuberance and promise. One can be assured that it was read with great care followed by much discussion by the trustees of Iowa College to whom it was especially directed. All it would take would be some small occurrence in Davenport to tip a majority of the wavering trustees over to Grinnell's side.

Early in 1857, the city council of Davenport unwittingly obliged Grinnell by providing that incident needed to convince a majority of the trustees that the continuance of the college at its present location had become impossible. The council informed the college that again the rapid growth of the city had made it absolutely essential to extend Main Street, which lay between Brady and Harrison streets, on up to the top of the bluff. This promised to be a much more serious intrusion through the campus than had been the earlier street extension which had forced the college to move from its original site.

This time the college did not quietly acquiesce. The Executive Committee of the Board of Trustees prepared to bring suit against the city. "Before anything could be done," Magoun reported to the full board, "the order was executed, the fence broken down, and a pass of forty feet opened in line with the west side of Main Street, by destroying the trees in that part of the grounds. ... This waste and destruction are irreparable, but the trespass was committed before your committee could act."[18] Many of the trustees were ready at that point to give notice that the college would leave Davenport, but at a meeting of the Board on 20 April, a reluctant majority agreed to wait until the courts had decided the issue.[19]

The district court issued a temporary injunction halting the actual construction of the street until an appeal by the city to the Iowa Supreme Court could be adjudicated. While awaiting that decision, the college was courted by some eight communities with serious proposals of what they could offer in the way of a dowry to effect such a happy marriage. The town of Grinnell, of course, was the most persistent and generous of the suitors.

Just prior to the trustees annual meeting and the Commencement exercises of 1858, the Supreme Court handed down its decision. It upheld the right of eminent domain. The interests of the public must prevail over private property rights. The street would go through the campus. For the first time, the people of Davenport realized that it might very possibly lose Iowa College. A small group of leading citizens headed by Hiram Price fully appreciated what this loss would mean both economically and culturally to the town. They made a desperate appeal to the Board of Trustees not to move. They asked the Board to give them the reasons why it felt compelled to leave. This request Magoun, speaking for the Board, answered with a bill of indictment against the city of Davenport for its "want of interest in co-operation with us ... that has been both painful and amazing considering the importance and value of such an institution to the city." Even at this late date, however, the trustees did not slam the door in the face of those asking them to reconsider their decision. They informed Hiram Price and company that Davenport would be placed in the same status as the other eight communities who had made bids for the college and the trustees would then decide as to who most wanted their institution.[20] The town's response was to offer Iowa College still another location in the city: "thirty-five acres of a beautiful bluff in the lower portion of the city, commanding one of the most magnificent views on the river, [seemingly, Davenport had an inexhaustible supply of bluffs] at the low price of $100 per acre, with twenty years to pay it in, at ten per cent per annum."[21] This was hardly an attractive enough offer to keep

Davenport in the running. In fact, the race was already over. J. B. Grinnell had won handily, and both the town of Davenport and the trustees knew it.

The faculty, however, had not been a party to the trustees' deliberation throughout all of these long months of controversy. Although as upset as the trustees by the prospect of a major street invading their campus, none of the faculty except Daniel Lane could imagine the college abandoning its beautiful campus and superb facilities. All four of the faculty had bought homes in the city and they had fully expected to remain in Davenport for the remainder of their lives. Bullen and Sheldon had especially strong hopes for the future of the college at Davenport. While the trustees were mulling over Grinnell's repeated bids, these two professors of mathematics and science, with the active cooperation of William Salter, had been wooing a wealthy iron manufacturer of Burlington, Charles Hendrie, to provide sufficient funds to enable the college to establish a "Scientific and Mechanical School" at Iowa College in Davenport. These efforts had paid off handsomely, and Hendrie in the spring of 1858 pledged $15,000 of Burlington and Missouri railroad bonds to endow a "Professorship of Civil Engineering and Scientific Mechanics." This gift would be lost if the college should transport itself to Grinnell, far removed from the mechanics in Burlington whom Hendrie wanted to educate.[22] The faculty was quite willing to put up with a street through the campus in order to keep the college in Davenport.

The faculty never fully understood that the trustees' unhappiness with Davenport had far deeper roots than the city's unpleasant habit of running streets through the campus. When belatedly they realized in early July that the decision had been made to leave, their response was immediate and bitterly angry. On 8 July 1858 the faculty minutes reported, "The Faculty were unanimous in their opinion that their resignation should be tendered to the Trustees ... and Prof. Ripley was appointed to prepare a report on this subject." Apparently not even Daniel Lane dared to vote against his colleagues by whom he was already regarded as a pariah. Two days later the faculty met and approved of Ripley's report "Resignation of the Faculty of Iowa College" in which Ripley accused the trustees of having no faith in the faculty and regarding them as being "unfit to teach in a college."[23]

On 28 July a letter to the editors, signed only "X," appeared in the Davenport *Gazette*. It raised the interesting question as to "whether the trustees morally and legally can use this donated property in any other locality in the State. ... Would it be a violation of trust? I make this suggestion for the consideration of the wise and just."[24] Although the identity of X was never revealed, the trustees generally believed that Ripley was the author.

The town never followed up on X's suggestion. Perhaps a majority of the citizens were as unhappy with the college as the trustees were with the town. An editorial in the Davenport *Daily Morning News* more accurately expressed town opinion than did Hiram Price and his associates:

> We think we can do without a College just now, especially such a one as is now soon to depart forever from our midst. The free schools of the city afford the means of obtaining a good practical education ... without undergoing a four year's process in humbugging at a one-horse College, for sake of getting a disregarded commission in the army of letters, written in a tongue [Latin] which nine-tenths of the holders cannot read in three weeks after they get them.[25]

As for the students, there is no evidence that their views on the move were ever sought by either trustees or faculty. Commencement was held on 14 July as scheduled, but no mention was made that this would be the last collegiate exercise to be held on the Iowa College campus. The only mention of the students was a sneering comment in the same Davenport *Daily Morning News* editorial that "we hardly suppose there are ten parents ... who, in this enlightened age, would think of sending a youth out there to receive an education that would fit him for the battles of this world."

The paper's conjecture proved overly generous in its estimation of ten. The students essentially responded as had the faculty. Not a single student transferred along with his college to "out there."

Final arrangements for the merging of Iowa College with Grinnell University were soon made. A committee of the trustees, headed by Magoun and Reed visited the town of Grinnell in the late summer, and the marriage of the two institutions was quickly and easily arranged. The assets of both institutions would be pooled into a single endowment. J. B. Grinnell would provide the land he had promised for a campus, and Iowa College would provide the name for the institution and essentially the same traditional classical curriculum. Both institutions would provide members to the newly constituted Board of Trustees. It must have pained J. B. to have to give up the proud name of Grinnell University for the less distinctive name of Iowa College, but he was never one to sacrifice practical advantage for personal vanity, big as his ego was. After all, it had been essentially the name Iowa College, with all that that name conveyed in terms of historical precedence and religious affiliation, that he had been eager to purchase.

On 27 September 1858, the Board of Trustees of Iowa College formally voted "to remove Iowa College to Grinnell at the commencement of the next college year or as soon thereafter as the interests of the institution will permit."[26] The trustees cast their vote with varying degrees of enthusiasm. Nearly all accepted the inevitability of this move, however. Of those who had held positions of influence during the Davenport years, only William Salter of the trustees and Theron Baldwin of the Society for the Promotion of Collegiate and Theological Education at the West remained irreconcilable to the decision. There is no record that Salter attended any further meetings of the Board and within five years he resigned as trustee, never again to return in spite of strong urging from J. B. Grinnell and others. Nor could the college any longer expect Baldwin to be its strongest supporter within the Society.[27]

J.B., of course, was exultant. As soon as the vote had been taken, he dashed off a quick note to the editors of the New York *Independent* informing them, "An important event related to Education and Religion has just occurred in Iowa. It is the removal of Iowa College from Davenport to Grinnell. ... This is the merging of two interests in one, at a central locality which now enlists, it is presumed, the sympathies of 150 Churches, not to mention a large class of intelligent, enterprising Citizens who associate the first College of Iowa and the high standing of her allumni [sic] with the success of the Colleges of New England."[28]

On 4 August, the trustees sold the college building and grounds to the Bishopric of the Episcopalian Church of Iowa for $36,000. It was this impressive asset which Iowa College had promised to contribute as its share to the endowment of Iowa College in Grinnell after any outstanding debts the college might have incurred had been paid. That stipulation proved to be more burdensome than either Iowa College or Grinnell University had anticipated. In making the last audit of the college books, Julius Reed discovered that his fellow trustee and for the past several years treasurer of the college, Joseph Lambrite, through malfeasance and/or stupidity in his investment of college funds had created an outstanding deficit which would consume most of the college's assets. How much Lambrite may have pocketed for himself and how much he had simply lost by giving the college's endorsement to bank notes for those who could not pay the loans they received and for which the college was now held responsible has never been revealed. All that Reed knew was that after all of these outstanding debts had been paid, only $9,000 remained of the $36,000 Iowa College had hoped to bring as its contribution to the endowment at Grinnell.[29] This loss was the final cruel blow to befall the college during the troubled Davenport final era.

In mid-November, Julius Reed shipped off to Grinnell 1,000 feet of lumber and 8,000 laths to be used in finishing the college building on its new campus and to build library shelves. He himself brought with him in a wagon "our scanty library, our few pieces of apparatus, our meagre nucleus of a museum, and the old safe containing the college papers, and $9,000."[30] There had been no room in the wagon for the prized college bell, so it was left behind for the Episcopalians.

All of Iowa College's worldly goods packed into one wagon—not much of an estate to show after twelve years of labor and sacrifice and prayer; not much return for Ephraim Adams's travelling thousands of miles picking up a dollar here and a dollar there; not much for a minister's wife with a bare subsistence household purse to buy food, squeezing a few cents out of that purse each week to meet the pledge she had made to give fifty dollars a year to the college fund; not much for a professor teaching six or eight courses a day on a salary of $500 a year. Eight years of college operation, and only ten graduates of the Bachelor of Arts program. There must have been those who wondered as that one little wagon came down Brady Hill and headed west if these years had been simply "a tale full of sound and fury, signifying nothing."

The worth of an ideal and its translation into action, however, cannot be measured with an accountants' precision by the listing of credits and debits in dollars and cents. Who could measure the worth of the education which the seven ministers, three lawyers, and one college teacher had received and prized after their four years at Iowa College?[31] Or what that education would mean to the communities to whom they offered their services? And those who had received their secondary education at the Academy—twenty times the number of those who had a B.A. degree—and went into small Iowa towns to offer the fundamentals of grammar and arithmetic—who could begin to evaluate their worth?

Iowa College had had its necessary beginning in Davenport and in spite of all its difficulties had established a reputation and an influence among the collegiate institutions of the West that would endure. Those were assets that far exceeded the value of the packing boxes in the wagon, assets on which several towns in Iowa were prepared to place a monetary value.

It had also been in this decade at Davenport that Iowa College had made two of the most important decisions of its history, decisions which would determine the nature of the institution and would never be revoked or even questioned. The first decision came in 1852 at a moment when the college desperately needed funds to increase the size of the faculty and was at the same time under great pressure from Baldwin's Society to bring about a closer relationship with the New School Presbyterians. An offer came from the Presbyterian Churches of Iowa to contribute funds sufficient to establish an additional professorship at the college. This offer seemed like a gift from Heaven until the trustees heard the conditions that must be accepted: The Presbyterian church would retain full control of that professorship in both the hiring and the firing of its occupants. This restriction the trustees could not accept. This professorship must like all other appointments be free of denominational control. Never would the college establish a religious qualification for any of its trustees, faculty or students. As Father Turner was wont to say, "We are a religious institution in spirit. We are not a sectarian college in practice." The offer was flatly rejected, and thus ended all further cooperation between the Congregationalists and the New School Presbyterians in the maintenance of the college.[32] As President John Nollen rightly claimed a century later, "From the first the founders of Iowa College were faithful to the legacy of liberty. ... They were determined that their new college should be free from ecclesiastical domination."[33]

The second decision of lasting significance was forced upon the trustees in December 1856 when nine young female graduates of the Davenport High School, having met all the admission requirements, applied to Iowa College for admission. With surprising little dissension, the trustees accepted

110

their application. Father Turner apparently spoke the sentiment of a majority of the trustees when he wrote to Magoun in his usual forceful and colorful style:

> In regard to the plan you propose. I should go into it with all my heart. I believe it is the way to do good. It is demanded by the spirit of the age, by the good of the rising generation, and the interests of our great state. And truly by the Cross of Christ. ...
>
> Our brethren could do almost twice as much as teachers if our institution was open to both sexes, for it would very much double the number of students. ... The female class will in after years exert more influence for the college than the male class. A woman never forgets the object of her love—her home, her church, and places where she obtains her education are always close to her and will always be remembered. Men become absorbed in their own affairs and think less of those who have fitted them for their stations. Suppose you educate 100 young ladies in the college. Most of them will soon become wives and mothers, soon have sons and daughters to educate and in a few years they will come back to their alma mater bringing their children with them, and the institution would come to have a warm place in their families. Let them multiply.[34]

Alden Robbins, president of the Board, was even more blunt in his affirmation. "We must go in right away for a Female Department at Iowa College. We can do three times the good with about the same means. ... If we don't go in for doing good the devil will get us all into the net—as he has our Presb. Brethren. ... To my mind the more contact & intercourse of the honorable kind, of course (& no matter if *some* are married & this is not dishonorable before coming to Davenport), of the two sexes, the better it will be for both & for the Trustees."[35]

The young women were admitted to the college, but it was a very qualified admission. They could attend recitation classes with the men if they had their parents' consent, but they were not allowed, curiously enough, to attend the morning prayer sessions or any other formal exercises of the college. By the time the college closed at Davenport there were eighty-two students in the college of which sixteen were women.[36]

The decisions made to keep the college free of sectarian control and to admit women established basic principles of merit which would give to the college its distinction. The ten years at Davenport would be remembered for these decisions if for nothing else. It would be a tale of accomplishment as well as sound and fury, signifying a great deal.

5

Suffering the Trials of Job at Grinnell:

First Trial—The College at War

1861–1865

There was disappointment for both parties to the merger when the wagon carrying Iowa College's material possessions arrived in Grinnell in early December 1858. The metal safe contained not the $36,000 Grinnell had anticipated but only one-fourth of that amount. The library collection was not impressive; many of the books in Iowa College's library had belonged to its faculty and had been reclaimed by them when they resigned. The College's scientific apparatus had been easily accommodated in two small trunks for shipment.[1]

Grinnell University, on the other hand, was not the going concern that J.B.'s circular of 1 January 1856 had promised it would be before the end of that year. The college's one building was still unfinished and the students in the Preparatory Department continued to meet with their instructors in whatever makeshift rooms could be secured in the village. There was no sign or mention of a Normal Department that the circular had promised would be in operation by the spring of 1857. J. B. Grinnell's expectations had far outrun their realization. The difficulties experienced in importing building materials, in finding laborers not otherwise occupied in building houses for the incoming settlers and inspiring them with J.B.'s sense of urgency had seriously delayed these plans. There were not the hundred or more children enrolled in the Preparatory Department; there were at most only one-third that number; and it would be at least two more years before any of them could possibly meet the requirements for admission to the college.[2] The impressive roster of faculty members available and competent to teach in the college as stated in the circular was in reality nothing more than a list of local people whose names came to mind as Grinnell was drafting his circular. Iowa College, as far as being an operating institution, was back where it had been in 1847 when the Articles of Incorporation had been approved by the State of Iowa. Starting de novo was hardly what the trustees had had in mind when they voted for the merger. Of necessity there would have to be a hiatus in the operation of the college for three years. It was not a prospect to warm the trustees' hearts, but if not warm, their hearts were stout, which would prove to be the college's greatest asset in the rough years that lay ahead.

In October 1860, Theron Baldwin, still disgruntled over Iowa College's move to Grinnell, wrote Julius Reed asking for a report on the status of the college in its new location in order that the Society could consider providing further aid for the next academic year. Reed had answered that "I presume in our quiescent state a general statement is all that they [the Directors of the Society] would desire." By "quiescent" Reed obviously was referring to the absence of any college instruction at Grinnell. It was hardly a fitting descriptive adjective to apply to the feverish activity of the previous two years to get classes underway once again. Reed was happy to be able to report to Baldwin as to what had been accomplished since the physical remnants of Iowa College had arrived in Grinnell in December 1858:

> The removal of Iowa College to Grinnell has been consummated. A beautiful site on the north side of town has been secured embracing seventeen acres. The College Building is of brick, three stories high, besides high basement, and forty feet in width and seventy feet in length. It

has cost over $9,000. Two stories are now occupied and the remainder will soon be completed.

The property of the College, of all kinds, at a fair estimate, we think a low estimate, is worth $40,000 above the remaining liabilities of the College.

The Preparatory and English Department were organized in September last and during the present term there have been 77 different pupils, 35 of whom are studying Latin, and of these 35, fifteen are studying Greek, ten are expecting to enter the Freshman class next fall. ...

We are making efforts to organize a Faculty & expect to reopen the College proper next fall, with the confident expectation that Iowa Coll. will at once become highly useful.[3]

J. B. Grinnell's optimism and go-ahead spirit was obviously contagious. Before the college could open its doors for its first freshman class at Grinnell in October 1861, however, much would have happened on the national scene to dampen that optimism.

However absorbing their own internal crises had been to the trustees and faculty during the last years of Iowa College at Davenport, it must have paled to insignificance to them as compared to the crisis that enveloped the nation. The college community, in general committed to the newly organized Republican Party and more specifically to its more radical element of abolitionists, had watched in morbid fascination the country's drunken stumbling toward disunion and Civil War. After the defeat of Free Soil, Free Men and Fremont in 1856 followed by the incredible decision of the Supreme Court in the Dred Scott case of 1857, these Congregational radicals no longer had faith that they could expect justice from Washington—not from that Democratic dough-face President, James Buchanan, not from that slave-holding Chief Justice, Roger Taney—and they wept and prayed for their doomed country. In 1858 they had cheered for that rising political star, Abe Lincoln, in his Senate campaign debates with the Little Giant of the old order, Stephen Douglas, only to be once again bitterly disappointed in American politics. Both their cheers and their tears but further alienated them from their neighbors in Davenport and made their college's departure even more certain and desirable.

What a blessed relief it was in 1859 to have their college safely removed to a community where the trustees and the new faculty they would employ would be accepted as part of the prevailing majority, not as cranks on the lunatic fringe. No need to campaign for a local prohibition option as the college community had futilely done in Davenport. In this town if ever a glass of grog was sold, J.B. would take your land back as his own. No need here to hide one's abolitionist sentiments. In Grinnell one could actively carry on the battle against slavery by providing a way station in one's own home for fugitive slaves from Missouri on their perilous trip northward to freedom in Canada. Ever since the founding of the town in 1854, the people of Grinnell had been eagerly awaiting the promised arrival of the Mississippi-Missouri Railroad line which was laying its track westward from Davenport to Council Bluffs, but a good eight years before the surface railroad finally reached Grinnell in 1863, the town had quite a different transportation line in operation. It had become an important stop for the well-organized Underground Railroad in carrying its precious and illegal traffic eastward to the Great Lakes toward freedom across the border.

Within two months after Iowa College had established itself at Grinnell, there occurred one of the most exciting and historic events in the town's history—the weekend visit of John Brown in late February 1859. Brown had first crossed Iowa in the fall of 1857 on his way to Kansas. Then largely unknown to the general public, Brown had been warmly received in Quaker settlements across Iowa from Springdale in Cedar County to Tabor in the far southwestern corner of the state. Now a year and a half later, Brown was heading back East and the whole nation knew his name, and regarded him with either fear and loathing or admiration and loving. More than any one man he had turned Douglas's "Popular Sovereignty" in Kansas into unpopular slaughter. Convinced that

116

only a great servile insurrection could forever eradicate the cancer of slavery, he was ready to carry his holy crusade into the very heart of the slavocracy. If he could seize the federal arsenal at Harpers Ferry, he would arm the slaves of Virginia and succeed where Nat Turner had failed thirty years earlier. The last demonstration of his fanatical zealotry in the Midwest was a quick foray into Missouri, where he and his small band of fellow raiders killed a slaveholder, stole his horses and filled two wagons with slaves eager to go north. Brown arrived in Tabor with blood on his hands and a price on his head. This time, he received a very cold reception from the peace-loving Quakers, so he hurried on. Arriving in the vicinity of Grinnell on Saturday afternoon, 25 February, he secured his entourage in a grove at the edge to town and then paid a call on J. B. Grinnell, whom he knew to be a dedicated abolitionist. Here he did get a warm welcome. Grinnell not only was willing to house Brown and his company in Grinnell's large wool-storage barn, but so confident was J.B. of the town's sympathy, he dared to show Brown off at the Congregational church on Sunday evening.

The whole town turned out to see the notorious Brown. Among the spectators was a fifteen-year-old girl, Joanna Harris, who had come with her parents from western Pennsylvania in 1852, and after first settling in Lee County, her father had been attracted by J. B. Grinnell's advertisements for settlers in his colony. James Harris had purchased a farm from Grinnell a mile west of town. Ardent abolitionists, the Harrises made their farm home one of the "safe stops" on the Underground Railroad. The child Joanna would later recall, "One night when I came home I found a colored woman with a baby in her arms sitting by the fire. We heard mother and father whispering to one another and realized that preparations were being made. In the morning she and the baby were gone. My brother had taken them on their way. Needless to say all this gave a peculiarly exciting turn to life for us and made us all as alert as crickets to the course of public events, especially those relating to slavery."[4]

The entire Harris family was in the church that Sunday

117

evening to see and hear their hero. Seventy years later, Joanna would relate that dramatic incident to her son-in-law. "I do not recall much of what he [Brown] said, but he denounced the oppression inflicted upon him. I particularly remember the harsh features, the cold, relentless eye and hawklike look of the hero of Osawatamie. He kept men and children alike in a state of awe and in this fact, I suspect, lay much of his ability to do things that most men would not dare to try to do."

Joanna recalled much more vividly Brown's stopping by their school a day later to see their teacher, Leonard Parker. The children followed Parker out to the street.

> We all scurried out and huddled about, a cluster of excited children, and saw the much talked of man sitting in the wagon seat holding the reins of the horses. Again that cold, stern eye held us in awe and silence. We were much excited to see a number of woolly heads and flashing black eyes and rows of white teeth greeting us through the cracks in the wagon cover where it had been lifted by some of the irrepressible pickaninnies crowded in the back of the wagon. We were all a tiptoe to see, and agog with suppressed excitement.[5]

Over the years ahead, the college and the town would host many famous visitors, but none would ever create quite the stir as did John Brown. J. B. Grinnell was excoriated by the conservative press and the Democrats of Iowa for having openly harbored, aided and abetted a wanted criminal. His familiar initials, "J.B.," would for years after be translated into "John Brown." J.B. remained blithely unperturbed by these attacks, and ultimately his support of John Brown's ill-fated trek to Harpers Ferry would earn for Grinnell an honored seat among the Radical Republicans in Congress. Nor did John Brown forget the hospitality extended to him by Grinnell. He sang the praises of the Grinnell community when he arrived in Springdale to spend several months training his followers in the art of surprise attacks.[6] There is a legend that he also remembered J. B. Grinnell in a more material way. It is said that Brown at the time of his execution in Virginia requested his friends to send one of the pikes used in the attack on the arsenal to his friend in Iowa and that as long as J. B. Grinnell lived this pike was carried at the head of the academic Commencement procession at Iowa College. If there is indeed truth in this story, then the pike has long since disappeared, but the legend has remained.

One thing is certainly true, however. With John Brown's visit the college and the town had established a statewide reputation for radicalism. The trustees of Iowa College had not escaped the passions of sectionalism and involvement in those forces pushing the country toward disunion and war by having moved their college from River City to that remote village known as Saints' Rest.

If the college was to open in the fall of 1861, there was much more to attend to than the discussion of John Brown's visit and the aiding of fugitive slaves. The first item for consideration by the trustees was the employment of a faculty. The persons J.B. had listed as faculty for his now defunct Grinnell University, including J.B. himself, were either not available or were not competent to fill the positions to which the 1856 circular had assigned them. The trustees of Iowa College may have had some concern that in merging with Grinnell's university, he would attempt to run the college. If so, however, those fears proved groundless. Surprisingly enough, Grinnell distanced himself from the reorganization and operation of the college. Having obtained his objective of getting Iowa College to move to his town, he seemed content to let others take charge. He remained on the Board of Trustees, but he apparently never insisted that his support of an Oneida style of a practical, nonclassical curriculum including agricultural science and teacher training should prevail. J.B. was so preoccupied with his own business affairs of selling land, promoting the production of wool in Iowa, and investing in railroads that he had little time to give to the college. Then, too, he was politically ambitious. In 1856, he had been elected to the Iowa Senate where he led the drive to establish a public school system in Iowa, and it was his bill that became law in 1858. Four years later, Grinnell sought higher office in being the Republican candidate for the U.S. House of Representatives. Following the census of 1860, Iowa's representation in the House had been increased from two to six members. In the Congressional election of 1862, all six of the Republican candidates were victorious, and only in Grinnell's race was the contest even close. The John Brown visit continued to be J.B.'s political albatross, but with the solid Quaker and Congregational support in his district, he won out. Once safely seated in the House, he was quickly brought into the inner circle of the increasingly powerful Radical faction of the party, which loved him for both the enemies and the friends he had made at home.

Office holding in Des Moines and later Washington kept Grinnell away from his town and college during a great part of the time that Iowa College was getting started again.

Increasingly, the real power in directing the college affairs had become centered in one of the newer members of the Board of Trustees. George Frederic Magoun had become a member of the Board in 1856, but during the previous five years that he had lived in Iowa, he had become well known to all the trustees and to the Congregational ministry of the state. Born in Bath, Maine, in 1821, to a family of wealth and prominence, Magoun had never experienced the hardships that most of his fellow ministers in Iowa had known as youths. His father was a shipowner, bank president and mayor of Bath, and as a member of the Maine legislature had been co-author of Maine's celebrated law prohibiting the sale and use of intoxicating liquors—the first statewide prohibition act in the nation. A graduate of Bowdoin College in 1841, and a student in theology at both Andover and Yale seminaries, young Magoun had gone west in 1844 as a teacher, first in Galena, Illinois, and then in Platteville, Wisconsin, prior to his ordination in 1848 and his acceptance of pastorates in both Wisconsin and Illinois.

Magoun came to Iowa in 1851 to study and then practice law in Burlington, where he became a friend of William Salter and James Grimes. In 1855, he succeeded Ephraim Adams as the Congregational minister in Davenport. A man of commanding physical appearance, with his great leonine head and flowing beard, he appeared to his associates as someone who might well have served as the model for Michelangelo's portrayal of God, giving the touch of life to Adam, on the ceiling of the Sistine Chapel. When Magoun entered a room, the others present instinctively felt obliged to stand, if not to bow, before him. In whatever capacity he chose to employ his considerable talents, be it classroom, church or court, he took command. John Nollen in his history of the college, called Magoun "the unmitred bishop of Iowa Congregationalism" and asserted that "the word 'compromise' was not in his large vocabulary."[7] Once Magoun was on the Board of Trustees, the earlier leaders—Ephraim Adams, Asa Turner and Julius Reed—became secondary figures in the management of the college. It would be largely his great strength of will that would sustain the college through the many crises that lay ahead.

With the powerful advocacy of Magoun, the trustees insisted that the traditional classical liberal arts curriculum must be maintained in the new setting. There was no further talk of J. B. Grinnell's grandiose plans for a "practical" education that would include an Agricultural Science Department and a Normal School for teacher training. The Great Three disciplines of the New England liberal arts college would continue to dominate the instruction, and a knowledge of Greek, Latin and Mathematics would remain the hallmarks of a truly educated man. Henry Adams's sarcastic comment about a liberal arts education in the mid-nineteenth century would have been as applicable to Iowa College as it was to Adams's own alma mater, Harvard, at the same period, "The story will show ... that in essentials like religion, ethics, philosophy; in history, literature, art; in the concepts of all science, except perhaps mathematics, the American boy of 1854 stood nearer the year 1 than to the year 1900. The education he had received bore little relation to the education he needed. Speaking as an American of 1900, he had as yet no education at all."[8] To this sentiment, J. B. Grinnell, as a graduate of the ill-reputed Oneida Institute, would have given a hearty amen, but before the magisterial presence of the graduates of Bowdoin, Amherst and Yale, who were the trustees of his college, he kept a discreet silence.

Even so, however, when Iowa College reopened in 1861, some minor changes in curricular structure gave the faint suggestion that the old order could be altered and that those self-evident truths concerning the liberal arts might not be eternal verities, world without end. Within the classical four-year college curriculum which culminated in the granting of the Bachelor or Arts degree, the Greek and Latin courses previously required in the senior year were dropped in order to give greater attention to science courses. Of even greater significance to a changing order was the introduction of two new curricular courses: the Scientific Course, a three-year program, which when successfully completed earned for the graduate a Bachelor of Science degree; and the Ladies Course, which eliminated Greek and as substitutes for the classics, offered courses in "Belles Lettres" and modern foreign languages. For the first time also, students were admitted to take so-called Optional Courses, but the college actually meant "occasional students," not "optional courses"—that is, students who had no intention of earning a degree could sign up for a course or courses in the regular college programs and earn credit. This was an early experiment in adult education. These innovations introduced in 1862 were motivated, however, more by a desire to attract to the college a larger number of students than they were by any change in educational philosophy.[9]

With the introduction of a separate course for the ladies in 1862, the trustees quite unwittingly admitted a Trojan horse within the hitherto stoutly maintained walls of the classical liberal arts college that made inevitable the destruction of the hallowed preeminence of the classical languages. With the typical attitude of the male supremacist of that day, the trustees sincerely believed that females were so delicate in both mind and body as to be unable to endure the rigors of instruction in Greek. The women, of course, could not expect to receive a B.A. degree for this watered-down education—only a diploma. Nevertheless, an important first step had been taken in broadening the scope of the liberal arts that eventually would be as meaningful to the male students as to the delicate females whom the trustees sought to protect.

To implement this program of three separate collegiate courses with eight constituent departments of Greek, Latin, Mathematics, Belles Lettres, Physical Science, Mental Science, Political Science and Christian Science the most pressing need was to recruit a faculty. Once again, Iowa College was back to "the day of small things" in respect to having available a competent faculty. Fortunately, there was at hand a man who was capable of fulfilling the role that Erastus Ripley had played in Davenport in 1850.

Leonard Fletcher Parker was that man. Born in Arcade, New York, on 31 August 1825, Parker was left fatherless at the age of four. In his early youth, he was obliged to provide the main economic support for his mother, doing the chores on the family's small farm, and at the age of sixteen, beginning his career as a teacher in a country school. Not until he reached the age that most students graduate from college was he able to pursue the higher education he sought by enrolling in Oberlin College in 1846. While still a college student, he became a tutor in classics. Following his graduation in 1851, he entered the Oberlin Theological Seminary, intending to go to Siam as a missionary, but ill health forced him to leave the seminary. His health restored, Parker married his Oberlin classmate, Sarah Candace Pearse, and for two years taught in Brownsville, Pennsylvania.

In 1856, the Parkers came to Iowa to join the Grinnell

colony. Parker was promptly employed as teacher in the local primary school, and when the Grinnell University Preparatory Department opened the following year he became its first principal. In 1858, he added a third job to his busy schedule by being appointed the first superintendent of public schools in Poweshiek county. Parker demonstrated the courage of his abolitionist convictions in 1860 when he, along with Amos Bixby, resolutely resisted a mob who attempted to prevent four male fugitive slaves from enrolling in the town school.[10] Abolitionism in the abstract may have been the prevailing sentiment in J.B.'s colony, but there were many citizens who did not favor Parker and Bixby's insistence upon racial justice as a concrete reality in their town.

As a successful principal in the Preparatory Department, Parker was, like Ripley before him, the obvious choice to be the first professor of Iowa College in Grinnell when twelve students, whom he had prepared, were ready to enter college in the fall of 1861. Parker recruited two other local men to join him on the faculty: the Rev. C. B. Smith to be professor of Rhetoric and English Literature, and the indefatigable Julius Reed to serve in his place as principal in the preparatory school, which now had ninety-nine students in attendance.

With the academy and the collegiate department once more well launched, the trustees were able to turn to an important item that had been left as unfinished business in Davenport—the selection of a president for Iowa College. As was previously the case, they once again had high aspirations for the office. They first asked one of the most distinguished liberal theologians in America, the Rev. Horace Bushnell of Connecticut to take the post. When he declined, they attempted to interest another well-known Biblical scholar, S. W. S. Dutton, but he too refused.[11] At this point, Father Turner in his usual blunt manner told the other trustees, "I am getting discouraged in looking after great men. If we can get a good man at the head, we can get along. ... We can find Professors as we need them."[12] Although

124

Turner did not mention a name, it was clear to the others as to whom he was referring. Leonard Parker had demonstrated his ability as an administrator in establishing the Preparatory Department and as county superintendent of schools. Of even greater importance to Turner were Parker's holding views on slavery and higher education for women that were entirely consonant with his own. Some of the other trustees were equally enthusiastic about his choice. Parker, unlike his predecessor, Erastus Ripley, who had turned down the presidency in 1848, would have been happy to accept, but a majority of the trustees felt that he was too imbued with the radicalism of his alma mater to be acceptable to the general public. The term "Oberlinism" still carried a stigma that frightened many Congregationalists. So, to his deep chagrin, Parker was passed over.[13]

Turner's suggestion of looking for a candidate close at hand did, however, inspire the trustees to consider one of their own number. In July 1862, Magoun was offered the presidency. Quite wisely Magoun replied that he would accept the office only if and when the Board had secured a special endowment that could pay his salary. John Holbrook volunteered to go East to raise the funds as quickly as possible.[14]

Before Parker in the fall of 1861 could begin to offer instruction in the classical languages to his newly admitted college students, the nation was at war with itself, and the Union forces had suffered their first defeat in the Battle of Bull Run. With that defeat at Manassas, Virginia, the North realized that this conflict, unlike the Whiskey Rebellion of 1793, was not a minor insurrection which would easily be crushed before the end of the year but a full-scale war, whose outcome could no longer be confidently predicted.

General William Sherman's memorable statement, "War is all hell," was particularly applicable to the conflict in which he had played so conspicuous a part.[15] On 4 January

1861, two months before Abraham Lincoln was to be inaugurated as president, the outgoing president, James Buchanan, had decreed the day to be a national day of prayer and fasting for the welfare of the nation. In his church in Burlington, William Salter on that day preached a sermon on "Our National Sins and Impending Calamities." He eloquently defined the terrible meaning of a civil war: "All war is a terrible barbarity. ... It Makes men fiends and devils. A civil war is worse than all others, because those who have been closest allied to each other have the greatest facility for attacking and destroying one another, and their passions become most exasperated. The record of such a war constitutes the bloodiest chapter in history."[16]

Salter spoke as an Old Testament prophet in foreseeing what lay immediately ahead for the American people. In terms of the actual number of casualties, more Americans died or were wounded in the Civil War than in all of our other wars combined prior to World War II, for it was the only war in which it was necessary to count the casualties on both sides as being American casualties. It has been the only war in our history that left vast sections of the country devastated. More than any other event it was the great determinant of political affiliation in both the Midwest and the South for more than a century. What the Trojan War was to the ancient Greek world, the Crusades to the Middle Ages, and the Wars of Religion to central and western Europe in the early modern period the Civil War has been to the United States. It is the American Iliad—the continuing fount of romance and tragedy for the generations following. No individual, institution or community that experienced those fateful four years was left unscarred by its "terrible swift sword."

Colleges were particularly vulnerable to the insatiable demands of a nation at war to put young men into uniform. Nearly all colleges in 1861 were exclusive preserves of males, conveniently collected in accessible locations, engaged in activities that could in no way be regarded as vital to the war effort, and peculiarly susceptible to peer pressures and patriotic propaganda. Campuses were bountiful hunting grounds for recruiting officers. The few colleges, including Iowa College, that were coeducational by 1860, could now thank their good fortune, not their prescience, in having admitted women students. During the next four years, it would be the "delicate ladies" upon whom these colleges would largely have to lean for support.

Enrollment figures as given in the Iowa College catalogues reveal how important to the institution the female students were during the war years. The full impact of the war on the student body was not, of course, immediately felt. When the college reopened in 1861 after its three-year hiatus, the twelve students in the traditional classical course, all males, were as many as could have been expected or the college prepared to instruct even if there had been no war. In the Preparatory Department, open to both sexes, males outnumbered the females by nearly two to one, so that in this first year of war, there was a total enrollment in the institution at both the secondary and collegiate levels of seventy-six men and thirty-five women.

For the second year of the war, there was a rather dramatic shift. By 1862 the Ladies Course was in operation. There were seven men in the collegiate department—all sophomores. There was no freshman male class, an ominous portent of what lay ahead. In the newly opened Ladies Course there were twenty-one students, the females in college thus outnumbering the males by three to one.

By the fall of 1863, in the two collegiate courses open only to males, the Scientific Course had seven students and the Classical Course had no sophomore class and only five entering freshmen. The Ladies Course, however, had thirty-two women enrolled, and of the twenty-six students in the Preparatory Department, fifteen were females.

The college did not publish a catalogue for the year 1864–65, but in the fall of 1865, with the war having been just concluded, there was no senior or sophomore class in the Classical Course; there were four juniors, who may have in-

127

cluded some men who had returned to college after military service. Most significantly, of the eight entering first-year students, two were women, admitted for the first time into the Classical Course. Evidently the exigencies of war were such as to convince the trustees that women were strong enough to undertake the study of Greek. In the other hitherto male preserve, the Scientific Course, there were no students at all.[17]

A far more sobering table of statistics, forever immortalized on a stone tablet in the college chapel, is the list of eleven men who died serving the Union cause. Of these eleven, five were killed in battle: Benjamin Cassiday, Benjamin Holland, Eugene Jones, James Loring, and Joseph Shanklin. Six died either of wounds or of disease: Thomas Craver, James Dowd (who died in the infamous Andersonville, Georgia, prison), James Ellis, Francis Ford, Albert Hobbs, and Samuel Thompson. These men had died in such far away places as Mississippi, Tennessee, Alabama, Louisiana and Georgia—as remote and alien to this generation of midwestern soldiers and their families as would be San Juan Hill, Chateau-Thierry, Bataan and the Mekong delta to those student warriors who were to follow. Eleven fatal casualties in four years of war is not an impressively large number unless one considers how very small the student numbers were during this war. Only then can we realize that Iowa College's casualty list for the Civil War looms as large or larger in proportion to the percentage of casualties among the students as for any of the succeeding wars in which the nation would be engaged.

Although the Grinnell community was distant from the major theatres of war, the nearest battles taking place in Missouri, yet like every community in the nation, it was confronted with the ugly reality of war enough to know, without the benefit of General Sherman's observation, that war was indeed all hell. In 1863, the long-promised railroad finally reached Grinnell—the westernmost point of any railroad line in the North. So for the last two years of the war, the little town became a major terminal for recruits from farther west to board trains to take them to battle, and for scarred veterans returning home. In the eager young faces of those heading by rail east and south the townspeople could read the glory and pride of war, but in the gaunt faces of those who were thankfully heading west by stagecoach or by foot, if they still had two legs, they saw the suffering visages of those who had experienced hell.

The ever observant Joanna Harris, whose four older brothers and fifty-eight-year-old father enlisted in the army, had been admitted to the Ladies Course in 1862. She remembered the impact of the war on college instruction. "Our college class work was more or less erratic ... by constant excitement from news of the events, by our concern for our loved ones facing the dangers at the front, and by the intermittent reports of victories and then of defeats with horrible destruction. Systematic and serious study was very difficult, or rather impossible." Often the entire recitation period would be devoted not to the parsing of French verbs, but to the latest news from Vicksburg and Gettysburg. She recalled one incident when the most vocal local Democrat, R. M. Kellogg, insisted that the flag on the college campus should be flown at half-mast on the death of Stephen Douglas in 1862. He was stoutly resisted by the college boys in his effort to lower the flag. It would not be the last time that there would be a struggle between town and gown over the campus flags in time of war.[18]

Another town youth, James Hill, whose father as member of the Iowa Band had given the first dollar to Iowa College, would remember the crowds that gathered daily to hear the latest news of the war read aloud:

Individual families did not have individual papers in those primitive days, and so you might see the crowd gather silently around the post office door from all quarters as if the birds of the air had spread apprehension. Sometimes an individual man would be seen to stagger as if he had been hit, and sometimes a women seemed attacked by faintness, as if it were herself and not her husband or son that was in danger of being struck down.[19]

Even without benefit of radio or television, this distant war was brought directly into every home in the land.

In the midst of the war, the trustees' commitment to the ideal of racial equality was to be forcibly tested by the application of a young black woman for admission to the Ladies Course at Iowa College.[20] Only the last name of Alexander from Muscatine was given. The young girl had received the education requisite for admission to Iowa College. Parker had fought for the right of blacks to enroll in the local primary school. As county superintendent of schools he felt that he had the authority to order their admission. In this instance, however, he found it necessary to poll trustee opinion before making the decision, for he was aware that her admission to the college might mean the withdrawal of some white students and might adversely affect Holbrook's fundraising efforts in the East.

Over the next several weeks Parker received in general the answers he had hoped to get. Daniel Lane, who still had some doubts about coeducation, gave a somewhat qualified response: "If ladies are to be admitted to the college, there is nothing in my policy to prevent the admissions of *colored ones.*" But he added, "If the colored girl can go to some *colored school,* perhaps it would be *pleasanter* for her to do so."

Most of the replies were strongly supportive of her admission. The president of the Board, A. B. Robbins, who as pastor in Muscatine undoubtedly knew her, answered by quoting Acts 17: 26— "And hath made of one blood all people." To this Scriptural sanction, Robbins added, "This probably includes Jews, Arabians and Africans or Americans of African descent. All those [students] leaving because of the coming of these last [African Americans] are probably so deficient in brains that they would dishonor the institution by remaining. ... They had therefore better leave at once."

President-elect Magoun said he doubted if many students would leave if the young lady was admitted. There had been no problem at his alma mater [Bowdoin] when a black was admitted. Magoun quoted with pleasure the comment of one of the most conservative trustees: "Brother Guernsey writes me, 'I say let her in, and if some choose on that account to go, let them go. Let the principle be settled that a man's a man for a' that, and a woman's a woman, of course.'"

Especially reassuring was Trustee Holbrook's response that the refusal of admission to the Alexander girl "would be a damaging blow to my plans & efforts. I can think of scarcely any thing else that would so effectively bar my progress."

The highly respected trustee, General George B. Sargent, reached the height of approbation in writing, "If I should ever by my vote prohibit any of God's human creatures upon this earth from all of the advantages to be derived from Iowa College on account of their (his or her) color, I should pray that my tongue might cease its utterance and my right arm be paralyzed."

Only one trustee, J. M. Chamberlain, answered in the negative. He resented holding a vote by mail to answer so momentous a question. He wanted a full discussion by the trustees. "I do not think it necessary that they [African-American students] should be admitted to our college. There is a limit somewhere to social familiarity between the races & with Oberlin in its central position, I am inclined to think it not wise to establish another such institution." Here Chamberlain got in a purposefully cruel jab at Parker, a product of radical Oberlinism.[21]

Needless to say the young woman was admitted. Unfortunately, college records do not exist to ascertain how long she stayed in college, or indeed if she ever came to Grinnell. All that can be said with certainty is that she did not graduate. On the other hand there is no record that any student left the college because of her admission. The students who were leaving in 1863 went to fight for a Union which would be restored without slaves.

In 1862, as was the common practice among volunteer enlistees in the army during the Civil War, a group of college students formed their own company and asked Parker to lead them into battle. Parker was eager to accept the offer, but the trustees, insisting he was indispensable to the college, denied him a leave of absence. Two years later, however, when a new group of war-bound college students formed Company B of the 46th Iowa infantry and asked for a faculty member to serve as officer of their company, Parker was not to be denied an opportunity to serve. He took his erstwhile students of Greek classics off to the battlefields for a one hundred–day tour of duty. From Collierville, Tennessee, on 19 July 1864, Parker wrote back to the college's newspaper, *The News Letter,* giving an account of his war experience. Much of the letter was devoted to singing the praises of the black troops who were serving in the Union army: "They are our most trustworthy 'Union men' and furnish us the most reliable information as to the position and movement of the enemy, the location of rebel supplies, and the loyalty and disloyalty of citizens. ... Fifty thousand men of more soldierly bearing or more desperate valor cannot be found in the service."[22]

Two of the eleven Iowa College men who died in service[23] were from Company B during the time that Parker served as the company's lieutenant. James Ellis, who would have been a senior at the college during the coming year, died in a Memphis hospital on 16 August 1864. The second casualty, Francis Ford, died in Grinnell on 27 November 1864, after Parker had arranged for him to be sent home.

Even so severe a trial of courage and faith as the war, however, proved to be also a dark cloud that had a silver lining in the most literal sense of that familiar old adage. Holbrook, on his fundraising tour of the East in 1863, discovered to his delight that there was indeed silver to be found for the college as a direct result of the war profits being made by New England textile manufacturers and railroad promoters. Holbrook wrote to Salter in May 1863, "I am now ... in New

England prosecuting my mission of raising funds for our college. I find money plenty, & the country prosperous to an astonishing degree in spite of the war. ... I find a deep interest felt in Iowa. Our patriotism has done much to secure for us the affection of New England. I shall easily raise the $2,000 for the college—indeed I have got about half of it now, after the second sabbath; I have no doubt if I was to keep on 3 or 4 mos. I could raise $12,000 to endow our Presidency & even more. All feel that we ought to have one good Puritan College in Iowa."[24] Holbrook did keep on, but found he had to dig harder to find less and less silver. The old professional in money raising, Ephraim Adams, joined him in the summer of 1864, but the enactment of our first federal income tax "hedge up the way," Adams wrote his wife, "for getting money."[25] Holbrook, however, did raise enough to endow the presidential office at the college. Just as Adams had found his mother lode in Preserved Carter, so Holbrook found his in the person of Samuel Williston of Easthampton, Massachusetts, and it was an even richer vein of silver than that of Carter. Williston gave $10,000 to the cause, and ultimately after another decade of painful extraction, finally provided the college with an endowment of $28,500. Magoun could now come to Grinnell as the Williston Professor of Mental and Moral Philosophy as well as President of Iowa College, and he formally accepted both positions in July 1864.[26]

This increase in endowment enabled the college to do more than guarantee Magoun his salary of $1,500 a year. Additional faculty could now be employed. In 1863 a German immigrant, Carl Wilhelm von Coelln, who has the distinction of being the first professor at Iowa College whose educational background did not include any theological training, became Professor of Mathematics. He had married the daughter of a deacon of the Congregational church in the small town of Orwell, Ohio. In visiting his wife's parents before coming to Iowa, von Coelln had met the young pastor of the church, Samuel Jay Buck, a graduate of Oberlin, who in addition to his ministerial duties also taught science in the local academy. When von Coelln revealed to Buck that he was going to Iowa with the hope of finding a teaching job in some college there, Buck somewhat impetuously said, "When you are out there find a place for me." Von Coelln asked, "Would you come if I did?" To which, as Buck later admitted, "I replied, very rashly, 'Yes, I think so.' It was a reply made very much at random and with no expectation that anything would come of it. To our surprise, however, a few months later, a letter came asking if I would accept the principalship of the preparatory department of Iowa College."[27]

Buck accepted, and came to Iowa College in February 1864 to serve as principal of the Preparatory Department. In 1869, he succeeded von Coelln as professor of Natural Philosophy upon the latter's departure to become State Superintendent of Public Schools. Buck over the next four decades would become one of Iowa College's most distinguished and best loved professors, a leader of the faculty, and for three years (1884–1887) the college's acting president.

Other additions to the faculty during the war years were the Rev. Henry Webster Parker as professor of Chemistry and Natural Science and Charles W. Clapp, professor of Rhetoric and English Literature. At the end of the first four years of operation at Grinnell, Iowa College had finally assembled a faculty as large and even more distinguished in scholarship and teaching than it had had in Davenport.

In choosing the first principal of the Ladies Department, the trustees thought themselves fortunate to have readily at hand Professor Parker's wife, who accepted that position in 1862. Sarah Candace Pearse Parker was also the first in the college's history of what the historian of the women's movement in Iowa, Louise R. Noun, has aptly called "strong-minded women." At least the equal of her husband in education, strength of character and a talent for leadership, Sarah Parker was the pioneer force in the promotion of higher education for women in Iowa. She was to give to coeducation at Iowa College precisely the jump start it needed. During the three-and-a-half-month military absence of her husband,

Sarah Parker, being the senior professor of the college, acted as the unofficial acting president. She also assumed her husband's duties as county superintendent of schools during his absence.

Reaching the limit of her patient acceptance of a salary of $400 a year, only a little over one-third of that paid to the male professors, she abruptly resigned in 1868 and only agreed to return when her salary was raised to one-half that of her male counterparts.[28] For the seven years that she served as principal of the Ladies Department, she provided a much admired role model for the first women graduates of the college. Her forceful presence did not engender the same admiration from the male faculty and trustees, but their not-so-veiled criticism never deflected her from pursuing her mission. Many years ahead of her time, she effectively demonstrated that a woman could successfully combine marriage, including a family of five children, with a career.

Such a woman represented a real threat to the long established principle of male superiority. It was small wonder that when the Parkers in 1870 left Iowa College to accept positions at the University of Iowa and the trustees began a search to find their successors, one of the trustees, Jesse Guernsey wrote, "Don't get an Oberlin woman for Principal if you can avoid it."[29] The college never did. Even so, Oberlin did not have a monopoly on "strong-minded women," and if Sarah Parker was the first, she would not be the last such woman to occupy a position of power within the college management.

President Lincoln did not have the full support of the die-hard abolitionists until he issued the Emancipation Proclamation on 1 January 1863 freeing all slaves in those areas that were still in a state of rebellion. Men like Leonard Parker, Amos Bixby and Joanna Harris's father, James Harris, had been convinced that God would not give the Union forces victory until the nation had renounced slavery. This same sentiment was shared by many of the college's trustees—Asa Turner, Ephraim Adams, William Salter and Oliver Emerson in particular. Although Lincoln's proclamation was not as comprehensive as they would have liked, nevertheless his words, "henceforward shall be free" they saw as the deathblow to the hated institution, and made this conflict for the abolitionists a holy war sanctified by a righteous God.

If the proponents of abolition had expected an immediate divine intervention on behalf of freedom and justice, they were to be disappointed and would continue to be sorely tried for what Salter had called "the national sins." The war became ever more violent, and the casualty lists grew ever longer. On 4 July 1863, Ephraim Adams at his pastorate in Decorah recorded in his diary: "An old fashioned 4th of July celebration. ... Our armies now seem to be all on the move. Pennsylvania infested by Rebels, and Vicksburg not yet taken. ... This is the 3rd celebration since the war [started]. About two more there must be ere it closes. How many lives must meanwhile be lost?"[30] To Adams's rhetorical question there was an easy but terrible answer—many, many more. Of Iowa College's eleven fatal casualties, two-thirds occurred after the great victories of the Union at Vicksburg and Gettysburg. Adams's sister-in-law, Esther Douglass, wrote to Elisabeth Adams, "There have been great rejoicings within a few days over late victories, but there are many in this neighborhood [New Haven, Vermont] who are anxiously searching the papers for the lists of the killed and wounded, and I suppose 'tis so everywhere. I wish our officers would leave off sending back slaves to their masters, and then perhaps God would let us have the victory without such great loss."[31] In spite of Lincoln's proclamation, as long as some of his generals continued to ignore his edict, the nation's sins, the abolitionists believed, had not yet been washed away in the blood of its sons, and victory would still elude the North.

With the defeats of the South at Vicksburg and Gettysburg on 4 July 1863, however, the turning point in the war had finally been reached. Nevertheless, it would take the relentless scorched-earth drive of Sherman through Georgia and the slow, bloody advance of Ulysses Grant through the wilderness of Virginia extending for nearly two more years of battle before the Confederacy would accept the inevitable. It was not until 11 April 1865 that Adams could record in his diary, "Last week came the news that Richmond was taken. Today that Lee and his army have surrendered. So wanes the Southern Confederacy."

Two more entries Adams had to record in order to complete his diary record of the Civil War. One more terrible sacrifice was demanded as an act of atonement in the Great American Tragedy: "April 16 Rumors that President Lincoln was assassinated on Friday night last at the Theatre—also Secretary Seward in his sick chamber." And the following day: "April 17 Too true too true. Confirmed beyond a doubt."[32]

Three weeks later, on 4 May 1865, fifteen thousand Iowa service men marched in triumph down Pennsylvania Avenue in the reunited nation's capital. Iowa College was represented in that victory parade. "They looked," said one Iowa news reporter, "like lords of the world."[33] Salter in his sermon of four years earlier had put "national pride" as first among "Our National Sins," but perhaps even he, that stern Calvinist judge, would have excused pride in this instance. America had gone through its greatest trial, and with both those who had only endured and with those who had also triumphantly prevailed, there was the same realization that nothing that might lie ahead would demand a more severe testing of the survival of themselves or of their nation.

Ephraim Adams, Harvey Adams, William Salter,
members of the Iowa Band, half a century later.

Second home of Iowa College in Davenport, ca. 1855.

Josiah Bushnell
Grinnell, abolitionist,
statesman, promoter,
lured the college
to his town.

West and East Colleges; East, the first college building in
Grinnell, was destroyed by fire in 1871.

West College, ca. 1873, the second building, escaped the fire; [background right] Central College completed after the fire.

George F. Magoun, first president 1865–1884, eloquent orator for Salvation, sustained the college through fire and cyclone.

Chicago Hall, Blair Hall, and Alumni Hall, erected within
three years after the 1882 cyclone.

Jesse B. Macy, class
of 1870, professor
1885–1912, internationally
famous creator of new
department of learning—
Political Science.

Goodnow Hall, with tower for observatory,
completed in 1886. [Below] Library in
Goodnow in 1890s.

Martha Foote Crowe,
principal of the Ladies
Department 1883–1891,
made college more truly
coeducational.

Mears Cottage, built in 1888 for women;
first dormitory on campus.

George A. Gates, second
president, 1887–1900,
strong advocate of service,
led college into modern era.

George D. Herron, first
professor of Applied
Christianity, 1893–1900,
outstanding proponent of
the Social Gospel.

Clara Millerd, class of
1893, one of most bril-
liant graduates, professor
of Greek and Philosophy
for many years.

Carrie Rand, instructor in Social and Physical Culture, 1887–1900, would become Mrs. George Herron.

Rand Gymnasium, built in 1897, gift to women of the college from Carrie Rand; destroyed by fire in 1940.

6

The Trials Continue:

George Magoun

Through Fire and Storm

1865–1884

Iowa College had given sixty-nine of its students to the Union army for combat service during the four years of war, so depleting its student body that by 1864 there was not a single able-bodied male left on campus to attend its classes. In 1861, the first enlistees had marched off to war singing the rousingly patriotic, "Rally Round the Flag, Boys," but as the war changed these eager boys into weary, battle-scarred veterans, so also did their songs change to the tremulous "Just Before the Battle, Mother," and the hauntingly plaintive "Tenting Tonight on the Old Camp Ground," with its refrain, "We are tired of war on the old camp ground / Many are dead and gone." Sixteen percent of Iowa College's student soldiers would be dead and gone before the indefinite "When" in their song, "When this cruel war is over," had finally and blessedly become at Appomattox in April 1865 the definite "Now this cruel war is over."

Leonard Parker, in recalling "Iowa College in the Civil War" some three decades later, would write: "What did it cost the boys? Did they appreciate the sacrifice? It cost life for some; others lived on in broken health, life-long invalids. For still others the best years of preparation for high service were given to the country and life left was less influential than it would have been with four years of college instead of camp behind them."[1]

In addition to the sixty-nine who fought in battles there were four other students who served in noncombative roles: three Quaker men—Seth Arnold, Jesse Macy and Robert Haines; and one woman—Mary E. Snell. They too saw the ravages of war and were forever scarred by the sight.

When in September 1865, with the war finally over, and the academic year about to begin, the college in effect was for the third time in less than twenty years making still another fresh new start. A few veterans returned to finish their collegiate education that had been so brutally interrupted, and four former soldiers entered college for the first time as freshmen. Parker could proudly write, "It may be well to remember that the college was the first to give free tuition to disabled veterans."[2]

Along with the return of men to its classes, Iowa College for the first time had a president to direct its course. George Magoun as early as the winter of 1863–64 had been given the assurance he had demanded that there was now a sufficient endowment to support a chief executive officer. He had promptly resigned his pastorate at Lyons, Iowa, in preparation for his move to Grinnell. Before he could assume his new duties, however, tragedy struck his family. His wife, Abby Hyde, as well as their newly born child, died on 10 February 1864. Devastated by the death of his companion of sixteen years, who had given him nine children, Magoun asked for and was granted a leave of absence before coming to Grinnell as president. "My health was so broken, having buried wife and child, that all the assurance I could give the Trustees was that on my return, if I could do any work at all, I would see what could be done for the College."[3] Following his formal acceptance of the presidency in July 1864, Magoun left immediately for Europe where he spent the next eight months in travel and study.

There was never any doubt in his own mind, however, nor in those who knew him that Magoun would find the strength to assume the responsibilities that were now his. Magoun in fact had begun to assume the role of president as soon as he had first been informed in 1862 that he had been elected by his fellow trustees, two years before he finally accepted the position. He had written Acting President Parker stressing the importance of getting music instruction into the curriculum in order to attract young women to the campus and he had warned,

> Our most formidable competition is going to be with Cornell College. ... They have two large buildings & 381 students of whom *60* are in the College Course—40 freshmen. They are wise about teaching young ladies, and drawing multitudes to their Commencements, several thousands being present at the recent one. Also they have $60,000 worth of property a Trustee tells me and but $5000 of debts. It will be happy for us when we can say we will be out of debt on a certain day.[4]

Even while in deep mourning, just prior to his leaving for Europe, Magoun was busily writing to the trustees giving his views—which already carried the force of being edicts— as to "what could be done for the College." He prescribed the text books that should be used for the courses in Mental and Moral Science and in Political Economy and the Constitution of the United States. The major thrust of his administration, however, would be to expand the faculty and course offerings in the natural sciences. He pointed out how far advanced the best Eastern colleges were in this area as compared to Iowa College. "The day cannot be distant when, if the College has any respectable patronage at all, two instructors will be needed. ... There is no department in which the subject matter of knowledge increases so rapidly as in that of Natural Sciences. ... At Brown and Dartmouth Natural Philosophy is taken from the Math. Dept. and combined with Astronomy in a separate professorship, and at Brown there are two instructors in Chemistry besides—(one of Applied Chemistry)." Magoun looked forward to the day when Iowa College could also offer courses in Applied Chemistry, Botany and Zoology, and possibly some work in Metallurgy.[5]

Magoun was inaugurated as the first president of the college at the Commencement exercises in July 1865. In his inaugural address he made his commitment to the awesome responsibility he was now assuming. "Surrendering a most happy pastorate, and declining other posts of honorable and more gainful service, I have heeded this call as the voice of God."[6] In the years that followed, Magoun would never question his assertion that he had heard and heeded the voice of God. Indeed, to his associates at the college, it often appeared that Magoun regarded his own voice and God's voice as being synonymous.

Never would the college have a more magisterial presence in the presidential chair than it had with Magoun over the next twenty years. During the eight years he had served on the Board of Trustees prior to his coming to the presidency, Magoun had been the most powerful figure on the Board. His fellow trustees, accustomed to following his lead, were quite prepared to continue their unquestioning support of him in his new role. Few if any of Magoun's successors over the next century and a quarter would enjoy as compliant a Board as did he during most of his tenure in office. To the degree that the trustees recognized his regime as being despotic they appeared to welcome it, and gave him loose rein, checked only by financial stringency.

There were, however, among the faculty, the students, and within the larger community others who did not view Magoun as being quite the benevolent despot whom the trustees admired. The first to challenge the president's authority were the Parkers. Their response might well have been expected. From the day the college had reopened in Grinnell in 1860, Leonard and Sarah Parker had provided the on-campus leadership it sorely needed. Leonard Parker could never be reconciled to the fact that the presidency was not his. It should have been and would have been, he believed, save for the bigotry of a few trustees in their hostility toward Oberlinism. For five years, Parker had been acting president, both de jure and de facto, and within her own, more limited sphere, his wife Sarah had also ruled supreme over the Ladies Department. There would have been opposition from Parker to any one who might have assumed the title of president without that hated qualifying adjective "acting," but when two such superegos as Magoun and Parker met within the same small arena, the resulting confrontation proved to be historically memorable.

The outcome, however, was never in doubt. The only surprise was that the Parkers lasted as long as they did. It was not until the late summer of 1870 that they submitted to the trustees their resignations as professor of Ancient Languages and as lady principal. The trustees were not happy to receive these notices less than a month before classes were to resume for the fall term, without the necessary time—or so the Parkers hoped—for the college to find suitable replacements. Parker had accepted his appointment as professor of Classical Languages at the University of Iowa some time previously. The trustees and Magoun saw these late resignations as the final thrust to wound Magoun.[7] Even that attack, however, was parried by Magoun. He quickly found a replacement for Leonard Parker and took great delight in announcing the appointment of a "truly distinguished philologist," John Avery.

Prior to Magoun's arrival in Grinnell to assume the presidency, another Parker, Henry W. Parker, had joined the faculty in 1864. Enough money had been raised by Holbrook and Adams not only to endow the presidency but also to make possible a second professor in the natural sciences as had been strongly urged by Magoun. A graduate of Amherst College and Auburn Theological Seminary, Henry Parker had held pastorates in Brooklyn, New York, and New Bedford, Massachusetts, before abandoning the ministry to come west in 1864 to seek a career in teaching. Upon his arrival in Iowa, he applied for a position as professor of Natural Science at Iowa College and was quickly accepted.

Henry Parker was to have a relationship with President Magoun quite different from that of Leonard Parker. The newly arrived president quickly discovered that in Henry Parker he had that ideal Renaissance man that every liberal arts college president could fantasize about having but rarely if ever could find in the flesh. Parker's intellectual curiosity embraced the entire scope of human knowledge and *mirabile dictu,* his competency to perform matched the catholicity of his interests. He was prepared to teach, and to do so superbly well, courses in chemistry, physics, botany, geology, mineralogy, physiology, and even a course in domestic science for the young women students.

His awestruck colleagues could hardly have been more impressed if the great Alexander von Humboldt, who, it was said, had a mind that encompassed all knowledge of natural science, had consented to accept a chair at Iowa College. Nor was Henry Parker restricted to the field of science, broad as that was. He was a published poet of no mean ability, and could and did teach the first courses the college offered in studio art. His young colleague, Jesse Macy, would also later recall Parker's interest in architectural styles: "Simple and plain were the public buildings and dwellings in these early days. Professor Parker made a serious and persistent attack upon the architecture of the town." According to Macy, "his artistic eye demanded more consideration for man's natural and cultivated love of beauty, and he strove to teach the people in practical ways to seek for beauty in their surroundings, to build in graceful forms, to use the harmonious colors of natural woods in their interiors, and to follow nature's leading."[8] Thus did Parker anticipate the Prairie School of American Architecture a generation before Frank Lloyd Wright was to give Parker's architectural views a name and a reality in brick and stone on the midwestern prairies.

Parker's wife, Helen Fitch Parker, also contributed her own considerable talents to the college community. Her beauty and charm captivated the entire town. Here was a Helen who the more literary-minded Grinnellians could compare to another Helen who in ancient times had precipitated a major war, or to that beauty who inspired Poe in writing an ode "To Helen."

Never having been west of New York state until her husband brought her to Iowa, Helen Parker would remain, in the words of one chronicler, "incorrigibly and quite consciously 'Eastern.'"[9] Poet, novelist, author of children's books, painter—she ranged as widely in the humanities as did her husband in the sciences. The trunk loads of bright clothes she had brought with her to Iowa were the admiration and envy of all the town ladies, dressed in their "plain dark delaines, black silks, etc." Observing his wife at a tea party in their home, dressed in "green silk and green headdress," Henry Parker compared her to "a hummingbird among sparrows," which pleased her immensely.[10]

Mrs. Parker must have found the transition from New York to Iowa a difficult one, but she accepted it with grace and humor. She never resented her husband's transporting her to this primitive, alien environment, but she never attempted to become a part of it. She rather saw her mission as being that of elevating customs and manners of the frontier to her standards, not adapting herself to its mores. Her frequent letters to her sister provide a vivid insight into the life with which she had to contend. She could find true pastoral beauty in the landscape, "The country was fine," she wrote in describing her trip west across Iowa, "like an old cultivated farm district—not like a new country ... with one field of 250 acres of ripe grain. You can see nothing of this magnificence at the East." If the countryside could become so beautifully cultivated, she was convinced, so also could the people. "Never mind, all these ways of the backwoods will disappear in time. I do what I can by example and advice when it is asked. But there is one hopeless western fashion which will only die out in the next generation. Borrowing! ... Much cake being left at my tea last week, a neighbor who is wife of one of the richest here, offered to take it in exchange for fresh beef as they 'had been killing' and she wished to have some company!!! Henry cannot get over that. Well, it is something pleasant to live where your notions get a shock occasionally. One gets broader ideas." Then she added that she must close her letter: "A neighbor has just sent in to borrow pen and ink."[11]

Helen Parker was an important collaborator in her husband's work as teacher. She joined him in teaching classes in drawing. Her collection of sea shells, accumulated over many years, was reputed to be one of the finest and most extensive in the country. It became the prize exhibit in the college museum of natural history which Henry Parker had assembled and served as curator.

The Parkers were generous hosts to both faculty, students and townspeople. Jesse Macy wrote, "No social event in the student life was more highly prized as privilege and pleasure than the annual party in Professor Parker's home, where among books, pictures, music and artistic natural object, the boys and girls from the Iowa prairies were made by the graceful hostess to feel that all of her possessions and her own gracious gifts as well were at their command and for their enjoyment."[12]

The two Parker families departed Grinnell in the same summer of 1870. Henry Parker's fame as a scientist-teacher extraordinary had reached far beyond Iowa College and the Midwest, and in the spring of that year he was offered a chair as professor of "mental, moral and social science" at the Massachusetts Agricultural College at Amherst. Believing that he and his wife had savored to the fullest the rustic simplicity and charm of the West, and homesick for family and friends in the East, Henry Parker accepted the offer.

President Magoun was as dismayed by Henry Parker's resignation as he had been delighted by Leonard Parker's leaving. He wrote to the Samuel Willistons, whose generous gift to the college had made his presidency possible:

> I am so saddened by Prof. Parker's resignation that I must add a word. It is the saddest thing for me and the college … that could be. The other Prof. Parker (the Prof. of Ancient Languages) was no loss; we have already more than supplied his place by securing Prof. Avery. … But Prof. Parker's loss *cannot be* supplied. The Agricultural College has dealt Iowa College the most injurious blow we could have received in getting him away. I am sorry, also, to be persuaded … that it is really Amherst College which

has done it, and to expect ... that the Agricultural College professorship is only a stepping stone and after a short tarry there he will be appointed to a professorship in Amherst as his final and real destination. Why couldn't these wealthy institutions let a struggling and poor Western College alone? Prof. Parker is *needed* 20 times as much here as there and would do 20 times as much good. It is the great mistake of his life, returning to the east, just as he laid so noble a foundation for usefulness ... he had already done many times more than any other professor had accomplished.[13]

Magoun was not exaggerating in his assessment of what the loss of Henry Parker meant to Iowa College in 1870. He was clearly the most valuable member of the faculty at that time, and Magoun's bitterness toward the two educational institutions in Amherst, Massachusetts, is quite understandable. On the other hand, his evaluation of Leonard Parker's services was grossly unfair. Parker was as important to the re-establishment of the college in Grinnell as had been Ripley's to the founding of the college in Davenport. It is doubtful if the college could have had as successful and smooth a second opening if he had not been at the helm. He and Sarah Parker (whose departure, interestingly enough, Magoun did not even mention in his letter to the Willistons) gave the college precisely the strong leadership it needed during the critical war years of 1861–65.

Leonard Parker made other contributions to the college as well—and not only in the classroom. In his other position as county superintendent of public schools, he visited the country schools throughout Poweshiek County and was always on the lookout for bright young students whom he considered intellectually qualified for a college education. It was he who discovered two of the college's most illustrious alumni. In the Bear Creek township school he found James Irving Manatt and in Lynnville, a seventeen-year-old Quaker farm boy, Jesse Macy. Manatt proved to be the best student of Greek and Latin that Parker ever taught and would become one of the country's most distinguished classicists, chancellor of the University of Nebraska, and then for many years professor of Greek at Brown University.

Jesse Macy's interests lay in the field of political economy, and he never sought any home other than Grinnell. One year after his graduation in 1870, he became principal of the Academy for fourteen years, and then professor of History and Political Economy until he established a separate Department of Political Science in 1890, two years before Harvard established its department. Of the hundreds of faculty members the college has had in its century and a half of history, John Nollen's assessment made fifty years ago that Macy was "the college's most influential teacher" is still valid. If Parker had had nothing to his credit other than the discovery of these two youths, his service to the college would belie Magoun's adverse judgment.

With the departure of the two Parker families in the summer of 1870, both the college and the town were much the poorer. It would not be the last that the community would see of either man, however, for interestingly enough, neither could forget or cease to care for the college to which they and their wives had given so much. Henry Parker never made the transition from the Massachusetts Agricultural College to Amherst College that Magoun had gloomily predicted. In 1879, following the death of his beloved Helen, Henry Parker, much to Magoun's delight, asked for his old job back at Iowa College. He would remain on the faculty for another ten years until in 1889 total deafness forced his retirement.

Leonard Parker waited until Magoun was safely removed from office and a new president had been installed in 1887. Then he also came back to Iowa College, this time as professor of History. No longer the radical Oberlinite whose political and educational views had barred him from the presidency, Leonard Parker would now be the leading spokesman for ultraconservatism. It was always his unhappy fate to find himself in opposition to the prevailing power on campus. Too radical in the 1860s to please a majority of the trustees and President Magoun, he would now find himself in the 1890s a lonely swimmer bucking the strong tide of Social Gospel radicalism which was engulfing the campus of his beloved Iowa College.

The year 1870 had been for Magoun a mixture of pain and pleasure. The loss of Henry and Helen Parker had been offset by the departure of the other two Parkers. Of even greater joy to Magoun was his second marriage on 5 July 1870 to Elizabeth Earle of Brunswick, Maine. Twelve years younger than her husband, Elizabeth Earle was a graduate of Mount Holyoke College. She was teaching at that college when Magoun first met her. Their romance was promoted by the Willistons, who were friends of her family. With this marriage, Magoun had found as strong a support to his career as the two Parkers had with their wives. One contemporary Congregationalist described Mrs. Magoun as "Cultured, refined, a brilliant conversationalist, a marvelous Bible-class teacher, a gifted speaker, glowing with enthusiasm, cordial in her social relations, zealous in missionary endeavor, she was for many years a woman of commanding influence in our denomination."[14] She was even more important to the college than she was to her church—a paragon of a presidential spouse which few of her successors in that important role could ever hope to match. She even stepped into the breach in 1882 to serve as lady principal for two years following the departure of the popular Mary Ellis until a more permanent successor could be found. The society women of the town paid her their highest compliment by changing the name of their social club from "Busy Women's Club," to the "Elizabeth Earle Magoun Club." They also stipulated that all future presidents' wives would automatically be members of their elite circle, never envisioning the day when the presidential spouse might be a husband.

The entire community, town and college had welcomed

the arrival of Magoun's new wife. They saw her as a needed leavening force in the president's life, but that Magoun could be dependent on anyone to provide strength to his administration his associates found difficult to believe. By 1870, his authority within the college was unchallenged and absolute. Unprotected by late twentieth-century rules respecting academic freedom and tenure, a faculty member was at the mercy of the trustees. Whenever the trustees were as compliant to the wishes of the president as was the Iowa College Board to Magoun, any faculty dissent was both dangerous and futile. Magoun made his power forcibly evident in 1871 when on the eve of Commencement, he summarily fired the popular and able professor of Rhetoric and English, Charles W. Clapp, who had been a member of the faculty since 1864. Clapp's family found the president's timing particularly cruel, coming as it did on the day before Clapp's son was to receive his B.A. degree. Clapp appealed to the trustees for a reconsideration of this action, or at the very least, to provide him with a reason for his dismissal which Magoun had refused to give, but to no avail. The lesson of this incident, which Magoun clearly wished to convey, needed no elaboration—either subservience to the president or separation from the college. The trustees twenty years earlier had expressed the desire to find someone who could bring an "unruly faculty" into line. In Magoun they had found that man. Whether or not the faculty loved their leader was, as Machiavelli had said centuries earlier, unimportant; what counted was that they should fear him.

As might be expected, Magoun got mixed reviews from those alumni and townspeople who dared to speak out. Irving Manatt, student and later instructor at the college, would say of Magoun that he was "the prince of college presidents." Manatt, who in his long career was to know many college presidents, and to become one himself, readily admitted that Magoun was an autocrat: "I think he never quite got over the notion that the college included the church and the community—included too, Congregational Iowa if not the commonwealth [of Iowa]; and he was president of the college. I am not saying this to his reproach; it was the most natural thing in the world for him to think so; and he, if any man living—had a right to think so."[15]

There were others—and they were numerous—who viewed Magoun as quite another kind of prince, more akin to Machiavelli's ideal. J. P. Lyman, a graduate of the college who had become a leading lawyer in Grinnell, wrote to a friend to explain why he, unlike his friend, would not contribute to the college. Lyman was a kinsman of Leonard Parker, and could never forget how his cousin had been treated by Magoun. "So long as they keep that prince of sinners at the head of the institution I shall never contribute one cent toward its support, and I wish others felt the same way. My interest is here, and I have a great interest in the college, but I feel that the sooner the head droops and dies, and even a wooden one is substituted, the sooner it will grow and take the position that we all desire to see it occupy. Every gift will in a measure sanction the President, and it seems to me that whatever does that is an injury rather than a benefit. Am I not right?"[16]

Another critic of Magoun would write Leonard Parker: "I have often seen (not read) his [Magoun's] unending denunciations of 'errorists' of every description in the Christian Mirror, meaning by 'errorists' every Christian man whatsoever who presumes to depart by a hair's breadth from the theology which it please His Sublime Arrogancy, George Frederick Magoun, to patronize. ... Deacon McClory, of my church at Wittenberg, said to me once, after returning from Grinnell, 'I have been talking with some of the students, and they complain that President Magoun exacts of them greater deference than they owe their Maker.'"[17] This deference obligated all male students, upon meeting the president on the streets, to step aside and remove their hats as a token of respect.

Magoun remained sublimely impervious to all such barbs of criticism. As long as he had the unflagging support of the trustees and the total obeisance of the faculty, as long as he could move audiences by the power of his oratory (Man-att called him "the incomparable orator" of his time), any adverse comment was but the annoying buzzing of a harmless fly about his head.

Faculty support for the president was not prompted only out of fear of his power. He was in meeting with both trustees and potential donors the faculty's ardent champion to raise salaries and add additional instructors. For these efforts on their behalf, the faculty could find benevolence in the depotism which they endured.

Faculty meetings seldom involved a debate on educational policy. Personnel issues of hiring and firing were strictly reserved as the president's prerogative. The faculty was small enough to make committees dealing with special areas of college administration unnecessary. There was only the occasional ad hoc committee, requested and appointed by the president, to deal with a particular issue. The minutes of regular faculty meetings reveal that they were almost exclusively devoted to what at a much later time would be delegated to such bureaucratic offices as the Academic Standing Committee and the Student Affairs office.

Magoun did not use his authority to make a radical revision in the overall curriculum of the college. The concept of parallel courses of study borrowed from Union College in New York and first introduced by Iowa College when it reopened at Grinnell would remain the basic organization of its educational program until 1893. This structure offered three tracks of study: male students had available to them either the traditional classical course with its emphasis on the Great Three of Greek, Latin and Mathematics or the Scientific Course, with its emphasis upon Natural Philosophy and Physical Science; female students were required to take the Ladies Course where Belles Lettres predominated, and originally gave to its graduates not a Bachelor of Arts or Bachelor of Science degree, but only a diploma certifying to a successful completion of the course.

It was not by revision of structure but rather by the emphasis and support that he gave to certain disciplines that Magoun was to have his greatest impact upon the college's curriculum. Although educated in the rigid classical curriculum of Bowdoin and strictly orthodox in his Congregational Calvinistic beliefs, Magoun must be judged a modernist in his enthusiastic promotion of the natural sciences in higher education. He was determined to have Iowa College in the vanguard of scientific advancement. Samuel Buck and Henry Parker had in the president a champion of their discipline.

In his vigorous promotion of the natural sciences as early as 1862, Magoun had little realization of its consequences, for in the decade that followed, he would unwittingly be pushing his college into the very maelstrom of scientific controversy that had resulted from the publication in 1859 of Charles Darwin's *Origin of Species*. Not since the publication of Isaac Newton's *Principia* in 1687 had a single book had such an impact upon western thought. Darwin's book, to be sure, lacked the originality of Newton's work—the idea of evolution had been a matter of speculation among scientists for at least a century—but its disruptive force to the established order was far greater than that of *Principia*. Darwin's accumulation of evidence was so massive and detailed as to change a hypothesis into an established law for many scientists.

Within liberal arts colleges throughout America, as Stow Persons points out in *American Minds*, "The theory of evolution, and especially Darwinism, came conveniently to the hands of scientists as a weapon in their struggle for institutional influence and prestige. They had merely to insist upon their right to pursue truth wherever it might lead to place the clerical academic authorities in an embarrassing dilemma."[18]

For Magoun this embarrassing dilemma was particularly acute. Seeing himself as "keeper of the flame" of religious orthodoxy for the whole state of Iowa, at the same time he wanted to expand the horizons of science within his own institution. Happily for him, he found an escape from this

161

dilemma in the writings of the highly respected Harvard geologist and paleontologist, Louis Agassiz, who saw science progressing within the grand fixed design of nature ordained by God, not in a random, haphazard progression from lower to higher species as envisioned by Darwin.

In the student newspaper, *The College News Letter,* Magoun wrote a lengthy review of Agassiz's twelve-lecture attack given at the Harvard Museum of Comparative Zoology on Darwin's "physico-speculative structure." Magoun concluded his article, satisfied that "Professor Agassiz showed ... that the evolution of Darwin and Spencer—out of one species into another and higher—does not exist."[19] With Agassiz's doctrine of a fixed design for each individual species, Magoun could have both science and religion, and in that faith he would remain content for the rest of his life. Inasmuch as Iowa College was his to have and to hold, he believed that his faculty and his students would see science as he saw it, moving forward but ever adhering to God's grand order for the universe.

Magoun's primary concern always was for the students, for they after all were the raison d'être for the college's existence. It had been relatively easy to bring the faculty into line once he had got rid of a few potential troublemakers like Leonard Parker and Charles Clapp, but Magoun had to be ever on the alert as to what the students were thinking and doing. In enforcing the social regulations governing student behavior, which had remained largely the same as those initially established in 1848, Magoun had the enthusiastic cooperation of the faculty, for they were at least as zealous as he in demanding strict compliance.

How did the students fare within this authoritarian regime? For them, the system was much more all-pervading than it was for the faculty, for the students lived under several masters. They knew, of course, that the ultimate power rested with the president, but their daily brush with authority came in the classroom where the instructor ruled supreme, or on the streets of Grinnell where they were very likely to come under the close scrutiny of a professor alert to catch some miscreant smoking a cigar, uttering a profane word, or—worst sin of all—walking with a person of the opposite sex.

We know a great deal more about student life at Iowa College after the appearance of the first student newspaper in 1871. *The News Letter* began as a single column which the local town newspaper, the *Grinnell Herald* agreed to publish monthly. It did not become a true journal of student opinion until July 1873, when it appeared as an independent, four-page paper, edited by the students and published on a monthly basis. The college has had many student publications over the past century and a quarter, but none has ever excelled and few have equalled in literary style, grammatical correctness, cleanness of copy and breadth of coverage, not only of the Iowa College campus, but of other colleges as well, as did its very first publication, *The News Letter*. Its editorials were concerned with more than a preoccupation with its own navel; here one could find lively debates over the great scientific battle of Agassiz versus Darwin, and positions on the national political issues of the day.

Within the pages of *The News Letter* one can also find some indication of student reaction to the regulated society in which they lived. Beginning cautiously and discreetly enough to satisfy Magoun, the paper over the years became bolder in its criticism of social regulations, and in so doing undoubtedly reflected the prevailing student opinion. Of the eight College Laws printed in the college catalogue regarding "Deportment of Students," the one which the students found the most irksome was Rule 3. (As the list of regulations grew longer, this later became the hated Rule 13). It stated, "Young gentlemen will be allowed to visit young ladies connected with the institution only during the vacation of study hours on Saturday afternoon, except by special permission of the Faculty." Parenthetically it must be added, special permission was rarely given. The catchall Rule 5, surprisingly enough, was seldom an object of attack by the students, at least as reflected in the paper. It stated: "Everything in the deportment and habits of students which will interfere with their highest mental and moral development is prohibited— not only profanity, obscenity, the use of intoxicating drinks as a beverage, or tobacco, and gambling, &C, but also attendance at balls or dancing parties, playing at cards or billiards, or at any unlawful games, absence from their rooms during study hours without permission, and violation of the courtesy due to fellow students and the respect due to instructors."[20]

Even more than the specific rules imposed by the college, however, the students resented the procedures established for their enforcement. The administration had faithfully preserved the tradition of public confession and punishment which had its origin in the cutty stool of John Knox's Presbyterian Scotland and the scarlet letter of Richard Mather's Congregational New England. Every Friday morning Chapel was public confession time, scornfully referred to by the students as "Come Forward Day," when President Magoun would ask each student to "come forward" to state publicly if he or she had attended church twice on Sunday, had been regular in chapel attendance, and had faithfully observed study hours. It was also the time to confess voluntarily more serious crimes—the violation of Rule 3 or Rule 5 with its list of other forbidden activities. The incentive for freely admitting one's sins was that the punishment might be somewhat mitigated. Following this voluntary baring of one's past week's behavior, time was given for anyone else—a fellow student, or more likely, a faculty member—to bring charges against an unconfessed sinner, and an immediate hearing and trial would ensue. This was Iowa College's first attempt at what might be termed "an honor system."

It was the public nature of these proceedings which the students most despised. Those few students who were familiar with Roman Catholicism must have envied the privacy of its confessional booth where only the priest and God were privy to one's sins and absolution was given at the moment of confession.

164

Student opposition to "Come Forward" chapel became so pronounced that eventually Magoun and the faculty were forced to yield to their protests. In 1880, the faculty voted to change the rule "on self-reporting." Rather than public confession in chapel, "Each student shall report once a week to his excusing officer, his attendance on Sunday services, and college prayers, and his observance of Rule Third, Chap. V, the ten o'clock rule, and the rule on leaving town. Voted that the Executive Committee [of the Faculty] be requested to furnish blanks for reports of students."[21] But even if confession orally in a public gathering had been replaced by written reports to a single excusing officer, the rules remained the same, and the system still promoted as much dishonesty as it did obedience. One student, D. W. Norris, class of 1872, was frank in his assessment: "The lying that the system developed was indifferent and amusing, and yet men who considered themselves competent teachers of young people for many years defended the system and opposed its abrogation."[22] The students continued to chafe under this system, and many trespassed upon forbidden ground whenever they felt they could do so without being detected.

That there were many violations of the rules is hardly surprising. What does seem strange to the academic world of the late twentieth century, and particularly to post-1960 students, is that the system was tolerated for as long as it was. This was an age, however, that not only accepted but fully expected the college to carry out its duty of being "in loco parentis," often with far more vigor than the students' own parents. Coeducation was still a novel and, many parents felt, very dangerous innovation in higher education. Iowa College attempted to minimize the potential risk of joining the two sexes on the same campus by having only the classroom and chapel coeducational. In all other social activities sexual segregation was the order of the day. This is what parents demanded if they were to send their sons and especially their daughters off to college. There is only one known instance where a father—a colonel in the army, no less—withdrew his son from Iowa College after the boy had been given demerit marks for some minor peccadillo. Colonel J. T. K. Hayward in a letter to Magoun censured the Faculty "for their laws and discipline" which he regarded as irrational.[23]

Much as the students themselves complained about the restrictions placed upon them, they knew that transferring to another college would provide no relief, for similar rules would be found everywhere. Actually, Iowa College was considered to be somewhat more liberal than many other colleges, especially those sponsored by the Presbyterians and Methodists, for at least Iowa College was nonsectarian, and a particular Sunday church service was not prescribed. Students were free to choose whatever available church in town they preferred. A motion by one faculty member to "incorporate the Bible as a textbook for one lesson per week for all students," was quietly tabled, where it lay stillborn.[24] Iowa College students were debating the validity of Harriet Beecher Stowe's portrayal of slavery within six months after the publication of her novel *Uncle Tom's Cabin* in 1852. They were never to suffer the restrictions on reading that the Mount Holyoke women knew under a regulation that stated that the reading of fiction was strictly forbidden, and the one suggested reading outside of the assigned textbooks was Washington's Farewell Address. And at least the hated Rule 3 was far more precise and understandable than Oberlin's rule that "Young men and young women may not walk together on the campus unless they happen to be going in the same direction." Other college administrators would agree with President Magoun when at the inauguration of his successor, he told the assembly, "Character, character, character—above scholarship, above refinement, or expression—character after the pattern of Our Lord is what this college was created for."[25]

The housing of students would remain a problem for the college throughout the nineteenth century. While still at Davenport, the college had made the decision not to build dormitories. The then all-male student body had to find lodging in private homes. The admission of women, particularly after the college moved to Grinnell, forced a change in that policy, but unfortunately policy did not automatically build dormitories. A Ladies Boarding Hall was built in 1874, but it could only provide rooms for a portion of the women. A few of the men lived on the top floors of the two college buildings, but the majority of the students continued to find their own rooms in private houses approved by the college, where the landlords were obliged to enforce the social regulations of the college. Boarding houses, strictly segregated between male and female clientele, provided meals.[26] It is the eternal prerogative of students since the beginning of colleges to complain about the food served, but if one student, D. W. Norris, is accurate in describing the meals served at his boarding house, student complaints in the 1870s were fully justified:

> The boarding houses were not only bad, they were villainous. The regulation breakfast was hash, or codfish; dinner [served at noon], a stew, supper, dried prunes and sorghum, though the latter was a luxury. Sunday dinner consisted of a dish called chowder, made of potatoes, milk, and scraps of meat, fish, etc. gathered from the plates during the week.[27]

It was small wonder that student illness, even death, from dysentery, typhoid, and ptomaine poisoning were all too frequent occurrences.

Such conditions were to prevail throughout the nineteenth century. The trustees would note with pleasure in their annual meeting in July 1893, that not a single student had died during the past academic year—a rare and memorable record. When Edward Burling of the class of 1890, one of the nation's most distinguished and successful lawyers and a generous donor to the college, returned to his alma mater in 1959 for the dedication of the new library which bore his name, he began his brief talk not with the usual platitudinous salutation given on such an occasion of how delighted he was to be back on the campus he had loved as a student, but rather with the blunt announcement, "When I was a student here, I was ill-housed, ill-fed and ill-educated." While the audience gasped at this unexpected candor, Burling graciously added praise for the college he now saw, so different from what he knew as a student.

Yet in spite of strict regulations and poor diet, most of the students not only survived but also received an education that would stand them in good stead in their future careers. Nothing the college imposed could suffocate youthful high spirits, which may be the youngs' finest attribute. As masterful artful dodgers, the students managed to find ways to live within the system, or perhaps more accurately outside it. Although faculty minutes were replete with accounts of the misdeeds of those unfortunate enough to be caught in their transgressions, the monitors of student behavior were always uncomfortably aware that their surveillance was but a poor net full of holes.

During the Magoun era there were only two incidents that the president and the faculty found so egregious as to become causes celebres to rock the college. That the ring leader of the first, Henry Carter Adams was the son of one of the college's founding fathers, the sainted Ephraim Adams, made his escapade especially noteworthy.

The incident involved the stuffed carcass of a walrus which the college had been given to be exhibited in Henry Parker's museum. When the building in which the museum was housed was destroyed by fire in 1871, only a portion of the museum's exhibits were saved, but unfortunately the walrus was one of those objects rescued and was placed in the entryway of the college's remaining building. Parker's successor as professor of chemistry and curator of the museum, Henry Carmichael, attempted to restore preservative on the fire-damaged beast in whatever free time he had, but these were rare moments and the work progressed slowly. As the months passed, the carcass began to ripen, and in the warm spring weather, the odor became ever more pungent and reached the top floor where Adams and a few other boys lived.

Appeals to Professor Carmichael for relief were unavailing, so Henry and his comrades decided to take direct action. On a warm May night, just before the ten o'clock curfew when all students were required to be in bed, these self-appointed undertakers stole out of their rooms, hastily dug a shallow grave and interred the decaying beast. Not content with this simple and necessary burial, Henry suggested that the poor corpse be given a decent farewell. What had originated as a mere act of sanitation quickly became a jolly lark. They placed a crude wooden monument at the head of the grave:

Hic Jacet

WALRUS BOANERGES

Oft called the iceberg's daughter
A
Member of
Prof. Comical's department
Died Aug. 7 1870

At the foot of the mound, they placed a card: "This walrus standing where it did was a public nuisance, offensive both to sight and smell. After bearing it for some time it was thought best to give him a decent burial."

The next morning the call went out that the perpetrators of this act should come forward and confess. This all of those involved willingly did. They were charged with four violations of college rules for which apology was required: first, they had broken the ten o'clock rule; second, they had violated the respect due to instructors (it was that reference to "Prof. Comical's department" that was particularly resented); third, they had no business to meddle with college property; and fourth, they had disturbed the public peace. The boys accepted this bill of indictment and apologized to Magoun.

Henry, in a letter to his father, gave details of the incident and told of Magoun's reaction:

169

We were led to believe that if this apology was made, the matter would be dropped. ... If such had been the case all would have felt justice had had her due. But I am sorry to say such was not the case as indeed such never will be the case as long as Pres. Magoun is at the head of this institution.

In speaking of the matter at chapel he was in such a rage that his voice trembled. His rage I suppose was because he could see that not a person in the house sympathized with him. The invectives which he hurled against us and the charges which he hurled against us ... were such as only the Pres. could wield. ... Not content with this—besides much more—he suspended one of our number who had no more to do with the affair than any other one. He was a freshman and all of his classmates have suspended themselves until he be restored or until the three weeks have expired. Also three from our class—those who were in the affair—have done the same, and I truly think that it is no more than is due to him, ourselves; and who will ever come to school here.

This mass voluntary self-suspension is the first recorded incident in the college's history of a student rebellion against the president.

Henry added a final note of apology to his father: "In all of this, father, there is only one thing which makes me feel sad, and that is that by my foolish love of jokes I have brought myself into a place where I may do some injury to an institution which you all your life have labored to build up. Yet at the same time I think it is no less than right that I should not receive every belaboring which one desires unjustly to inflict upon me."[28]

Henry's apology was fully accepted by his father. Indeed neither Ephraim Adams nor any other member of his family could ever again have the same high regard for Iowa College's first president as they previously had. President Magoun was the real loser in the affair. For the first time as president, he had been publicly humiliated, first by the stony reception his chapel harangue had been given by his audience, and even more pointedly by the entire freshman class's decision to go on strike.

The second major incident which was to put both the president and the faculty on the defensive concerned the student newspaper. *The News Letter,* since its becoming in July 1873 an independent paper under the auspices of the News Letter Association, with a board of managers consisting entirely of students, had established a reputation for excellence among students as well as with the general public who had access to its pages. The faculty had never been happy with this arrangement and felt that a student organization free of college control should not be allowed to exist. Magoun, however, had been surprisingly tolerant of this organization. The paper had generally been supportive of the president and had opened its columns to him whenever he wished to express his views on education, religion and evolution. Consequently, in this particular brouhaha, it was the faculty, not Magoun, who led the charge.

The professors had been assiduous readers of *The News Letter,* constantly on the alert to find something in its pages which would warrant faculty intervention into its management. In the November 1880 issue the faculty believed it had finally found the evidence needed to call the paper's editorial staff to task and proceeded to do so.

A careful line-by-line reading of the issue by this writer has failed to reveal what might have disturbed the faculty. It may be that as a fifty-year veteran reader of such diverse student publications as the *Scarlet and Black, Pterodactyl, The Paper,* and *Gum,* I have become so shockproof as to be rendered incapable of detecting what apparently violated sensitive Victorian propriety. Could it have been the expletive, "By gad, sir!" on page 10, or "Touche! That's a jigger" and "In God I trusted, in Trig I busted" on page 11. Perhaps it was the report on the Rev. Burbank's talk at the Congregational church which the reporter found to be "a marked exception to the dull and uninteresting grinds we generally receive under the name of missionary meetings." (p. 12).[29]

171

Whatever the spark may have been, the faculty was ablaze with anger. At its meeting on 29 November 1880, it voted that *The News Letter* be required to apologize in their [sic] next number for the profanity and low language permitted to appear in the last issue."[30]

The managing editor of the paper, F. H. Harvey, was a remarkably self-possessed and determined young man. He boldly asserted the Constitutional protection of the First Amendment guaranteeing freedom of the press. The News Letter Association by its charter was not subject to any outside dictation, including that of the college. The next issue appeared in December without either the apology or the promise of not again "indulging in language that even borders on profanity," that had been demanded.

The faculty was now prepared to take the action that most of its members had wanted from the beginning. On 20 January 1881, a motion was passed dissolving the News Letter Association and further ordering "the paper published be discontinued and that no College paper be thereafter published by any student or association of students except under an organization and regulations approved by the Faculty."[31]

Harvey and his staff simply ignored this faculty fiat. The February issue appeared on schedule, and the faculty, apparently advised by legal counsel that it had no authority to dissolve an organization independent of the college or to stop its publications, could only sit by in impotent rage as *The News Letter* made its regular appearance under the editorship of Harvey.

If the college could not stop the paper, it could at least punish its editors for, as students, they were subject to college discipline. By faculty vote, the other members of the staff aside from the managing editor received ten demerit marks, but Harvey was to receive fifteen demerits. This punitive action against Harvey was made more severe in June when he was expelled.[32]

Having successfully defied college authority for the past eight months, Harvey did not now intend to submit passively to expulsion—the college's equivalent to capital punishment.

He appealed over the heads of the faculty and the president directly to the Board of Trustees. Willy-nilly, the Board was forced to step in. A special committee of the trustees to look into the matter was appointed, headed by Ephraim Adams, who since his son's involvement in the walrus affair was no ardent supporter of the college's disciplinary methods.

In September, just prior to the opening of the new term, the committee made its report. It agreed with the faculty that in the future "The Faculty must in all cases be consulted by the students before organizing any literary, scientific or other society connected with the Institution; and in no case shall such society be formed without the permission of the Faculty of the College." The trustees enclosed a letter from the new board of the News Letter Association, who would take over the paper for the coming year, agreeing to this policy. In other words, the News Letter Association surrendered its independent status. The trustees urged that the faculty accept this capitulation and permit *The News Letter* to continue publication. This was a clear victory for the faculty, and this policy would prevail for all publications and other student organizations for the next eighty years.

As for Harvey's petition to be readmitted to the college, the trustees also enclosed his letter to them, stating that although his term as managing editor had ended, he too accepted this new policy, even though he offered no apology for previous actions. He formally requested re-admission to the college, to which the trustee's report added, "This also we recommend to your careful and we may say favorable consideration." The trustees did not find that he deserved special punishment but rather "should be dealt with on the same principle as that of others. ... The fact that a petition signed by 49 of our graduates is in the hands of the Ex. Com. praying the Trustees to investigate the whole case is not to be forgotten—and favorable action might obviate the necessity of the investigation." The trustees were also painfully aware that nearly the entire current student body had signed a petition demanding Harvey's reinstatement.[33]

Under such pressure the faculty reluctantly yielded. One

173

day after receiving the trustees' recommendation the faculty voted that "Mr. Harvey's request be granted ... and also Harvey's case be publicly announced. ... Thus also a petition for his reinstatement signed by many students of the College and Ladies Courses was favorably answered."[34] Even in victory, it was bitter humble pie the faculty had to eat in public. In an attempt to salvage something of its pride, the faculty informed Harvey when he returned to campus for his senior year that he had been reclassified as a junior. Even this petulant slap, born out of pique, was to be denied the faculty, however, for a week later, undoubtedly due to quiet trustee interference, the faculty voted that "Harvey be classified as a Senior ... and that he be explicitly informed that this implies no pledge to graduate him."[35] Harvey did graduate, however, as scheduled, and became a successful lawyer in Wyoming, being able to put to good use the excellent practical experience he had received at Iowa College in trial defense.

F. H. Harvey and Henry Carter Adams, who was to have an illustrious career as a leading economist at the University of Michigan, stand out as students in the early history of the college for their celebrated activities in the well-regulated society of the Magoun era.

Fortunately for the administration and faculty few other students aspired to and none achieved, such memorable notoriety. Most were content to find release from the stress of their studies and prominence on campus in activities sanctioned by the college. The most prestigious of the extracurricular student organizations, at least in the eyes of the faculty, were the literary societies which flourished well into the twentieth century. The first literary society was organized in 1853 by Professor Erastus Ripley while the college was still at Davenport. He gave the society its name, Chrestomathian (Useful Learning), and its program was devoted to training young men in the useful arts of debate and oratory.

Prior to the Civil War the major topic for debate was slavery—its existence and its extension. In the decade after the war, the most provocative political issue was woman suffrage. In 1870, a constitutional amendment passed both houses of the state legislature, and it appeared that Iowa might be the first state in the Union to grant women the vote. In Iowa, a proposal to amend the state constitution must pass the legislature in two successive sessions before submitting it to the voters for ratification. In 1872, the bill again passed the lower house, but was defeated in the senate by only two votes.[36] Jesse Macy would recall that in these years, "Woman suffrage was indeed a standard topic for debate, but it was not taken very seriously," neither by the male students at Iowa College, nor apparently by the Iowa electorate. Macy decried the fact the postwar student body "was not politically inclined. ... The questions debated were such as: whether conscience is a creature of education, or ... whether there is more pleasure in pursuit than in possession."[37] Such debates brought to the Chrestomathian Society collegewide renown, and it would remain the premier student organization until its demise in the 1920s.

During the Civil War, however, when there were few male students, this society became dormant. As in so many other areas of college life, the female students kept the concept of the literary society active by organizing their own society in 1863. Not to be outdone by the males, they too adopted a Greek name—the nearly unpronounceable Calocagathia (Beautiful Goodness) Society,[38] which was familiarly known as "the Calico Aprons." Because it was considered unseemly for women to engage in public debate, the activities of this society were largely restricted to the reading of poetry and presenting the members' own efforts at the writing of essays and verses.

The Chrestomathian and Calocagathia societies were Iowa College's democratic Greek-named substitutes for the exclusive and secret Greek-letter fraternities and sororities popular on many Eastern campuses. Anyone could join Iowa College's literary societies. Throughout the college's early history there would be sporadic attempts on the part of a few students to establish secret fraternities, but these efforts would always be vigorously stamped out, not only by the faculty but by an overwhelming majority of the students, who held fast to the college's tradition of egalitarianism.

As the student population grew in numbers, additional literary societies were formed: The Grinnell Institute for men in 1870; the Ellis Society (named for the popular lady principal, Mary Ellis) for women in 1882; and three literary societies for the students in the Academy—the Philologian (1867) and the Lewis Literary Society Association (1871) for males; and the Elizabeth Barrett Browning Society (1886) for females. The meetings of these societies were closed to any visitors of the opposite sex, except for once a year when each society could celebrate the anniversary of its founding and could invite friends regardless of gender. Anniversary days were immensely popular, for after the program the celebration frequently culminated with an oyster stew supper with oysters shipped in barrels by rail from the East Coast. These anniversary celebrations gave vitality to the literary societies; otherwise these organizations might have had difficulty in recruiting members. To many students, participation in the society activities was at least as demanding and time consuming as their regular class work. The students found the literary societies too closely allied to intellectual pursuits to provide much of a release from curricular pressure.

The male students found a needed physical outlet in a variety of activities that the mores of the day offered only to them. In the years immediately following the Civil War, there was a student military organization on campus, for a time headed by the professor of Civil Engineering and Military Drill, Arthur Hardy, in which all able-bodied men were expected to participate, but this prototype of later R.O.T.C. units on college campuses faded away with the departure of Hardy in 1873.

Most men, however, looked to themselves to find extracurricular pursuits that would give them exercise: hunting for game birds in the open prairies, or an occasional camping trip with friends during college breaks. There was no river close by, as there had been in Davenport, for swimming, boating and fishing. Many men got exercise in chopping wood, cleaning yards or house painting in order to pay for college expenses.

Organized team sports made their first appearance in the postwar years. A crude form of baseball had been played at Davenport, but it was the Civil War that gave to America's great national pastime its modern form and universal popularity. The veterans brought this game back from the war to many college campuses. At Iowa College in 1867, the former soldier, Michael Austin, class of 1871, formed the first baseball team ready to take on all challengers. The first intercollegiate game of any sport ever played in Iowa was a baseball game with the University of Iowa in 1868, which Iowa College won 24-0.[39]

The faculty was not happy with this intervarsity development. Intramural games were the preferred contests. Reluctant permission was given to meet with an outside team, but only if the game was played after 4:30 P.M., and was played in Grinnell. All games had to be home games, and an illicit trip to another college meant automatic expulsion. This restriction, if obeyed, meant a very abbreviated schedule. It was secretly—and not infrequently—violated.

The only other team sport to make its appearance on campus during the Magoun era was a game which was called "football." Jesse Macy always claimed credit for having introduced this sport in the late 1860s. From his description, it appears to have been more like the European form of football which we were later to call "soccer" than our present game of football which would shortly develop out of English Rugby.[40] Soccer proved to be no serious competitor to baseball in either player or spectator interest, and was to disappear as a team sport at the college, not to be resurrected for another eighty years. All other organized sports were totally absent either for lack of facilities or a knowledge of the game—no tennis courts, swimming pools or golf courses. Basketball would not be invented until 1891. The only activity even remotely resembling track sports, according to Macy, was due to the success that Mahlon Willett, class of 1869, had in persuading some of his classmates to join him for "a brisk walk or run into the country before breakfast."[41] Baseball ruled supreme at Grinnell as it did at all other American colleges in the 1870s.

College men were strictly on their own in the promotion of athletics. There was no gymnasium, and the idea of providing instruction in physical education and in providing a coach would never have occurred to the faculty, the president or the trustees even if there had been funds available for such luxuries. Games at best were simply tolerated and carefully restricted.

Physical activities for the female students were even more limited. Their delicate constitutions must be carefully protected both within and outside the classroom. Properly attired in heavy, many-layered and restrictive garments, women could find physical exercise only in the decorous, ladylike strolls, like nuns always in pairs, down to the village square, and from their rooming house to the campus. That the females survived this restrictive regimen designed to protect their innate weakness is, ironically, testimony to the strength of their constitutions.

For two decades, George Frederick Magoun ruled his college with some complaints but few challenges to his authority. Only before extraordinary natural calamities would he be forced to bow in submission. Two such disasters were to occur during his tenure to extract from him an admission that on those occasions he was powerless.

The first and lesser of the two trials to which he was subjected was the destruction by fire of East College, the older of the two buildings on campus. This occurred shortly after midnight on 24 December 1871. The Iowa College physical plant at this time consisted of only two buildings, West College and East College; to house all activities on campus—

classrooms, chapel, library, laboratories, and museums, as well as providing dormitory rooms for a few male students. By 1871, it was apparent that a third building was needed, and President Magoun had spent many long and arduous months seeking funds in the East, playing the uncomfortable and unaccustomed role of obsequious sycophant to potential donors—the one aspect of his job that he found distasteful. By the fall of 1871, Magoun had successfully raised enough money to begin construction of the third building, and then came that fire.[42]

Of the several accounts written of this spectacular fire, one of the most graphic is that of Benjamin St. John, class of 1876, which was published in the *Blue Book* of 1898:

> There had been a heavy fall of snow, and the weather was bitterly cold. Several of the students were spending their [Christmas] vacation in town, and devoting most of their time in keeping warm. On the day previous to the fire, one of the boys, a Jew by the name of Van Noorden, had gathered an extra amount of fuel in his room, and built a roaring fire, with the result that the partition behind the stove took fire. This was discovered and put out with a few buckets of water. It was watched until about 10 o'clock that night, and as there was no further sign of fire, the boys went to bed. Later, near midnight, they were roused by the smell of smoke, and crackling flames. Without stopping for elaborate toilets, the boys hustled out into the bitter night, the little Jew running through the deep snow to West College to give the alarm, shouting as he ran, "Jesus Christ has come for us! Jesus Christ has come for us!"

> My own room was in East College, just at the head of the second flight of stairs, but I was spending the vacation with my classmate, L. S. Keen, whose room was in ... West College. On the first alarm I was out of bed and saw the flames bursting out of the southeast room and the dense smoke pouring out of the building. Knowing that it was doomed, my only thought was to save my possessions if possible. ... I ran through the snow, and up the stairs, against the protests of the boys who had left their rooms but dared not return. But up I went, followed by Harry Adams (as we called him then, now Dr. H. C. Adams) who

179

had a bucket in his hand. ... Pressing my way on I burst open my door and ... rushed for my clothes, bedding, trunks and tossed them from the open window, ending by throwing down my stove. ... Filling my lungs with fresh air ... I made a dash for the stairs with the hot blast of the flames on my cheeks and the bannister almost blistering my hand as I touched it. ... I was so nearly overcome that I staggered as I came into the open air, not realizing till then the risk I had run to save a few dollars' worth of property. ... When the building was nearly burned down, I remembered that I had left all my books and a set of stencil tools, for which I had paid $25.00, to be burned up. ... One of the upper rooms had been used as an arsenal for storing the guns used by the military company, which Prof. Hardy had organized. A few of the guns were rescued but most were burned, together with a lot of cartridges which went off with a lively fusilade. The museum was on the lower floor, and the specimens [including the unfortunate afore mentioned walrus] were mostly saved. I remember the weird scene, the snowy landscape lighted by the flames, and adorned with various specimens of bird and beast scattered about in every direction, some of them in lifelike attitudes, while beyond the circle of light was the black and bitter night.[43]

President Magoun must have watched the destruction of one half of the college's facilities with a sinking heart in the realization he would have to begin anew his search for funds for yet another building. What is surprising, however, is not that a college building should have burned to the ground on that night, but rather that such a fire had not happened earlier. At a time when central heating was unknown and every student was required to provide and tend to his own stove in his college room, it was something of a miracle that a similar calamity had not struck other times with perhaps far more serious consequences.

St. John's account is of interest not only for its dramatic, first-hand description of the 1871 fire, but also for its providing the first evidence of a Jewish student's being in residence at Iowa College. If true, this revelation raises some interesting questions. How did a Jewish student happen to be enrolled in this school, totally committed to Christianity? Although Iowa College from the beginning had prided itself on being nonsectarian, the ecumenical reach of its teachings, its authorized religious services, and its general ethos had never extended beyond the Christian faith in whatever denominational form that faith might express itself. The college catalogue for the year 1871–72 lists David Van Noorden as a student in the English Department of the Academy, and gives as his home Brussels, Belgium; so this boy may have the distinction of being our first international student as well as our first Jewish student. How did Van Noorden fare in this overpowering gentile society? What, if any, special consideration had been given exempting him from the daily prayer services or from the rule requiring attendance on Sunday of church services in a town where there was no synagogue? We have no answers to these probing questions and can only surmise as to how serious were the problems he encountered in being a minority of one in this community. All that the catalogue reveals is that Van Noorden stayed at the college for only one year.[44]

Iowa College was slow in recovering from the fire of 1871. There were enough funds on hand to complete the new building, Central College, which had been under construction when the fire occurred, but any hopes that Magoun had for a quick rebuilding of East College dissipated as the nation was plunged into the depression of 1873, the most serious economic setback in our history up to that time. Gifts to the college dried up. Although the college catalogues throughout the 1870s continued to show three buildings on campus, it was only by reading the fine print under the picture of East College could the prospective student discover that it had burned in 1871, and was currently nonexistent. Only basement walls and a large hole in the ground marked its location.

Nevertheless, Iowa College could boast of an impressive campus. In 1867 the college had acquired enough land to the south of its two buildings to provide a semicircular front yard, forcing Sixth Avenue to make a gentle curve around the campus which still exists today in spite of efforts over the years by highway engineers to "straighten that road out." The trustees also authorized in February 1867, "the setting out of 300–400 elm trees at a cost of 25 cents each."[45]

In 1870, the trustees also granted the right of way to the Central Railroad of Iowa (later the Minneapolis and St. Louis Railway) to lay its tracks through college grounds. Undoubtedly this proposal was successfully pushed by J. B. Grinnell, who had an interest in that road, and one can only marvel at the docility of the other trustees in yielding to this pressure after their having fought so bitterly against the invasion of campus grounds by only a street in Davenport.[46] Of necessity, trustees were far more amenable to the wishes of railroad corporations than to the dictates of the Davenport city council. Indeed, the college for years would boast in its promotional literature that Iowa College was the only school in the country where a student arriving from either the north or the south could step off the train and be right there on campus. This busy little railway line still exists today (although now only a freight carrier) and is still being cursed by students, as in generations past, for delaying them in their mad dash to class, and still bemoaned by those attending concerts and lectures for drowning out programs with its blaring whistles.

Students felt their campus was being locked in by Sixth Avenue on the south, by the large town houses on Park Street to the west, and now by iron rails to the east. Ever optimistic about the future growth of the college, they raised a demand, from the 1870s on, that the trustees acquire more land to the north—the only direction in which further expansion could occur.[47] To these pleas, the money-strapped trustees and president turned a deaf ear. They sought only enough funds to complete a campus already planned. With the return of better times in 1880, they were confident they could at last rebuild the burned-out East College and per-haps raise enough money for the long-hoped-for Ladies Boarding House. Then within three minutes on the night of 17 June 1882 even these modest expectations were—quite literally—blown sky high.

The great storm that hit the village of Grinnell on that fateful night, which is always referred to as the Cyclone of '82, but perhaps more correctly should be called "tornado," has been elaborated upon so profusely in articles, memoirs, and even in songs, poems, novels, and in one dramatic "After the Storm" landscape painting by the Chicago artist, Emma Merrick, that it hardly needs another retelling. No history of this college, however, would be complete without some at-tention being given to what has been called the greatest na-tional calamity "ever to befall any college in the whole his-tory of education."[48]

Commencement in the year 1882 had originally been scheduled, according to custom, on the last Thursday in June, but in that year on Tuesday, 27 June, there was to be a statewide referendum on a proposal to adopt a law pro-hibiting the sale and use of alcoholic beverages in the entire state. Fearful that their Commencement might keep prohi-bitionists from the polls, the trustees decided to hold the graduation exercises one week earlier on Tuesday, 20 June. This abbreviated calendar resulted in a rush on campus to complete classes, final examinations and student orations before the close of the term. There was little time to take note of the abnormal heat on Saturday, 17 June, three days before Commencement. A vague sense of depression and instances of shortened tempers pervaded the busy campus, unrealized signs that the barometric pressure throughout a vast area of the upper Mississippi valley had dropped to a new low. By late afternoon and early evening people did notice strange cloud formations in both the east and the west, colored in green, yellow and red hues. Although the heat did not abate, these clouds gave promise of rain and a blessed cooling.

Grinnellians had no news of what might be happening in the surrounding areas, for in those pre-radio, pre-Doppler days, there were no advanced warnings to seek shelter. As the towering clouds grew thicker and blacker, the last choir rehearsal before Commencement was cancelled and the director urged his singers to hurry back to their rooms before the rain came. The rains did come, and then at precisely 8:44 P.M. the storm in all of its wild, whirling fury struck the town.

Accounts vary as to the course of the destructive whirlwind through the village. The most commonly accepted version is that a tornado touched down at the southwest corner of the city limits, heading northeast until it had levelled the college. Then abruptly it made a U-turn to the southeast to direct its fury for the destruction of the small village of Malcom, some nine miles away, as the tornado flies.

The story of this storm, however, is more complex than that of a single tornado making a U-turn as it passed through the town. The most scientifically sound analysis of the great storm that swept across Iowa that night has been given by S. Henderson Herrick, the son of Stephen L. Herrick, a teacher and trustee of the college. In his article written for the *Annals of Iowa* in 1897, Henderson Herrick gives a detailed description of the gigantic cyclonic storm wave. It originated in northwest Carroll County, some 150 miles WNW of Grinnell. In moving ESE across the state at a speed of from 45 to 60 miles per hour, it reached a width of at least 100 miles. Along its course, it spawned numerous tornadoes on its northern and southern sides. Many of these tornadoes never touched ground, others wreaked considerable damage, mostly to farm buildings in Greene, Boone and Story Counties. As the wide storm wave crossed southern Marshall County, it curved south into eastern Jasper County, gained force, and near Kellogg gave birth to its most violent tornado along its southern edge. It was this tornado that roared into Grinnell from the southwest and did most of the damage. Just at this moment, a second tornado made its appearance a few miles north of Grinnell. It too headed for the town, and there met its partner tornado, the exact spot estimated as being at the corner of Eighth Avenue and Broad Street, the northern most limit of the town. After a brief but terrible *danse macabre* over the college, the two tornadoes separated and continued on, headed in opposite directions.

The force of this tornadic collision had been sufficient to divide the huge storm wave that had mothered the whirlwinds. One section of the storm followed the course set by the tornado heading northeast. Greatly weakened by the impact, this section, nevertheless, continued in that direction, passing through Belle Plaine, where numerous small, identifiable articles it had picked up in Grinnell—photographs, letters and documents—were later found. It finally died out some ninety miles northeast of Grinnell.

The major section of the storm wave, however, continued on its original path, heading on a diagonal line southeast through six counties, and finally exiting the state at the Mississippi river a few miles south of Burlington, giving its last gust of wind in eastern Illinois. The storm had made its spectacular transit of 250 miles across Iowa from Carroll to Burlington in less than five hours. It was indeed a night to remember. Many communities, especially Malcom, had felt its fury, but it was Grinnell that had been pounded with two devastating blows, each of which, Herrick estimated, delivered a force of "not less than 200 pounds to the square inch."[49]

A tornado always leaves in its wake not only death and destruction but also innumerable stories of the storm's frequently capricious and merciful behavior. Grinnell had a rich store of such lore: that of a baby snatched from its father's arms as the family ran for safety, then gently deposited unharmed on the floor of a neighbor's roofless kitchen; of a locomotive coming through the campus picked up and then set down upright beside the tracks; of a family of five buried in the ruins of their house and then dug out by neighbors, not only alive but hardly scratched.

Such stories of miraculous escapes helped to ease the pain of the survivors who must now assess the damages wrought: thirty-eight dead, of whom two were college students—B. H. Burgett and Burritt Chase; thousands of dollars worth of property destroyed beyond repair, including some of the town's most expensive homes. Curiously enough, due to the paths taken by the tornadoes, the business section was left relatively unscathed. The biggest loss in property value was the college. The buildings were gone. West College was totally demolished; the walls of Central College, built of stone, had withstood the fury of the winds but bottles breaking in the chemistry laboratory had started a fire which gutted the building. All of the fifteen-year-old elm trees that had graced the campus were reduced to splintered firewood. The only objects left intact were the college bell, but no cupola in which to hang it, and the Civil War memorial plaque.

One student, Helen Campbell, with her poem "Nothing Left," became the college's poet laureate of the disaster:

> "Nothing left." Long years of toil,
> Lingering days of care and moil
> Bravely met, each one a token
> Of a home now crushed and broken.
> For the days to come can never
> Give back youth and youth's endeavor;
> And the soul, of all bereft,
> Sits in darkness, "Nothing left."[50]

President Magoun's home, out of the track of the tornadoes, was quickly converted into a make-shift hospital, and the schoolhouse nearby became a temporary morgue. Magoun's one thought was of his college and the students who might be trapped inside its buildings. When he finally managed to make his way through downed trees and across streets that had become rushing streams, he found the devastation more total than he had imagined. A crowd of students and townspeople, carrying lanterns, were standing in awe before the ruins while others were digging frantically into the fallen bricks to remove bodies, dead or alive. One student, Katherine Jones, would later recall the scene:

> When it was thought that all had been taken from the ruined buildings, Dr. Magoun stood on a pile of bricks ... that had been so important a part of the college to which

he had given his life work and called for silence. Against the background of the night, the heavens still densely covered with clouds, the only light coming from lanterns and the lightening, in the distance now—against the background of cloud and storm stood the notable form of the old president and his voice broke a silence as if he had been alone as he called the roll of the boys who might have been in the ruined buildings.[51]

Standing on the ruins of his college, Magoun could say in the words of Job, "The Lord gave, and the Lord hath taken away, blessed be the name of the Lord." To his audience, however, Magoun appeared less like the patient and submissive Job and more like the awesome Moses on Mount Sinai, tablet in hand, long white beard blowing in the wind, viewing the scene before him with horror and anger. The names of the boys in residence in the two buildings were called, those present at the scene responding and the disposition of the four wounded youths, including the two who would be dead before morning, being accounted for. There were a few names on the list, however, whose whereabouts Magoun had not ascertained. Before he could give the order for further digging into the ruins to find them, one youth hesitantly spoke up to inform the president that all of those boys who were marked as missing were members of the college's baseball team. In defiance of the strict rule against out-of-town games, they had gone early that morning to Tama to play that town's team and had not as yet returned to the campus. Only relief, not stern judgment, greeted this announcement, for if ever there was a moment to forgive transgressions it surely was now.[52]

Those who had assumed that Commencement would be cancelled that year, or at the least postponed, did not know President Magoun. The attributes of courage and determination with which he was splendidly endowed never were so fully demonstrated as during the next two days. He announced the exercises would be held the coming Tuesday as scheduled. Monday would be devoted to burying the dead. On Tuesday morning he would deliver the baccalaureate sermon, and in the afternoon the Rev. David Mears, the Congregational minister at Worcester, Massachusetts and the husband of J. B. Grinnell's daughter, Mary Grinnell Mears, would give the Commencement address. The twenty-nine seniors, the largest class Iowa College had as yet graduated, would then receive their diplomas.

Mears and his wife had arrived in Grinnell in time to be witnesses of the great storm.[53] Mears fortunately had his speech safely secured on his person, but Magoun's sermon, carefully prepared months in advance, had been left in his office, and was now, along with the office, gone with the wind. Magoun would be obliged to improvise as only he, Iowa's greatest orator, could.

Magoun entitled his sermon "And God was in the Whirlwind." He took as his text Psalms 148:8:

> Fire and hail; snow and vapour;
> Strong wind fulfilling His word.

All that Grinnell had lacked on that Saturday night was the snow. Magoun was convinced that God had not destroyed Iowa College as He had Sodom and Gomorrah because it was evil. As with Job, God had been testing the college's leaders to determine the strength of their faith and their commitment to carrying on their mission. Magoun left no doubt in his auditors' minds that the trustees, the president, the faculty and the students of Iowa College had that faith and they would carry on.

Buren R. Sherman, governor of Iowa, issued a proclamation calling for the people of Iowa to provide relief to the stricken towns of Grinnell and Malcom. The railroads agreed to run special trains into Grinnell to carry volunteers free of charge to aid in the relief work. Unfortunately, to the great resentment of Grinnellians, too many of these free-riders came not to clear away debris and nurse the wounded but to gawk at the ruins and to pick up souvenirs of Iowa's great storm.[54]

The trustees a month later were able to tally up the college's losses as being: $54,800 in buildings; $2,800 in heating apparatus; $10,000 in library materials; $4,045 in scientific apparatus; $8,000 in museum specimens; and $2,000 in furniture and fixtures, for a grand total of $81,645, not including the musical instruments and library belonging to the Conservatory of Music. Insurance covered only $9,975 of the loss. The trustees sent out "An Appeal for Aid To the Friends and Patrons of Iowa College," to institutions and communities throughout the country, asking for $125,000 to restore what had been lost and to provide funds for the Ladies Boarding Hall the college had long wanted.[55]

Money did come in, mostly in one and five dollar gifts from Iowans and even from unknown sympathetic friends from as far away as Canada, New England and even England itself. J. B. Grinnell, however, looked for richer sources who could provide more than these nickel and dime contributions. Believing that direct personal contact would be more productive than printed brochures, he headed East immediately after Commencement to call on rich friends from Illinois to New York. His first stop was in Chicago where in a highly unusual act, the Chicago Board of Trade suspended its frenzied business activities for a morning to permit Grinnell to make his appeal for funds. He was introduced to the traders by the mayor of Chicago, Carter Harrison. A reporter of this event was greatly impressed with J.B.'s performance:

> Mr. Grinnell made no claim to being an orator. But in a speech remarkable for its brevity, its force and its compelling appeal, he sent the hand of every man who heard it down into his pocket for money, or else a pencil wherewith to sign a subscription. In the long and notable history of the Chicago Board of Trade no more stirring thing has ever happened.

Some in the audience had gratifyingly bulging pockets. Among those whom the reporter listed were P. D. Armour, N. K. Fairbank, W. T. Baker, Samuel Allerton, and Zinn Carter, "who started the response."[56]

Following this smashing success in Chicago, Grinnell pushed on to New York where he again touched the hearts, and more important, the wallets of men of property. Accounts vary as to how much the college received as a result of Grinnell's trip, the college's printed appeals, and the wide publicity the press gave to this disaster. Grinnell would state in his autobiography that the Relief Committee received nearly $150,000, of which the college received only those funds designated for its use. The college catalogue of 1884–85 states that the amount Iowa College received for its rebuilding "is little more than $70,000 ... much less than the college lost by the tornado."[57] Nevertheless it was enough to start the rebuilding.

Within two years after the storm, Iowa College had arisen phoenix-like from its ruins. Where before it had had only two buildings and a hole in the ground, it now had three much larger edifices than it had ever enjoyed. The names given to these buildings reveal the major contributors to its rebuilding: Chicago Hall, whose existence was owed to J. B. Grinnell's celebrated appeal to the Chicago Board of Trade; Blair Hall, named for J.B.'s good friend, John Blair, the great railroad builder in Iowa, whose gift of $16,000 was the largest single donation received; and Alumni Hall, made possible by the contributions received from the alumni Iowa College had produced over the past thirty years. Though small in number and means, this group was large in generosity and loyalty to its alma mater.

The three buildings were marvelously eclectic in architectural style. Chicago Hall, a large three-story brick building, complete with tower to house the rescued bell, in its solidity and curved rooftop facade, was reminiscent of the eighteenth-century Dutch architecture of Amsterdam; Blair Hall was late-nineteenth-century Victorian Gothic in its vertical lines and its cathedral-like pointed, arched windows on the front facade; Alumni Hall was the smallest and ugliest of the three, but even it made a feeble gesture toward style with its quite superfluous French Renaissance tower à la Richard

Morris Hunt, the country's reigning architectural czar of high fashion.

Henry Parker, the self-appointed critic of the Grinnell community's architecture, had returned to Iowa College three years before the storm. He now undoubtedly found the college's new buildings with their imported architectural features as even more inappropriate to the prairie environment than the earlier buildings. He was so delighted, however, with the space provided in the new Blair Hall for his indispensable museum, which must now be restocked with an entirely new collection of specimens, that he kept a discreet silence about style. The great majority of Grinnellians were immensely proud of these new buildings. Now Iowa College for them had that physical appearance that a good college should have. As for their utilitarian value it can only be said that the college made do with them for the next seventy years.

The rapid resurrection of Iowa College meant to the faculty and students that their college would endure, no matter what befell it. To George Magoun it meant that the challenge hurled by God from out of the whirlwind had been answered. Faith and commitment had not been crushed but greatly strengthened—"Blessed be the name of the Lord." To the ever-optimistic and forward-looking J. B. Grinnell, the college's rebuilding was a tribute to and a justification for aggressive capitalism. The college was now known throughout the land. In its very destruction it had acquired new and wealthy friends. "That cyclone," Grinnell remarked with smug complacency, "was a real windfall."[58]

191

7

Secularizing the Mission

1884–1887

More than buildings had been swept away by the Great Cyclone of '82. More than buildings hastily constructed to replace the old would signal the emergence of a quite different Iowa College than that which existed before the storm. Few institutions in America would have quite so abrupt and dramatic an entry into a new society as did Iowa College, but the winds of change blowing across the land in the immediate post–Civil War years were not dependent upon the sudden terrible force of a tornadic whirlwind in order to metamorphose all that they touched. However reluctantly some may have been, colleges everywhere during the last two decades of the nineteenth century were to experience the same transformations that were to be effected in Grinnell. Fading away was the old Greek classical order that had dominated learning for the two and a half centuries since Harvard College had opened its doors in 1636. Crumbling also was the undisputed authority of a Roman law handed down from on high, as had been so beautifully exemplified by George Magoun. There would be new concepts of law and order, new texts in the canon of learning, new centers of power. Colleges could not resist but only reflect and respond to the transformation the entire nation was undergoing in those years as it became industrialized and urbanized.

It has been only too easy to date the transformation of Iowa College by one of two memorable events—either by the cyclone of 1882, or by the inauguration of a new president in 1887. Each to be sure was a force for abrupt change—the first, materially in a new physical plant for the college; the second, intellectually and socially in the life of the college. Both events, however, could have been foretold from the freshening winds felt in Grinnell: a Doppler scan, had it then been available, could have given warning of a tornado; and an astute analyst of human behavior could have predicted that the authoritarian and seemingly immutable rule of Magoun was a center that could not hold. Such foreknowledge could not have forestalled either approaching cataclysm, but it might have alleviated the shock of its arrival.

There was a restless shifting among all of the college's constituencies after 1865 that could not be ignored. The students were no longer the quiet, pious children who had dutifully attended Iowa College in Davenport and had humbly and gratefully accepted whatever instruction was offered them in the classroom. There were now in the student body men who had gone off to war under the command of company officers whom they themselves had elected to lead them. Now as battle-scarred veterans they would not go quietly back into a nursery. There were now women who had demonstrated during the war years when they alone had populated the classrooms that they were fully capable, physically and mentally, of doing as well as men in the same demanding courses of study. They would no longer accept as their only choice a shortened and watered-down version of the liberal arts for which they could earn not a meaningful degree but only a certificate of faithful attendance. Some women even dared to compare their status with that of the former slaves of the South. They demanded that Lincoln's Emancipation Proclamation and the newly ratified Fifteenth Amendment, giving the black man the vote, be extended to include women of all colors.

In 1873, the students had found a collective voice in the

pages of their own independent newspaper where they could air and share their grievances with the public. From the act of expressing their desires for reform it was but a short step to more direct action. They sent petitions to both the faculty and the trustees. If necessary, they were even prepared to go out on strike, as they did in the silly and trivial Walrus Affair, which President Magoun had foolishly magnified into a momentous cause célèbre.

Much as the complaining actions of the students may have disturbed their teachers, the faculty itself proved to be an agent for change. After nearly twenty years of virtual self-rule under the nominal aegis of the Board of Trustees, whose policy seemed to be one of benign neglect, the faculty in 1865 had not found it easy to accept an imposed order of presidential authoritarianism that supervised every detail of faculty performance. Two professors from among their preciously small number could not make the adjustment and departed from the college—L. F. Parker, voluntarily in bitterness, and Charles Clapp, involuntarily under protest.

Over the next two decades, the faculty's composition changed in regard to both professional training and practice. The early faculty both in Davenport and in Grinnell had been ordained ministers whose postgraduate training had been in theological seminaries and who had regarded themselves as being quite competent to teach in any of the disciplines that a liberal arts college might offer. Iowa College would not employ a nontheologically trained teacher until Carl von Coelln, a product of a German gymnasium and university, joined the faculty in 1863, but he was the rare exception, and for many years, the minister-turned-teacher would be the norm for most liberal arts colleges.

The ideal faculty member had been best exemplified at Iowa College by Henry Parker. His educational credentials—a B.A. from Amherst College and graduate study at Auburn Theological Seminary—were impeccable. His special competency in natural science and chemistry had been acquired without benefit of graduate study, but the catholicity of his

195

interest had extended his teaching repertoire to literature and art. Before Parker had ended his career in 1889, however, the ideal of universality was being replaced by the ideal of speciality. The venerable English universities of Oxford and Cambridge as the true Pierian springs of learning were being replaced by German universities, where the graduate student drank deeply from a single stream of inquiry and was rewarded not with a Master of Arts degree, but with a much more prestigious Doctor of Philosophy designation. Iowa College obtained its first faculty member holding this degree in 1871, when Henry Carmichael, Henry Parker's replacement, was appointed professor of Chemistry. The M.A. degree would remain for another forty years as a quite acceptable terminal degree in all fields, but before the end of the century, the Ph.D. was not the rare phenomenon it had been twenty years earlier.

The Renaissance scholar at home in all areas of human knowledge had become outdated and was no longer held in awe by the new generation of scholars. Such a universal scholar was now regarded with covert contempt as being a jack-of-all-trades, master of none. The fine old Italian word, *dilettante,* once meaning one who delights in the arts, had become an epithet to brand those to whom it was applied as being mere amateur dabblers. Henry Parker had been replaced by Jesse Macy as the model scholar and teacher. Macy's educational background, to be sure, was seriously deficient. He had never done graduate work at a German or even an American university, and his only advanced degree, an M.A., which he had earned by examination at Iowa College, was of dubious quality, but Macy would prove that one did not need an impressive pedigree to advance to the forefront of the new scholarship. Here was the specialist who would create an entirely new department of learning—political science—to accommodate his specialty, and would introduce into his classroom the most recent innovation in teaching borrowed from Johns Hopkins University—the seminar where students were required to make use of primary sources. Macy was the only Iowa College professor to gain international fame in the nineteenth century, one who could count James Lord Bryce and Sir George Trevelyan as friends and bring them to Grinnell as lecturers.

As the faculty grew in numbers and in its own self-esteem as the essential source of specialized expertise, it also became, like the students, more impatient with the old order. Members of the Iowa College faculty from the beginning had never been hesitant in presenting their needs to the trustees, earning for themselves the judgment by the trustees of being "unruly," but now increasingly they openly questioned the right of the trustees to determine the internal affairs of the college. They demanded and got the right to have a voice in selecting Commencement speakers and recipients of honorary degrees. They chided the trustees for mitigating the punishment they had imposed on the editor of *The News Letter*. They regarded the curriculum in particular as their exclusive preserve and expected the trustees to endorse whatever curricular changes they deemed appropriate. Above all, the faculty demanded from the trustees a commitment to change, giving concrete evidence that the college was moving forward into a new era of liberal arts education. "Come forward" was taking on a quite different meaning from that used by Magoun to designate a chapel hour when students must make public confession of their sins.

The third college constituency to play a role in this period of transition was the Board of Trustees. Not enough attention has been given by historians of higher education in America to the change in composition of the governing boards of colleges and universities in the post–Civil War period. The rapid proliferation of state universities and land-grant colleges with their secular leadership proved to be the innovating force in effecting a changing membership on governing boards of all institutions of higher learning. The legal curators were chosen in a variety of ways. In some states, the governor nominated and the legislature approved of trustees for the tax-supported universities; in other more populist–

197

minded states, like Nebraska, the trustees were elected by the people. Most private liberal arts colleges continued to hold fast to the original concept of a continuing self-perpetuating board. No matter what the process, however, by the late nineteenth century, all governing boards were becoming remarkably similar in composition. The men chosen—and except in some of the women's colleges they were almost always men—were persons of prominence in business and politics, men who could raise the needed funds, either from their own pockets or from those of their friends. One notable friend of Iowa College, Annie N. Savery, Iowa woman suffragist, in 1868 contributed money to be used for scholarships for women over a twenty-year period.[1] In the case of state schools, governing board members were chosen for their ability to pull the right political strings in the legislatures to get university budgets approved.

One needs only a quick run through of the listings of the Board of Trustees in the catalogues of Iowa College to appreciate what was happening to the composition of governing boards in liberal arts colleges everywhere. The original Board of Trustees chosen at Davenport in 1846 had consisted of eleven ministers and only one layman. In 1862, at the time of Magoun's election to the presidency of the college, the ratio stood at fifteen ministers and seven business and professional men. By 1880, the lay personnel on the board was nearly equal to the ministerial, nine of the former, ten of the latter. Ten years later there were thirteen business and professional men on the board and only eight ministers. As the college entered the new century, the triumph of the market place over the manse was complete—fifteen business and professional men as compared with only six ministers.[2] Property had replaced piety as a desideratum for college governance. Iowa College had the advantage over many other religiously based colleges in having a larger pool from which to select new trustees inasmuch as it had never required its trustees to be members of a particular sect. It could pick men of influence where it willed from those willing to serve.

The impact of this changing composition of governing boards on the educational goals and programs of colleges was far more profound than has generally been thought. In the beginning of Iowa College's history when the overwhelming preponderance of both trustees and faculty came from the ministry, there was a commonality of interest which prevailed over any minor differences that might arise between them. The two groups shared the same educational background—a liberal arts college and a theological seminary. Both groups believed the true undergraduate education could only be found in the classical curriculum of the Great Three disciplines. Although faculty and trustees performed different tasks in society, both believed that they labored in the same vineyard, sustained by the spirit of Christ, to achieve a greater glorification of God. Indeed so close was this bonding several of the trustees—Erastus Ripley, Daniel Lane, Julius Reed and George Magoun—moved easily from pulpit to classroom, while David Sheldon reversed the direction by going from the faculty to the Board of Trustees.

Slowly but inevitably this community of interest and purpose was disrupted as ministers were replaced by businessmen on the Board and subject specialists within the faculty. The transition did not mean either group opposed change from the old order, but by change the two constituencies quite often meant quite different and opposing things. The newer representatives of both groups were in agreement that the day of classics-dominated curriculum was over, but where the faculty was moving toward compartmentalized and, in the view of many trustees, highly esoteric learning, the business-minded trustees wanted more practical, utilitarian subjects taught—commercial subjects like stenography, accounting or marketing, and preprofessional courses in law and medicine. When the faculty protested that such "training courses" had no place in a liberal arts college, the trustees could argue with some credence that this criticism was nonsense. The liberal arts college had always been a training school, traditionally for ministers and teachers. Had

199

not the founders of Harvard College stated that they were establishing their school because they dreaded leaving "an illiterate ministry when our present ministers lie in dust"? Now in a new industrialized America colleges must prepare students for business and for professions other than pedagogy. Thus developed a fundamental difference as to what the liberal arts should include that would never be resolved. It must be said to Iowa College's credit or discredit, depending upon one's point of view, that it would hold more firmly over the next century to the more traditionally puristic interpretation of liberal arts than many other colleges, but the pressure emanating from trustees and students for more practical courses would persist.

The growing gulf in understanding the purpose of higher education between the two groups can be illustrated by the story of an encounter between Professor Harry Waldo Norris and a trustee in regard to the former's scientific research. Norris was a graduate of Iowa College, class of 1886. Like Macy, he received an M.A. degree from his alma mater and then, unlike Macy, did graduate study at Cornell University and the University of Freiburg, Germany. He was appointed to the Chair of Natural Science as a successor to Henry Parker in 1891, and became the father of the modern biology taught at Grinnell. He took as his specialized field the study of the shark's pituitary gland and won recognition as the leading authority on that particular subject. A trustee, trying to understand why anyone would be engaged in so esoteric a specialty as this, politely asked Norris if he hoped from this study to discover some practical application for his finding—perhaps something of medicinal value? Norris was astounded by the trustee's question. "Why no, of course not," he replied. "I study the shark's pituitary gland because I am interested in a shark's pituitary gland. That's reason enough."[3]

A puzzled trustee trying to understand what the teachers at his college were up to would be far more appreciative of the research being done by another early giant in science at Iowa College, Frank Almy. A graduate of the University of

Nebraska with a Bachelor of Science degree, Almy had joined the faculty at Grinnell in 1893 to head the newly established department of physics. Two years after Almy's arrival at Grinnell, a Bavarian physicist at the Wurzburg Physical Institute in Germany, Wilhelm Roentgen, on 28 December 1895 published a paper, *"Eine neue Art von Strahlen,"* in which he announced his discovery of X-ray. Within two months, Almy was to replicate that experiment and take an X-ray picture of his own hand, which surely was one of the first such pictures ever made in this country. Now here was a product of scientific research that even the most practically minded trustee could understand. Almy's experiment had obvious utilitarian value. There was no need to ask the purpose of Almy's research.[4]

It was in this period of growing differences in background and objectives between trustees and faculty that stereotypes of each group were created. The college teacher became the absent-minded professor, an impractical dreamer who had never had to meet a payroll and lived in an ivory tower isolated from the "real world." The businessman trustee, on the other hand, was the money-grubbing, ruthless entrepreneur, the prototype for Charles Dickens's Josiah Bounderby, a man whose interest in reading never extended beyond the balance sheet in his account books and who saw no value in any pursuit that did not return a monetary profit. Like all other stereotypes, these representations were grossly warped generalizations, but they were too often accepted without question by both sides in respect to the other group. The original communal "us" was tending toward a fission into polar "us and them," which at best could cause each side to reconsider its own position, but at worst could result in a confrontation.

It was in these years of transition for the liberal arts colleges that yet another constituency was to emerge at Iowa College as an influential factor. This particular group, starting with only two members in 1854, remained too small in number for several years even to consider itself as a distinct

201

group deserving to be recognized and listened to by those who were managing the college affairs. Not until 1879 did the alumni, growing in numbers with each passing year, coalesce into an association and become more assertive in promoting its own place within an extended college family.[5] As early as 1881, forty-nine alumni signed a petition demanding that the trustees investigate the faculty's actions in the much-publicized Harvey–*News Letter* contretemps. These alumni protested as individuals, however, and not in the name of the Alumni Association, for rarely, if ever, could the Association speak as one voice on any issue. The only common bond that the alumni had was that they all had once belonged to the student constituency. They had mixed memories of their collegiate experience and mixed aspirations for their college's future. Those who remembered only the good in the good old days of their youth wanted the college to stay just as it had been when they were students. Those who were inclined to emphasize the word "old" of "the good old days" felt that the past was truly passé, and they welcomed and even urged reform. It was alumni of this ilk who took the initiative during the early 1880s in pushing for a forced retirement of President Magoun and the selection of a vigorous young man to be a leader who could move the college forward.

College administrators and faculty could never quite decide as to whether the alumni constituency was a blessing or a curse. The college needed the help the alumni could give in monetary contributions and in the recruitment of students but would always resent and fear any overt alumni interference in daily operations and in projected plans. Neither interference in the name of tradition nor that for reform was welcomed. Lack of unity among the alumni collectively and lack of any individual alumnus with wealth great enough to exert undue influence over the college made such fears groundless. The preponderance of Iowa College graduates had chosen careers as teachers, ministers, small-town lawyers or housewives, vocations not noted for their munificent pecuniary rewards.

Poor as most of Iowa College's alumni were, however, they had responded eagerly and generously to the college's great need following the tornado of 1882. In recognition of their contributions to a devastated alma mater, the trustees named one of the three new buildings Alumni Hall. Of greater import to the Alumni Association was the privilege of electing, from 1884 on, three alumni to the Board of Trustees.

In granting to the Alumni Association the privilege of se-lecting members of the Board, the trustees were not setting a precedent of allowing other than the Board itself to elect new members. In order to stimulate a greater interest in the college among the Congregationalists of Iowa, the trustees had earlier granted the state General Association of this de-nomination the same right. It was through this latter group that Iowa College in 1883 got its first woman trustee, Louise Stephens, the widow of a former trustee, R. D. Stephens of Cedar Rapids. She apparently found her place on the hith-erto all-male Board a lonely one, and she resigned before completing her term. It would be another thirty years before a second woman was to enter the select company of this male governing board when in 1914, the Alumni Association fi-nally elected a woman to represent their organization. Mary Chamberlain, class of 1892, was the daughter of J. M. Cham-berlain, a long-time trustee, treasurer and librarian of the college, and like her father, she was a generous donor of property in Grinnell adjacent to the college. She stayed on the Board through her term but did not seek a second term. Again a hiatus of female trustee membership existed for an-other quarter of a century until Florence Kruidenier, the daughter of Gardner Cowles, a former trustee and owner of *The Des Moines Register,* was elected to the Board in 1935, followed the next year by another woman, Mrs. Frank Hixon of Lake Forest, Illinois.[6] Only four women trustees over a fifty-year period for a college that had been coeduca-tional since 1857 was not a record that the alumnae could point to with pride, but Iowa College was hardly unique in its sexism.

Among those agents contributing to changes in the college during the 1870s, the president of the college, George Magoun, must also be included. By 1880, to be sure, he had become the epitome of die-hard reactionaryism to most students, who objected to his stringent enforcement of outdated social regulations; to the younger faculty who resented his authoritarian rule; and belatedly, to some trustees who viewed with alarm dropping enrollments, resulting in a graduating class of only four students in 1878. Nevertheless, it should not be forgotten that it had been Magoun who had pushed for an expansion of course offerings and staff in the natural sciences. It had been he who had brought a little flexibility into a heretofore rigidly and fixed uniform curriculum by introducing the principle of elective courses first adopted at Harvard; and it was he who first permitted women to take the same courses as the male students if they so wished, and receive a Bachelor of Arts degree for their successful efforts. Magoun was a complex person whose contradictory actions were never easy for his contemporaries to reconcile or for later interpreters of his career to evaluate. That he too had played a significant role in the modernization of Iowa College and in the secularization of its mission must be conceded.

By 1880, however, to all but his staunchest supporters, it had become apparent that he should retire from the office he had for so long held firmly in his grasp. Never having liked fund-raising, an essential part of any president's duties, he became ever more ineffective in beating the bushes for what few dollars he might possibly raise. It had been J. B. Grinnell and the venerable Ephraim Adams who brought in the money to rebuild the college after the great storm. Magoun after 1875 seldom left the campus to renew contact with previous donors or to find new friends for the college.

It is ironic that Magoun should be forced out of office soon after the destruction of the college for, in what must be regarded as his finest hour, he had demonstrated that courage and determination essential to the college if it was to continue its mission. Standing on the ruins of his beloved college on that dreadful June night of 1882, he had appeared as the very embodiment of the Biblical patriarchal leader prepared to take his people forward across the desert, but like Moses, he was not destined to lead them into the fruitful valleys of the Promised Land. No longer was there a place for this Old Testament figure in the Book of Kings. What lay ahead for him was an unwanted Exodus from the throne.

There were many who were eager to do the toppling. It was a curious alliance of disparate elements whose pressure against Magoun would soon prove irresistible. There were Leonard and Sarah Parker, nursing old grudges from their exile in Iowa City and continuing to foment opposition against the man whom they held responsible for their banishment. Among the alumni were Henry Carter Adams, class of 1874, and Albert Shaw, class of 1879, both just beginning their respective brilliant careers in academia and journalism which would add luster to Iowa College's roster of graduates. They remembered their president as an irrational tyrant. On the Board of Trustees was John Meyer, a former colonel in the Union army and now a money-minded merchant in Newton, Iowa, who believed Magoun's continuance in office was losing for the college needed revenues in gifts and student tuition. There was in Grinnell an influential lawyer, J. P. Lyman, who regarded Magoun as "the prince of sinners." There were Congregational ministers throughout the state who resented Magoun's arrogance in assuming that he was the "unmitred bishop" within a denomination that for two and a half centuries had held to the complete autonomy of each individual congregation. And there was virtually the entire current student body who were becoming ever more restless under the old regime.

In June 1881, Magoun asked for a six-month leave in order to go East for study and travel. It was a request the trustees were happy to grant, and undoubtedly many held an unexpressed hope that he would find his native New England so attractive he would not return.[7] In this hope they were to be sorely disappointed. Magoun returned on schedule, rested and vigorous, giving every indication that he expected to continue in office until death forced his departure. By 1883, however, criticism of Magoun was becoming too open and pointed for the trustees to ignore.

In the minutes of the annual meeting of the Board on 23 June 1883 there appears a cryptic entry which begs for further elaboration: "Trustees to pledge they will never make any incriminating remark against any other member of the board. If any trustee does, he must be called to order to apologize."[8] It is very tempting to infer that this action was prompted by certain indiscreet remarks made by some trustees against Magoun. It would take more than a formal motion, however, to silence the criticism of the trustees directed toward their president, and certainly the Board could not hope to quiet the even louder anti-Magoun clamor coming from outside the Board.

The annual meeting of the trustees held on Saturday, 21 June 1884, proved to be a momentous one. President Magoun had absented himself from this meeting—the signal of what was to come. He had sent a letter to the Board which was read aloud. Magoun first took care to point out to his fellow trustees that his relationship with the college was three-fold: (1) he was a member and presiding officer of the Board of Trustees; (2) he was president of the college with all of the prerogatives that that office entailed; and (3) he was professor of Mental and Moral Science. He was now prepared to offer his resignation from his first two offices, but he desired and expected to retain his "third relationship" with the college. He wanted an assurance from the Board that funds would be "obtained from outside sources for his life support." A committee delegated to consider this letter and to make its recommendations to the full board at its second session on Monday, 23 June, was appointed, consisting of Ephraim Adams, Harvey Adams and J. H. Merrill. The committee recommended that President Magoun's resignation as trustee and president of the college be accepted effective immediately. As to Magoun's request that he be given life-time support from a specially obtained endowment, the committee was more cautious: "if the funds can be secured, he may continue as Professor during his life, [providing] that he stay on as Professor til in the judgment of the trustees, his personal consideration on his part, or the interests of the College on its part require otherwise." The committee further recommended that "until the funds can be secured, he be paid his present salary from general college funds." The trustees quickly accepted the committee's report. If there were any dissenting votes they were not recorded. The trustees immediately elected three of their number to serve as the presidential search committee: Ephraim Adams and A. B. Robbins, who had been on the Board since the founding of the college, and as the third trustee, Samuel Merrill, former governor of Iowa, to give further prestige to the selection process.[9]

All of this suggests that plans had been readied for the eventuality of Magoun's retirement some time before it had been finally realized. The trustees wanted no delay in finding Magoun's successor. The ending of a notable era in the history of the college was thus summarily effected.

As if to give emphasis to Iowa College's entering into a new era even before another president had been selected to lead them, the trustees met twice more in special session during that busy summer of 1884 to consider some pressing reforms presented to them by the faculty and by the students. The faculty wanted major revisions of the separate and distinct curricular tracks which had been established in 1862. The basic concept was kept, but there were alterations in the individual tracks within both the college and the Academy.[10] Within the college curriculum, the Ladies' Course was replaced by a Literary Course of four-year duration, emphasizing modern languages and literature, open to both men and women. The Classical Course was kept essentially the same as first established in 1850. Both of these curricular courses would terminate with the granting of the Bachelor of Arts degree. A new curricular track, the Philosophical Course, with a broader sweep than the other two in the liberal arts was introduced. Graduates of this course of study would receive a new designation—the Bachelor of Philosophy degree. Within a very short time it would become the most popular course of study with the students. The Science Course remained a three-year program resulting in a Bachelor of Science degree. It was considered the most utilitarian and masculine-oriented course of study and attracted few women.

Iowa College Academy had been from its beginning in Grinnell on a two-track system: the three-year Classical Course for those who planned to enter Iowa College; and a four-year English Course for those not intending to go on to college but wanted a secondary education which would be sufficient for teaching in public primary schools. Two departments were now added to the Academy's offerings: a Literary Course of only two years, which gave a smattering of a secondary education, primarily in the humanities, and was of particular interest to adult women who had never had the opportunity for a secondary education; and a four-year Music Course designed to prepare students for careers in the teaching and/or the performing of vocal and instrumental music.

Music as a discipline had always been something of an orphan child, adopted by the college only for its usefulness in the recruitment particularly of female students. The faculty had insisted that music had no proper place within the liberal arts at the collegiate level, and its courses for years had been taught on an ad hoc basis by whatever local talent might be available. In 1875, however, the college had employed a regular, full-time instructor, Willard Kimball, who proved to be an able musician and an ambitious promoter of his discipline. By 1877 he had been so successful in attracting students to his program that he persuaded the college to authorize the establishment of a Conservatory of Music which would be under the college's jurisdiction but separate from the Academy and the college. Now, in 1884, Kimball's program was given academic status as a fourth track of study within the Academy.

After the faculty had obtained what it had sought in respect to curricular changes, it was next the turn of the students to push forward their demands during this remarkable summer of reform. The students had many grievances directed against the social regulations imposed upon them, but the most obnoxious restriction of all—even more than the hated Rule 3—was the ban against playing or attending any out-of-town athletic contest. This rule was frequently violated, to be sure, but the prescribed Draconian punishment of expulsion was an omnipresent fear, capable of dampening even the joy of victory for both players and spectators.

Before they had any inkling that President Magoun's continuance in office would be under consideration at the Board's annual meeting in 1884, the students were prepared to present to the trustees their demand that the rule against intercollegiate games played off campus be repealed. A petition, couched in language that conveyed more earnestness than it did diplomacy, had been circulated and signed by nearly the entire student body. The faculty was infuriated by the effrontery of the students and sent to the trustees its own response to the petition, demanding that the Board rebuke the students for their disrespectful statement. The faculty also wanted the Board to make clear to the students that they had no right to communicate directly with the trustees over the heads of the administration and the faculty.

The trustees found themselves in a very uncomfortable position. The Harvey–*News Letter* fuss had revealed how very sensitive the faculty was to trustee interference in matters of student discipline. On the other hand, there was a growing conviction among the newer trustees that Iowa College's regulations were overly restrictive and should be reconsidered. Businessmen on the Board, in particular, were cautious about unduly antagonizing the students. These trustees were inclined to view a college as being the same as

209

any of the commercial enterprises with which they were associated, except of course the college never made a profit. They equated the faculty with employees in business, mere wage earners under the management of the trustees, while the students were the customers, who, within reason, should be given satisfaction. Moreover, any issue involving athletics touched upon a particularly sensitive spot. Success on the playing fields brought prestige and more students to the college, and by the 1880s, Iowa College had won fame as a baseball power. To avoid allying themselves completely with either the faculty or the students would require considerable adeptness in tight-rope walking on the part of the Board.

Magoun's letter of resignation had first priority at the annual meeting in June so the trustees were able to postpone any consideration of the students' petition until the special meeting in July when happily most of the students would be away for the summer.[11] A majority of the Board was not prepared to ride roughshod over the faculty's position by flatly rejecting the existing ban on out-of-town games. In a rather clever compromise, the trustees voted to change the rule to state that students hereafter could take part in any intervarsity game that had the approval of the faculty. Thus the onus of decision was shifted from the Board to the faculty. The faculty would have to face the students directly, unprotected by the higher authority of a sacred rule carved in stone.

As a sop to the faculty, the trustees mildly chided the students for the intemperance of the language used in the petition. They also gave to the faculty that which it had long wanted and which the trustees quite wisely were now happy to concede. Hereafter the question of student discipline would lie exclusively with the faculty. Don't come running to us with your petitions, the Board was in effect telling the students. Look to your teachers for compassion and understanding.

The trustees did hope, however, to create a less adversarial relationship between faculty and students. In a carefully and gently worded statement directed to the faculty, the trustees attempted to create such a climate:

> Trustees regard the recitation room the chief place of governmental power, as students who are faithful in study seldom need to be governed. ... Daily study is a chief factor in College government to be carefully watched. ... The Trustees propose to leave large discretion with the Faculty and largely to the honor and sense of propriety of students. It is hoped that students may be more disposed to confer with the Faculty and that all possible inducement and encouragement may be offered by the Faculty by seeking such freedom with students on all occasions. Let the law of love and sympathy have its fullest expression and exert its fullest power on the administration of the College; not so much by Faculty action as by the personal care and effort of each instructor.[12]

The existing policy requiring students to confess weekly their sins of either omission or commission in private to their faculty advisor, which in turn had replaced Magoun's "Come Forward" public confessions in chapel, was now itself abolished. Hereafter there would be no student self-reporting. Faculty members would be required to keep records of their advisees' deportment without the aid of confessions.

The trustees' reevaluation of college social regulations did not give complete satisfaction to either the students or the faculty, but it was a masterful high-wire performance by the trustees. They had successfully traversed their way over the pitfalls without totally alienating either group of petitioners waiting below. In daring to redefine college governance of the students, the trustees' rulings marked a fundamental shift in attempting to replace stern commandments handed down from on high with sympathetic understanding and cooperation between faculty and students. It was a noble ideal, a major break with the past.

The trustees were well satisfied with their successful

211

handling of both the faculty and the students in this busy summer of reform. One more issue remained unresolved when the Board finally adjourned in late August 1884—the procurement of a successor to George Magoun. This task of paramount importance was not to be marked with the same degree of proficiency that had distinguished their other efforts, however. Indeed, it would be difficult to imagine a more inept and bungled presidential search than that which was to ensue over the next two and a half years. Only part of the blame, to be sure, rested with the trustees. A major cause for the indecision, the protracted negotiations and long delay in reaching a successful conclusion was the responsibility of the trustees' first two choices for the position.

The search began with briskness and dispatch. It was the trustees' naive hope that they would have a distinguished occupant of the office within the coming academic year. Only hours after receiving Magoun's letter of resignation, three of the most respected members of the Board had been chosen to serve as the Committee on the Presidency. Shortly thereafter, the senior member of the faculty, Samuel Jay Buck, was appointed acting president. None of the trustees—and certainly not Buck himself—imagined the long tenure in office Buck would have, but after this propitious start, all involved would experience little but trouble and vexation.

Given that a quick resolution of the issue was the major consideration, it is ironic to note that from the beginning there was someone in the wings, waiting eagerly for the cue that would take him on to front center stage in the starring role. David O. Mears, the pastor of the Piedmont Congregational Church in Worcester, Massachusetts, had, at least in his own view and in those of his close friends at Grinnell, all of the necessary credentials to make him the obvious choice for the presidency of Iowa College. He was a theologian of some repute, and perhaps of greater importance, as the husband of J. B. Grinnell's daughter, Mary, he had close ties to the college. He had made a very favorable impression in the community when he delivered the Commencement address amid the ruins of the devastated town one week after the cyclone. As an added bonus, he would not come to the presidency empty-handed. He had been assiduously courting the wealthiest member of his congregation in Worcester, the shoe merchant Edward A. Goodnow, and had extracted from him a pledge of $10,000 to Iowa College for the construction of a library/observatory. J. B. Grinnell was able to announce this splendid gift just as the trustees began their consideration of the presidency.[13] Obviously Mears was a man who would be able to raise money for the college, for Goodnow's initial gift carried with it the implied promise that more would be forthcoming in the future if the relationship between him and Iowa College proved to be harmonious.

On 26 June 1884, A. B. Robbins, a member of the trustees' search committee, wrote Mears to inform him that only he was under consideration by the trustees. This proved to be somewhat hasty upon Robbins's part for to Mears it seemed clear that the trustees had accepted the obvious and that an official call would shortly be forthcoming. Mears very much wanted the position, and feeling confident that it was already his, he made the mistake of playing the game of being hard to get. By so doing, he would force the trustees to accept him on his terms rather than on theirs. As a minimum, he wanted a salary double that of Magoun's $1,500 a year. He also wanted the Board to agree that an endowment of $200,000 was essential for the survival of the college and to assure him that this could and would be realized in the very near future. Mears' closest confidant on the Board, even more than his father-in-law, was J. M. Chamberlain, the treasurer of the college, and Mears had been in communication with him before receiving Robbins's very encouraging letter. He had made clear to Chamberlain that he was very happy in his present position, that coming to Grinnell would be a tremendous sacrifice on his part for he was currently earning a salary of $6,000, and that the only reason he would accept would be out of a sense of duty and a desire to serve the college he had learned to love.

Mears was abruptly taken aback when one week after

hearing from Robbins, he received a quite different letter from Ephraim Adams, chairman of the committee, informing him that "other names had been presented and would require deliberation." Apparently, the trustees were not unanimous in the opinion that Mears was so obvious a choice that they need not look any further.[14]

To say that Mears was surprised and grievously disappointed would be an understatement. Even Goodnow's munificent gift of a library/observatory was being given careful scrutiny by the Board, as it carried with it the condition that out of the $10,000 benefaction, the college must provide ten scholarships of $60 each per annum to deserving young ladies, for Goodnow was a strong proponent of higher education for women. Indeed, so committed was Goodnow to the principle of coeducation that Mears was able to inform the trustees that their benefactor had also pledged an additional $5,000 toward the erection of a Ladies Hall, which had been a high priority item for both the trustees and the faculty for the past twenty years. This second gift also gave substance to Mears's assertion that Goodnow's interest in Iowa College would extend beyond his initial gift of a library. The only stipulation attached to this donation was that the hall must be named for Mary Grinnell Mears.

The trustees were pleased to name the Ladies Hall for Mears's wife, but the condition attached to the gift of the library of providing ten scholarships for women each year was a matter of some concern. The trustees wanted to make these grants as loans rather than outright gifts. This form of financial aid had been offered to Iowa College women students by the Ladies Education Society of Davenport, established in 1857. After the college moved to Grinnell, another Ladies Education Society, also providing only loans, was founded there in 1862. Over the years, the young women who received aid from the Society had been most faithful in paying back the money given to them. The Society still operates today, making it the oldest continuing educational organization in the college's history, but since 1970 it has given scholarships instead of loans.

To discuss this question of scholarships versus loans, Mears was invited to attend a special meeting of the Board on 21 August 1884.[15] This meeting would also give the trustees an opportunity to reevaluate Mears as a potential candidate for the presidency. In respect to the new buildings to be funded by Goodnow, the meeting went well. Mears was sure that an agreement could be reached on financial aid for women. There was also agreement on the location for Goodnow Library which was to be built just north of Chicago Hall, facing on Park Street. The trustees also agreed to employ as architect for both the library and Mears Hall Goodnow's choice of Stephen C. Earle, a Worcester architect of some national prominence. Earle had received his training from the distinguished architect Calvert Vaux, and was currently designing handsome buildings in the Romanesque style of H. H. Richardson, America's most admired architect at that time.

The promotion of Mears's candidacy for the presidency, however, did not fare as well. In a letter to Chamberlain after his trip to Grinnell, Mears wrote of his conversation with Chamberlain's father-in-law, Stephen L. Herrick, who like Chamberlain was one of Mears's strongest supporters on the Board:

> I had the first conversation with your honored Father, Mr. Herrick. ... I have never known such an hour as that spent in his room. He told me what he thought proper to say, the first gleam of light as to what the Trustees had done, etc. Two days later you came. Relying on the information given, I did not wish the Trustees to elect me, and then have the invitation refused. I repeated to you that nothing but duty, clear and plain, could call me from the ministry in which I have stood in Cambridge and Worcester for 17 years, and to which I have given my life. During the last week of my visit in Grinnell, members of the Faculty, prominent people in the town and several trustees

215

spoke to me in very strong terms as to what my duty was; but of course the strongest statements are the facts involving the financial and other questions of the College.

On leaving Grinnell, I left word with Father G. [J. B. Grinnell] to withdraw my name if there seemed the least doubt on the part of a single Trustee, or if any Trustee would desire any other man. ... In his last letter he told me that he had withdrawn my name, as Dr. Robbins advised delay. Since that letter my mind has been at rest as to what my duty is.

But, Bro. C., I can't help feeling (shall I say injured?) that after all that has been said to me and written ... , that nine weeks or more should have been spent in conversations behind my back, by those who certainly could not be afraid of questioning me most closely as to any fitness or unfitness I may have for the position. ... Ever since I saw your College ruined by the Cyclone, I have felt like working with you in its rebuilding. ... I am heartsick—not that I am not the President (I have coveted none of the burdens) but I cannot feel it a privilege to labor as I had done before any action on your part was contemplated with reference to me or before I had suspected such a thing.

To give pointed emphasis to his words of how much he had done for the college, Mears enclosed in this letter Goodnow's check with the request, "Please acknowledge to Mr. Goodnow personally the $10,000 he sends by me."[16]

This letter of aggrieved renunciation should have marked the end of Mears's troubled relationship with Iowa College, but Mears could not let the issue die. More letters to Chamberlain were to follow as the trustees continued to write, in Mears's words, "to any and every one they thought best in New England and elsewhere."[17]

In December 1884, the trustees were unanimous in thinking they had found "the best in New England," and they elected to the presidency the Rev. Charles F. Thwing, the distinguished theological scholar and pastor of the North Avenue Church in Cambridge.[18] Thwing, in response to this action, expressed the same concern over the college's financial situation as had Mears. Quite possibly he had heard of the on-again, off-again relationship with Mears in nearby Worcester, and he too wanted assurance from the Board that a campaign drive was underway to produce within a relatively short time an endowment of at least $200,000. The best that the Board could promise was that it would immediately employ a special financial agent and that the individual trustees would themselves be engaged in soliciting funds. They could give no definite date, however, as to when this Herculean task of raising the endowment to a $200,000 level would be realized.[19] Even the faculty got into the act by sending to Thwing a resolution stating that it was the faculty's "unanimous and earnest desire that the Rev. Mr. Thwing should accept the Presidency," and offering its help "in raising the money to meet his condition for acceptance."[20]

Thwing was interested enough to visit Grinnell in the winter of 1884–85 to look over the college of which he was now the president-elect. What he saw apparently did not bring forth a favorable response, and the issue remained in doubt for several more months.

Even the election of Thwing did not silence Mears. He continued to write Chamberlain and his father-in-law, making deprecating remarks about "the President-Elect," and pronouncing quite justifiable criticism about the entire selection process. Mears was especially irate over hearing that some of the trustees had accused him of "cooking up" the gift of Mr. Goodnow.

> I have no desire "to cook" any more. In fact, the man [Thwing] who has coyed you on & used you for a stepping stone to himself suggests that the Trustees roll up their sleeves & put on their aprons to cook $200,000 themselves. I had made every arrangement to secure for the College $100,000 for buildings, &c. this winter and spring; had spoken to Mr. Beecher [Henry Ward Beecher], meaning to go among his people who know me ... ; but lest I should be again accused of "cooking," have gone on my way in my church, leaving the College in the hands of those who profess to know its needs.[21]

After a delay of nearly six months, the trustees finally had Thwing's formal response to his election—a firm no. By now, the Board was so weary of the entire search that even Ephraim Adams was ready to concede that Mears was the only name under consideration. Mears and Goodnow were invited to come to the Commencement exercises in June 1885 where they would be given a royal welcome, and at the trustees' annual meeting held just prior to graduation, David Mears was elected president of Iowa College.[22]

Despite his repeated protestations to the contrary, Mears at last had what he had long sought, but his expected, immediate acceptance was not forthcoming. Now that he finally had the call, Mears was busily "cooking" again, preparing a pièce de résistance so magnificent as to enable him to enter into office with a fanfare of triumph. As early as May 1885, Mears had informed Chamberlain in confidence that he was sure he could persuade Goodnow to give Iowa College $50,000 in cash.[23] As president-elect, Mears would spend the summer working out with his patron the terms by which this gift would be made. In late August the search committee received word from Chamberlain as to what the trustees would have to accept along with the $50,000—nothing less than a change in the name of Iowa College to Goodnow College.[24] This proposal set off a flurry of letter writing between members of the search committee and the other members of the Board. Most of the trustees were shocked by the proposal, and a majority agreed with Adams, who wrote Chamberlain, "my first thoughts are $50,000 is a small sum for which at this late day to change the name."[25]

Various counter proposals were suggested. Perhaps Mr. Goodnow would accept the name Goodnow Iowa College, thus keeping the old name intact within a larger nomenclature. Or better yet, given Goodnow's great interest in female education, renaming and expanding the existing Ladies Department into the Goodnow Ladies College Institute. None of these suggestions was acceptable to Mears and Goodnow.[26]

There was, of course, a valid reason for changing the

name of Iowa College. It was so generic a name within the state as to invite confusion with Iowa State College at Ames or Iowa University at Iowa City, and the question of a name change would continue to be an issue long after Goodnow's proposal was forgotten. But if so venerable a name with its forty-year history as the pioneer institution of higher education in the trans-Mississippi West was to be exchanged for that of an individual, surely there were others more deserving of that honor than that of a man whose only association was that of a donor who so far had given only $15,000 to the college. There was Asa Turner, for instance, who more than any other single individual could be given the accolade of "founder of the college," and who had died at the age of eighty-six just as the trustees were considering Goodnow's bequest; or J. B. Grinnell, who had given the college its present home in the town bearing his name. In the weeks and months that followed the formal presentation of Goodnow's offer to the Board at its special meeting on 20 November 1885, the trustees heard from alumni, townspeople and Congregational churches throughout the region and the sentiment was overwhelmingly negative to the proposal.

Mears, however, was not willing to wait weeks while the trustees polled all of the many far-flung groups who had an interest in Iowa College. Having fully expected the Board to leap at the chance to get its hands on this princely contribution to the college's endowment, he was both surprised and angry that there should be any delay in accepting his and Goodnow's proposal. Apparently Mears had no understanding as to what to him seemed so bland and undiscriminating a name as Iowa College meant to those who were attached to it. In December, he sent a telegram to the Executive Committee of the trustees with the brief laconic message, "Under circumstances best for me to decline call. Will write." Chamberlain was then authorized by the committee to write Mears asking him to "leave the matter open for the present."[27]

Mears did delay sending his formal letter declining the presidency, for neither he nor the trustees were yet ready to break off negotiations. The trustees were still hopeful that Goodnow could be brought to reason over this name-change controversy. A majority of the Board was willing to accept the proposal providing Goodnow would state unequivocally that the college would be the major beneficiary in his will. This Goodnow refused to do, even though he was begged to do so by various delegations from Grinnell, including Magoun, Chamberlain, Governor Merrill and Ephraim Adams throughout the winter of 1885–86. "It is a good deal better to surprise them than to let it go the other way," Goodnow told Mears.[28] The trustees, however, did not want surprises, they wanted written certainties.

Mears, on the other hand, was not ready to call a final halt to negotiations in spite of his telegram in December declining "the call." He was certain that in the end the trustees would have to yield, for there had been a second stipulation in Goodnow's offer: David Mears would first have to be inaugurated a president of the college before the money would be forthcoming. Chamberlain had repeatedly impressed upon Mears how desperate the college was to get a new president, and by now it had no other choice but Mears. Mears just as repeatedly emphasized to Chamberlain and the trustees that he would not come to Grinnell as president unless the trustees had first accepted Goodnow's proposal. Mears readily admitted that the name change had been his idea, not Goodnow's, but once suggested, it had become for the proud old man an unalterable condition. Nor did Mears want his patron to consider any alternatives, for Mears had pledged his own honor on the assertion that Goodnow would, of course, be exceedingly generous to the college in his will. For the trustees to demand a written pledge to that effect would mean that they had no faith in either Goodnow's or Mears's word.

So the impasse continued with neither side yielding until finally at their annual meeting in June 1886, the trustees sent Mears what would prove to be their final word on the matter. First, they stated that "An unqualified acceptance on

his [Dr. Mears's] part of the invitation to the Presidency extended to him a year ago would be gratifying."

The trustees then gave their final answer to the Goodnow proposal:

> We feel that in the circumstances as they now exist,
> the way is not open to any action as to the change of name
> for the following reasons—
>
> 1st Because the sum named does not in our view by
> any means warrant it. It seems to us a serious step, and
> there are grave and weighty objections thereto, a step not
> to be taken unless the amount to be secured is enough to
> make it in the minds of people generally a clear case.
>
> 2nd Because such action in the present attitude is no
> certain advantage to the college. ... Our action would put
> us in a false light before the public, and subject us to a last-
> ing chagrin in case our hopes should not be realized, which
> is to say the least possible. ...
>
> As to this whole matter we very much regret that the
> question of change of name has ever been raised. We are
> truly grateful for the kindness of Mr. Goodnow in the gifts
> already conferred, and should highly appreciate any fur-
> ther gifts that he should be disposed to make. ... But as the
> question of name has arisen, we would say this: that
> should the circumstances ever occur in which some larger
> gift, say from $150,000 to $250,000 be conditioned on a
> change of name, that question would be favorably consid-
> ered.

The report concluded with the request that there be "a
speedy conclusion to the main question involved, and that
conclusion be that Dr. Mears accept our invitation. ... If in
this direction our hopes are not to be realized, it is for the interests of both parties that this should be known."[29]

Here was a candid answer to Goodnow's proposal. The
name of the college was for sale, but the going offer was not
high enough. No further bid was forthcoming, however. Apparently Goodnow did not think his name was worth more
than that already offered.

Mears was infuriated by this rejection. As the trustees

feared for themselves, he had been subjected "to a lasting chagrin" because his "hopes had not been realized." Indicative of his anger, he would not respond immediately to the trustee report, but had his wife do it for him. On 3 July 1886, Mary Grinnell Mears wrote,

> Mr. Mears was obliged to go away ... and he left me a duty which it is far from pleasant to perform. He thinks now under the circumstances it will not be wise for him to accept the Presidency of Iowa College and wished me to inform you of the fact. He did not decide until Friday and since then has been too busy for a word. ... The whole affair makes my heart ache.[30]

Some ten days later, Mears himself finally wrote his own letter of declination:

> As the matter rests, I know Mr. Goodnow's gift is now out of the question. This decision of yours has simplified the question before me, and in its light my duty seems plain. ... In response to your invitation it becomes my painful duty to decline your generous "call." ... Of his [Goodnow's] interest in the College far beyond any mere gift, I have absolute knowledge; but he will not allow himself to be put in the light of bidding for the name. All sure things are not legally written down at just the time we wish, but I know Mr. Goodnow too well to be deceived in him.[31]

On that aggrieved note of "what might have been," the protracted quest for David Mears as president ended in failure.

Edward Goodnow had one last gift to bestow upon the college that had refused to take his name. On 21 September 1886, the Executive Committee of the Board passed a resolution to "express thanks to Mr. Goodnow for the marble medallion of himself" which he had kindly sent to the college.[32] It would be for a time displayed in the one place on campus that did bear his name—Goodnow Library.

It had been extremely painful for the trustees to bid farewell to $50,000 in hard cash, but it was also difficult to realize that they still had no president for Iowa College, nor even a viable candidate to whom they could turn. They were where they had been in June 1884 when they had happily accepted the resignation of Magoun and had naively believed they would have his successor in place within six months.

In their despair they perhaps found some consolation in knowing that they had learned how not to conduct a presidential search from this dreadful experience: Don't elect someone without first ascertaining the willingness of the candidate to accept an offer unencumbered by any conditions he might impose.

Perhaps some trustees now realized the full truth of Ephraim Adams's words when the college first opened, "It is baptized with the Holy Ghost," for indeed it did seem that a special Providence had prevented David Mears from becoming president of Iowa College. As the negotiations had dragged on, even so loyal a supporter as Joshua Chamberlain had become distressed by some of the statements Mears made to him: "Pardon me, I am not set to criticize the actions of your Trustees, but the welfare of the College cannot endure much more work of such a sort as you have done."[33] And again, "While you say they [the trustees] have acted under the inspiration of prayer, that may all be so; but I do not yet believe that all your proceedings for the past two years have been the outcome of prayer; if so, praying men are not always to be trusted are they?"[34]

Mears made abundantly plain he had little respect for the Board, and relations between him and the trustees would have been strained from the outset of his tenure. His letters also revealed a man who was vain and stubbornly insistent on either having his own way or not playing the game. Nor is there any indication from the evidence available that Mears would be the innovative reformer that many of the trustees and the alumni as well as the faculty and students were looking for. The fact that Magoun saw Mears as being the only acceptable choice as his successor did not give promise of providing a break with the past. The college had indeed been fortunate when Mears gave his final "no" to its offer.

In his last communication to the Board, Mears had written, "This letter is written in the prayerful hope that the College and 'the right man' may speedily meet."[35] That was at least one prayer of Mears that was promptly fulfilled. In a surprisingly short time, the trustees did find "the right man."

Existing records do not indicate who first proposed George Augustus Gates, the Congregational minister of Upper Montclair, New Jersey, as a man whom the trustees might wish to consider. The first official mention of his name is to be found in the minutes of the Executive Committee of 31 December 1886 where it was reported that "Ephraim Adams presented correspondence had and information gained respecting the Rev. George A. Gates of Upper Montclair, New Jersey as a suitable person. The Committee is to pursue investigation in such a way as seems best to them."[36]

There are several possible sources for the initial suggestion of his name. As early as September 1885, George Magoun and Samuel Merrill, commissioned by the Board to go East to further the negotiations with Goodnow and Mears, had stopped off at Upper Montclair to consult with Samuel Wilde, who had offered a telescope for the observatory atop Goodnow Library. It is quite likely on that visit that these two men first heard of Gates from members of his congregation who sang the praises of their young minister. What these two emissaries from the college might have heard was impressive, for Gates had a quite remarkable educational background.

Born in Topham, Vermont, on 24 January 1851, Gates had attended St. Johnsbury Academy and then Dartmouth College, from which he graduated in 1873. After two years of teaching, he had begun his theological training at Andover Seminary, but had interrupted his studies there during the years 1878 and 1879 in order to study at the universities of Göttingen and Bonn, Germany.

There he was introduced to the "realistic idealism" of the famous philosopher Rudolf Hermann Lotze with its rejection of sterile, abstract theological doctrines and its emphasis upon the merging of idealism with practical activism for social reform. When Gates returned to Andover in the fall of 1879, he was quite ready to be converted to the Social Gospel teachings of William Jewett Tucker, who had only that year joined the faculty at Andover and would shortly make Andover "the storm center of theological controversy in the country."[37]

Upon graduating from Andover in 1880, Gates was denied ordination by the New England ecclesiastical council for being "a subversive radical," who fully accepted the heretical science of Charles Darwin. Even without the official sanction of ordination, however, Gates was invited by the newly organized Congregational church in Upper Montclair to be its first minister in the fall of 1880, and two years later, a reorganized council, chaired by the liberal theologian, Lyman Abbott, unanimously accepted Gates for ordination as a minister of the gospel.

It is doubtful if either Merrill or Magoun inquired into Gates's background as a possible presidential candidate in 1885, for they were then hot in pursuit of Mears along with Goodnow's money, but if they had bothered to do so, Gates's record as a radical evolutionist would hardly have endeared him to Magoun. A year later, however, when Mears had rejected the presidency, the name of Gates was brought to the attention of the presidential committee. Two alumni of Iowa College are very possible initiators of this Gates-for-president movement: Henry Carter Adams, who had been Gates's roommate during their freshman year at Andover Seminary; and Albert Shaw, alumni trustee, who had been one of the most outspoken critics of President Magoun, and who was now hoping to find just such a young progressive reformer as Gates to be the successor of the deposed old king. Adams's support would carry great weight with his father, the chairman of the selection committee, and Shaw's influence would be the most forceful within the Alumni Association.

No matter how the Gates candidacy was initiated, once the Presidential Committee was authorized "to pursue investigations," it moved very quickly. Two months later, on 22 February 1887, with a letter from Gates securely in hand assuring the committee that if asked, he would be happy to accept the presidency, the trustees in a special meeting unanimously elected George A. Gates as the second president of Iowa College.[38] Ten days later, the trustees received Gates's brief letter of acceptance:

> Yours of Feby 22nd reporting to me the official action of the Trustees in electing me to the Presidency of Iowa College, is received. The conditions stated in your letter concerning salary and the time of commencing service are satisfactory to me. I accept the office to which your Trustees have chosen me, and will be at Grinnell as soon after the first of May of this year as I can. Faithfully yours,
>
> GEORGE A. GATES

In three brief sentences, Gates had accepted the mantle of office—no hesitations, no complaints over personal sacrifice, no conditions as to his acceptance. For the weary trustees, this letter was worth infinitely more than $50,000.

In a somewhat longer letter, Gates responded to the equally unanimous vote of the faculty in support of his election.

> The unanimity of the action of the Trustees in electing me to the presidency of your college was a most cheerful bit of news to me; the unanimity of the vote of the faculty expressing their satisfaction with the work of the Trustees is, if possible, yet more cheering. For, after all, my work and nearest association must be with you. The trustees are our occasional guests; you and I must keep house together. ... Such words are a sure pledge that we can begin our proper

226

work together at once, wasting no time in feeling our way toward each other. ... I come to you to give my life for that college. I want no grander work than to be permitted to contribute what I have, be it little or much, to that work. The more I have seen and learned of the college, the more I have come to believe in a glorious future for it. ... My part in this great work humbles me. ... But forgetting self in love toward God and fellow man, we may be able to do something.[39]

Something would indeed be achieved over the next thirteen years. The "right man" had at last been found.

8

"Thy Kingdom Come on Earth":

The Social Gospel Era

1887–1900

On 21 June 1887, George Augustus Gates was inaugurated as the second president of Iowa College. Standing at the podium to deliver his inaugural address, this slender young man looked even younger than his thirty-six years—more like a junior instructor or even a mature college senior than as the long sought for chief executive officer of the college. More than one member of the audience must have taken a quick appraising glance from the stripling standing before them to the great leonine head of the old deposed king seated so conspicuously in the front row. The contrast between callow youth and majestic age was so great as to be shocking. One could not help but wonder if the trustees had been so eager to break with the Magoun past that they had gone too far in their revolt—or, what was more likely, they had grown so weary of the long presidential search that they had finally grabbed the first willing boy to come along and now expected him to do a man's job.

Then this boy wonder began to speak, and very quickly the differences between him and Magoun in physical appearance and age paled to insignificance as compared to the distinction both in style and substance between this inaugural address and that which had been given twenty-two years earlier.

Magoun had been the product of an age in which oratory was as highly prized as it had been in the Athens of Demosthenes or the Rome of Cicero. The greatest popular heroes of antebellum America had not been warriors or industrialists, and certainly not actors nor athletes, but rather Daniel Webster, John Calhoun and Edward Everett—men who could hold an audience enthralled for hours by the sheer power of voice and the magic of language. George Magoun had brought to the western prairie land the art of the spoken word, and for thirty years among ministers, lawyers, teachers and politicians he was renowned as Iowa's greatest orator. Within his college, oratorical skill was second only to character as the attribute to be developed in the students before sending them out into the world with degree in hand. Every senior was required to deliver at Commencement an oration which had been laboriously created and painfully practiced for months prior to the moment when it must be delivered. And always before the student was the magisterial image of the great Magoun, a role model certainly to emulate but never possible to approach.

On the long awaited and dreaded day, the trembling candidate for the degree would deliver orally to the assembled multitude those distilled bits of wisdom garnered from four years of study. It was a grim rite of initiation for the seniors, endured more or less patiently by anxious parents and bored spectators. The trustees, the faculty, and of course, President Magoun, insisted on its continuance, for no college worthy of that name could allow the noble art of oratory to wither and die for lack of cultivation.

If George Gates had had to undergo a similar ritual at his alma mater, Dartmouth—which he probably did—he would not have been regarded as a star pupil in elocution at his graduation. His voice lacked the deep, sonorous quality so essential to a great orator—"wispy," Magoun would have called it—so thin that a large audience would have to lean forward in an effort to hear him. He eschewed the sweeping gestures of the emotive thespian which nineteenth-century

230

audiences demanded for their entertainment. Nor did he put his auditors at their ease with the comfort of recognizing cliché-ridden phrases and classical allusions, familiar to them all. No Horatio stood at the bridge, no Achilles sulked in his tent in Gates's orations. In the novelty of his metaphors and in the unexpected twist of his phraseology, however, there was a Lincolnian quality of originality that still gives to his published addresses a freshness and time-lessness a century after they were delivered.

In this first public appearance at Iowa College, Gates was at his very best. His inaugural address can and should be read today by trustees, administrators, faculty and students for their own edification. His ideas and ideals are as relevant to the college today as they were in 1887.[1]

Gates began his address conventionally enough by paying the generous tribute expected of him to those who had preceded him in the building and maintaining of the college. He turned first to the Iowa Band, to those eleven young men who had come to Iowa in 1843, "each to found a church, and together to build a college." Seven of the eleven were still living; four were in the audience on this day, and three still sat on the Board of Trustees after forty years of service. "The Immortals," Gates called them. "Could I gather into one garland the flowers of grateful feelings, which are in the hearts of this assembly, I would make it your crown of rejoicing."

"My second word is due to you, sir," Gates said in direct salutation to his predecessor,

who have given to this college the best years of your life. I should do you dishonor, and not honor, to speak your praises to your face. It would imply that you needed to be praised to have your praise known. The national reputation which this college has won is due in large measure, we all know, to yourself. ... You took it in the weakness of infancy; you see it grown into strength and beauty. To be called upon to succeed the work of a man like yourself is regarded by your successor as laying upon his shoulders heavy responsibilities.

Upon hearing these gracious words, the proud old man must have allowed a small smile of pleasure to soften his stern visage, but such satisfaction would be of short duration, for there would be little else in Gates's message inaugurating a new era that would meet with Magoun's approval.

There followed equally pleasing tributes to the Board of Trustees, the faculty, the alumni and the students. He singled out for special attention the speaker who had preceded him at the podium, Martha Foote Crowe, the principal of the Ladies Department. Mrs. Crowe had taken full advantage of the opportunity offered by her address of welcome to President Gates to give a brief history of the long struggle of the women students to obtain equal opportunity for a liberal arts education at Iowa College. "Although Iowa College is said to be devoted to the doctrine of co-education," the indomitable lady principal asserted, "it is, I am told, a fact that the Trustees have never formally adopted this principle." Even though "there were not wanting opposers ... to tremble lest woman should depart from her sphere," the women at Iowa College had prevailed. "Good causes have always progressed, even against the opposition of the good," Mrs. Crowe assured her audience, and she pointed out the notable successes among the 125 female graduates of Iowa College: Mary Apthorp, the first woman to receive a regular B.A. degree, now a professor at Oshkosh Normal School; Mary Raymond, author of children's books; the Snell sisters

who have founded the celebrated Snell Seminary on the Pacific coast, ... and Dr. Martha Cleveland Dibble, practicing medicine in Kansas City. ... It must be admitted, by this time, that woman can pursue the higher education without detriment to her mental and physical well-being. ... Pointing to such a record as this, ... it is with the deepest earnestness we commend this part of the work to our President, and to all friends of the College. It is our desire that here on the prairie, these earnest and aspiring young women of the West may forever have a place where they can obtain the best and most thorough education, where they with their brothers may learn not only to prove all things, but also to hold fast that which is good.[2]

President Gates very wisely responded to the challenge which his lady principal had thrown forth. He did not equivocate as to his own position on the issue presented. "To you on whose woman's shoulders is the care of the ladies' department," he answered Mrs. Crowe,

> I thank you for your cordial word just spoken here. I believe that the ameliorating influence of co-education far more than counterbalances any objections to it. ... I believe in Women's Rights, at least to the extent of her having all of them she can get. The history of this college proves what woman can get. The college opposed her having them, she has won them in spite of the college. If need be she can probably keep them similarly.

It was with this flat assertion, so bold and unexpected, from the college's chief executive officer that the audience first began to lean forward to catch every word that would follow.

What followed was nothing less than a pronouncement of a new order for the college. It was customary at that time for the president of a Christian college to select a text from the Bible around which he would construct his formal address. Gates selected his text from the words of Mark—in this instance not the Saint Mark of the Gospels, but Mark Hopkins, the long-time president of Williams College—a clear indication that here was no ordinary minister-turned-president delivering the usual homiletic message to his congregation. Mark Hopkins, Gates informed his audience, had given an address the previous year on "the fiftieth anniversary of his accession to the presidency of Williams College [and] on that occasion, he stated ... these four things as constituting the essential elements of a complete education: A sound body, a disciplined mind, a liberal education, and character." Here was the text which Gates had found the most appropriate for the further secularization of the college's mission.

To a college audience accustomed to hearing their president speak only of the mind and the soul, with no mention of the base body, it was startling and perhaps even shocking to hear this president say:

> First, a sound body. The day has gone by when the scholar's stoop is a mark of honor. ... Greek civilization deified the body. The perverted Latin Christianity of the Middle Ages devilized it. The modern age has learned to do neither. It has been discovered that there is a strong physiological basis for all mental and physiological phenomena, and therefore, unless the foundation be good, the superstructure is in danger. ... Therefore do I believe thoroughly in the cultivation and encouragement of college athletics of all sorts. In the gymnasium and on the campus, games and sports, rivalries, field days are a tremendous educational power. ... The comparative lack [in Grinnell, Iowa] of attractive wild scenery, winning rambles by forest, mountain and stream, emphasizes the need of cultivating the love for out-door activity of every possible variety. There should be no sympathy with the feeling which would rob young men of what Prof. Young, the astronomer, calls "the frolicsome freedom, fling and exhilaration of out-door sport. In the play of organized games the youth gets voluntarily impressive lessons in prompt decision, quick obedience, manliness, self-control and self-sacrifice. ..." It is better that superfluous physical vitality be wreaked on a ball, foot-, base-, or tennis-, than on college or town property. I would not give much for a youth who has not some stock of that sort to dispose of in some way.

Raised eyebrows from the faculty, a stony stare from the former president, and broad grins from the students must have greeted this pronouncement that a sound body stood first among the essential elements of a complete education.

> Second. The disciplined mind ... It is one of the chief objects of a college training to take a crude mind and teach

it how to use itself. Many such minds need to be inspired with a love for mental activity. ... No small part of the training is the pruning down of its errant activities. The young mind has to be taught that everything that flies through the head is not thinking. ... When the mind is in full chase after an antelope, it must be able not to stop and follow up every rabbit-track that chances to cross the trail. ... Fogginess must be taken out of thinking. ... It is a great part of a college training that one learn to say, without apologizing first, "I do not know." ... Here we see one of the greatest needs of our time: The cultivation of the scientific, as over against the dogmatic spirit. The world needs Bacon yet to teach the beauty and power of the inductive as opposed to the deductive method. The scientific spirit is modest, reverent, docile, frank; the dogmatic is imperious, assertive, authoritative, and it has had its day. [Was not, perhaps, Gates again addressing his predecessor this time in a far less flattering way?] ... Alas for that man who conceives himself to be in the right and everyone else wrong. His usefulness as a trainer of young minds is very little; he does about as much harm as good. ...

Third, a *college* education must be pre-eminently a liberal one. This as over against the special work of the technical training or the work of the professional schools. ... I would I had the power adequately to express my abhorrence of the bread-and-butter idea of a college education. ... Most of the current criticism of college work starts from that low premise. The value of Mont Blanc is not computable by the number of cafés it can supply from its glaciers. ... The object of a college education is not to fit one to get rich more quickly, or to win a sordid success over another. Were it so, the curriculum would be very different. The *aim* of a liberal education is to *give* larger life. That was the mission of the Son of God to earth. ... The Christian college is to take up that work and in the Master's name carry it on.

As for the content of a liberal education, Gates was quite traditional in his adherence to a three-fold division: "The study of language and literature, that is God in history. The study of science; that is God in his works. The study of philosophy; that is God in the thoughts of men. Such is the substance of the curriculum of a liberal education the world over. Under that general division there is ample room for the greatest variety of order of sequence and proportion of attention."

Strong advocate that he was, especially of Darwinian evolution, Gates nevertheless feared that "the marvelous advance in our time" of science would exert such pressure to dominate all learning that "we need to cling firmly to the study of history and literature lest we forget what has been already attained in our exhilaration over new discovery. The new baby must not make us forget all the other children. They too have rights. ... There is great conservative value in the study of language and literature,—and I think no age of the world was ever in greater need of that element of true conservatism than ours. By that is not meant the conservatism of ignorance or prejudice or intolerance. Much that masquerades under the title of conservatism is of that stamp."

For Gates, a liberal education was the most practical of all forms of higher education—not in the "bread-and-butter" sense of obtaining wealth for one's self, but in giving service to society:

> Physical riches are death, unless there be stalwart ethics alongside adequately dominant,—to determine the use to which the wealth shall be put. ... A class of men and women must be raised up, strong enough and in numbers enough, and with patriotism enough, to step into the arena of practical life ... [to] still the noise of this low and materialistic clamor.
>
> Who are these men and women? Whence are they to come? Whence, indeed, but largely from the rank of the liberally educated? From those who have been trained to broad thought, ... from those who are capable ... to put a strong, guiding hand on current events. ... From these ranks is to come, if at all, purification of our politics. ... They must some time be cleaned, or this nation will die of the typhoid malaria of political bribery and corruption. From these same ranks must come the power to hold the

church to its mission of practical salvation; for the church is larger than its ministers.

Set a potent Christian college in the midst of a state, and in time it will make the difference between having "the scholar and the ignoramus in our teachers of common schools; it will make the difference between the jurist and the pettifogger in our courts; between the scientific physician and the murderous quack beside the bedside of the sick; between the healthy leader of public opinion and the blockhead editing our newspapers; the difference between the statesman and the demagogue in the legislative halls; the difference between the rational believer, and the declaiming charlatan in our pulpits; the difference between the glory and liberty of the kingdom of God, on the one hand, and the perpetual reign of superstition, injustice and oppression on the other."[3]

That difference marks the value of the right kind of college to its geographical constituency.

Gates felt that he need not spend much time on Hopkins's fourth element in college teaching. "What I have said of the nature and design of a liberal education has involved so much of what would come under a consideration of *Character* ... that I need not use many words for that. Character means one thing for us; to possess the 'mind of Christ.' ... Two things seem to us more than all else to mark the Christian character. Reverence, deep and serene, the peace of God. ... The other thing is the conception of life as an opportunity for service. That is the driving power of the soul ... ; he is not yet educated who has not learned that all he is and has is for the *service* of fellow man, thus serving God. God does not need us to help him swing the planets, nor to take care of his authority; but he does ask us to help him help men."

It was only toward the end of his address that Gates gave specific attention to aims and needs of Iowa College as he saw and defined them.

I come to this college believing in it just as it is. ... I believe in having the work done by professors rather than tutors. This is one of the advantages of smaller classes and smaller colleges. ... As to discipline—I am both surprised and gratified to find a college so thoroughly reformed in the matter of self government. ... Iowa College is far ahead of many of the older colleges of the East in this regard. Some modifications may quite probably be needed. But in general we are on the right track. It is ten thousand times better that young people should learn to govern themselves, than that they should be governed in any best way whatsoever. ... I have boundless confidence in putting students on their honor. If we expect great things of them, they will give us better than we expect.

Not that Iowa College was perfect "just as it is." Even though Gates believed "everything is bright," he quickly added, "There are needs enough and pressing enough, but we shall meet them." He then proceeded to list the needs: a series of Ladies Halls similar to Mears Hall; "a good gymnasium, with bathrooms, all above ground, light and cheery." [The existing so-called men's gymnasium was located in the basement of Alumni Hall. It had no showers, only two old cast-iron bathtubs which were rarely cleaned.] "We want two or three more professors, and to pay them all a living salary." [Those were the words the faculty had been waiting to hear.] "We want more money for all these, and we are going to have it."

What should be the long range goal of Iowa College? Gates had a simple and not very original answer to that fundamental question: "This—to hold Iowa College in the forefront of colleges between Chicago and the Western Ocean. We believe that it stands side by side with the foremost now. (Some would say more than that,—but I think hardly with wisdom. Let our words be well within the truth.)"

And how to attain and maintain that goal? Again, Gates's answer was brief:

Hold our standard of education high, and press it ever higher. No word I say today is of deeper significance. ...

The direction in which we move ... is to be toward making
our diplomas cost more work, not less. The more we can
make the diplomas of Iowa College mean, the better in
every way in the end for our college ... I know some will say
differently. They say we must have students, and we must
adapt our standards to their capacity. I dissent most em-
phatically from that estimate of the college. ... We shall
raise our standards of admission in our next catalogue. ...
That college which helps hold them [educational stan-
dards] and push them higher still ... will have the honors
by and by. This is our best opportunity. We must not waste
it.[4]

If history had provided us with no document from the
Gates era other than the text of this remarkable inaugural
address, we would still understand the meaning of his presidency. We would know of his ideals, of his views on higher education, and the goals he set for the college which he was to
lead into the twentieth century. We would also know him as
a person: the seriousness of his commitment, lightened by
his casual asides of subtle humor; the shy diffidence of his
manner contradicted by the assertive, almost cocksure confidence in the college's future under his guidance; the biting
pessimistic critique with which he assessed America's Gilded
Age alleviated by his optimistic faith in the curative powers
of a liberal education. His message is a fascinating study in
paradox. Here can be found those key words which were to
become the hallmarks of his administration: a sound body,
developed and maintained through healthy exercise; a
trained and disciplined mind; the liberalism of needed
change; the conservatism in the preservation of the good and
the beautiful; above all, the bringing of the Kingdom of God
to earth through service to society.

One might well wish for the exit poll so favored by today's political analysts to ascertain the audience's response
to President Gates's address. Surely in the broad sweep of
the presentation, there were views expressed both to elate
and to irritate almost everyone there. The students present

would have been the most generally enthusiastic in their response. Even the relatively mild reforms in student regulations enacted by the trustees in the summer of 1884 had been hailed by the student newspaper at the time with the triumphant cry: "All things are become new. Yes, our so-called foolish day dreams have become more than realized."[5]

Now as they heard their new president say, "It is ten thousand times better that young people should learn to govern themselves," they knew the millennium had truly arrived. The students, however, must have had certain forebodings over what Gates had meant in saying "our diplomas must cost more in work" and admission standards must be raised.

The faculty found joy in the promise of more faculty and "a living salary" for all. They trusted his confident assurance that "we want more money, and we are going to have it." Many of them, however, were less than enthusiastic in the emphasis Gates gave to athletics. At the very least, he need not have given "a sound body" first place among the essential elements of a complete education.

Upon hearing Gates give his first formal address, the trustees knew that they had found the vigorous young leader they had been seeking for the past three years. There were those among them, however, who were disturbed by some of his remarks: his "abhorrence of the bread-and-butter idea of a college education," and his rejection of the aim of college education to "fit one to get rich or to win sordid success over another." These barbs struck home, inflicting wounds that would continue to fester over the next decade. The trustees had wanted change, but some now for the first time began to wonder if perhaps they had obtained not a reformer but a populist revolutionary, a little too eager to attack the very sources upon whom the college must depend to obtain the money he had promised to get.

The ministers in the audience, of whom there were many, were the most perplexed and disturbed of all by what they had heard. Gates had not given them a biblical text with which to introduce his remarks, but no one could doubt the genuineness of the reverential tone of his message or the sincerity of his commitment to the Christian faith. The Congregational ministers of Iowa had long resented Magoun's attempt for an imperial domination of their church. They liked Gates's attack upon "that man who conceives himself to be in the right and everyone else wrong." They could applaud his call to service, and most of them also had fears of the crass materialistic excesses of their society. But they also knew that Gates had initially been denied ordination for his acceptance of Darwinian science. At least some of them knew that he had been a student of the German philosopher Lotze and was a devoted disciple of that Andover radical, William Jewett Tucker, who was attempting to divert Christianity from what was still generally considered its primary mission, the eternal salvation of the individual soul, to a concern for a temporal salvation of a collective society. There were some uncalled for thrusts at "the charlatan in the pulpit," and few of the ministry present were sure as to what Gates meant when he said the church was "larger than its ministers," but they assumed it was not meant as a compliment. Both the clergy and the laity at that moment were prepared to reserve final judgment on this man, but the seeds of questioning had been broadcast. Gates by the time he had concluded his address had already appeared as a figure of controversy.

These incipient doubts were put to a temporary rest, however, by the brilliant success of Gates's administration during the first five years of his tenure. Reform always generates interest, and interest in turn helps to generate money—money in this instance from rich donors and from poor small-town Congregational parishes, and money also from the increased tuition receipts from an expanding student enrollment.

A nadir in post–Civil War enrollment at Iowa College had been reached in 1878 when there were only fifty-seven students in the various college programs, including twenty in the non-degree-granting Ladies Course, and only four seniors who graduated. By the time that Gates was inaugurated in 1887, there had been some recovery. Eight seniors graduated in the Commencement exercises that followed the presidential inauguration from a total student body of eighty-seven. During the next four years, the growth in student population was nothing less then exponential. In 1891, forty students graduated and the total student population of 262 was nearly five times that of 1878, making Iowa College one of the largest private liberal arts colleges in the country at a time when few of the state universities had more than five hundred students.

Gifts to the college during these years also showed a most gratifying increase. The Gates administration had a most auspicious beginning, for at the very first meeting of the trustees which he attended as president of the college, a gift of $20,000 from a Grinnell merchant, Alonzo Steele, was formally accepted by the Board to establish the Myra Steele Chair of Mathematics and Natural Philosophy to honor the memory of Steele's daughter who had died while a student at the college.[6]

As soon as he took office, Gates launched the campaign to raise the college's endowment to the $200,000 level, which both Thwing and Mears had regarded as the sine qua non for their considering the presidency of the college. For a brief time in the early 1890s, the college catalogue published the names of the contributors to this endowment fund along with the amount each had pledged. The pledges ranged from $25,000 from Mrs. E. D. Rand of Burlington (the first appearance of that notable name in the college's history); and $20,000 each from Steele, former Gov. Samuel Merrill, and Edward Manning of Keosauqua, Iowa; down to a lengthy list of $25, $20 and $5 gifts in cash from ministers, school teachers and housewives throughout Iowa.[7] Thus within three years after starting the $200,000 endowment fund campaign, the goal had been reached—at least on paper. It would be the responsibility of the administration, however, to convert these pledges and notes into hard cash on hand, which would prove to be a more difficult task than simply obtaining a promise.

Gates brought to the task of fund-raising not only a rare skill of persuasion but also amazingly good luck, an equally valuable attribute for such an undertaking. In 1894, for example, the long, drawn-out battle over the Reickoff estate was finally resolved in the college's favor. This dispute involved a very sizeable bequest which William Reickoff of Orange City, Iowa, a former student at the college, had made to Iowa College in his will. After his death, his other heirs had disputed the validity of this provision, but now, after a decade of suits and countersuits, the court had finally awarded Iowa College $35,000.[8]

With such gifts as these from Rand and Reickoff, the $50,000 the college had lost for refusing to take Goodnow's name no longer evoked painful memories of what might have been. For that reason even the most conservative and materialistically minded trustees could forgive Gates for what they considered his idealistic, impractical view of a college education. They could even overlook his radical political stance and dismiss as unimportant the rumor that he was a crypto-Democrat.

Gates enjoyed a honeymoon and a sustained love feast with his various constituencies that would last from 1887 until 1893. To the faculty—both to those whom he had inherited from the previous regimes and to the new ones whom he recruited, he seemed nothing less than a miracle worker. For many years, the size of the faculty had remained static. It stood at ten when student enrollment had dropped to its low point in 1878, and it remained at ten when Gates took the presidency in 1887. Gates had said in his inaugural address that "we want two or three more professors ... and we are going to have them." He more than kept that promise. By 1890, there were fourteen full-time members of the faculty, and by the end of the decade, the faculty size was double that which it had been when Gates took over.

The promise to pay all the faculty "a living wage" which

243

Gates had also made was not as easily realized, however. Faculty salaries showed little improvement during these years over the annual maximum of $1,200, which had finally been reached during the last years of Magoun's administration. When Gates left office in 1900, the highest salary paid was still only $1,500.

The faculty, as it had from the beginning of the college when Erastus Ripley had received $500 per annum, had never ceased in its annual reports to the trustees to push for higher compensation. In its report of 1888 during the first year of Gates's presidency, the faculty presented the following memorial to the trustees:

> The Professors in the College ... receiving a salary of $1200, per annum and less, are constrained by their necessities to appeal to the Trustees for adequate compensation for their work. Salaries in the institution, except those of President and Financial Agent, were fixed at the present low figures many years ago. Meantime the expenses of living here have increased. ... No one can possibly do justice to such work as ours on $1200 per annum. ... It is a common thing for our pupils, upon graduation, to receive several hundred dollars up to twice as much as their instructors do, for services not superior in quality and value, we can modestly say, to those which they enjoy here, and which prepare them to be better paid than we are.[9]

In its continuing pleas to the trustees, the faculty was fortified by the knowledge that it had the full support of its president, for Gates was as relentless as the faculty in exerting pressure for higher salaries. His report to the trustees in 1894 is typical of the messages he sent annually to the governing board:

> The strength of any college resides chiefly in its board of instructors. ... We beg again with most deference to refer to the matter of salary. The expense of living in Grinnell is higher than in some college towns; the salaries are lower. For comparison Beloit and Carleton both may be used in both of which salaries are larger than in Iowa College. [The

comparative salary studies that Professors Alan Jones and John Dawson have provided the administration and the trustees in recent years did not originate with them.] The spirit of every college should be to get the best and keep the best. ... There is no question of more immediate and vital importance than the adequate support of the teaching forces in the college. The teachers connected with Iowa College do not ask large salaries; they do expect, however, a reasonable support. Under present conditions they are able to do justice neither to themselves nor to their positions.[10]

The great fear that haunted both presidents Magoun and Gates throughout their tenures was that they would not be able to keep their best faculty because of being unable to match competitive offers. Bowdoin College, in particular, was a dangerous raider, taking two of Iowa College's most distinguished faculty: John Avery, who had succeeded Leonard Parker as professor of Ancient Languages and had been rightly praised by Magoun as being "our specimen scholar, pure and simple"; and Joseph Torrey, Jr., a brilliant chemist, who was offered a high-paying position with a steel company but chose to go to Bowdoin. Gates himself in 1892 refused an invitation to become president of Dartmouth, his alma mater. The faculty passed a resolution, strongly urging him to stay for the good of the college.

Considering the college's low salary scale it is not surprising that Iowa College was to suffer continual loss of some of its very best instructors. What is surprising, however, is that the college had been able to engage them initially, and that some stayed. Both Magoun and Gates are to be commended for the several excellent appointments they made. Torrey, for example, was succeeded by Walter Hendrixson, a Harvard graduate, who came to Grinnell in 1890, and during his thirty-five-year tenure sustained the college's outstanding Department of Chemistry.

John Crow, Avery's replacement, was yet another example of excellence being succeeded by even greater excellence. When Crow joined the faculty in 1883, the classics were in decline. Greek and Latin no longer dominated the curriculum, even within the Classical Course track. By the sheer excellence of his teaching, Crow brought about a Greek revival on campus that had nothing to do with architecture, and was as remarkable as it was unexpected. Students flocked to his classes without being driven there as they had been twenty years earlier by inescapable requirements. It was generally accepted by students that if you had not taken a Crow course you hadn't really attended Iowa College.

The arrival of Crow meant not only that the college had acquired a truly great classics scholar, but it also got as a bonus a remarkable female addition to the staff in the person of his wife, Martha Foote, who proved to be a worthy occupant of a position first firmly established by Sarah Candace Parker. Yet another of the many "strong-minded women" who have served the college throughout its history, Foote was a graduate of Syracuse University and was among the first women in the country to earn a Ph.D. degree. After teaching English at Wellesley College, she came with her husband to Iowa College in 1883, and the following year she accepted the position of Principal of the Ladies Department, roughly equivalent to the later title of Dean of Women. An ardent feminist, she was to battle throughout her seven years in office to make Iowa College truly coeducational. She had refused at first to take her husband's name, but when she was advised quietly but pointedly by the college that it was unseemly for a couple living together not to have a common name, she reluctantly accepted his surname but preserved her individuality by adding the letter "e" to Crow, an addition which the college catalogues deliberately failed to observe. According to John Nollen, Crowe was "a source of some amusement to the students [as she] always marched briskly ahead of her husband as they walked to their work at the college. She could wax sweetly lyrical about the blue gentians on the campus, and then pour out the vials of her disapproval upon young ladies who departed from her accepted norm of conduct."[11]

Nollen should have added that her most vitriolic effusions were dispensed upon a patriarchy which was reluctant to grant full equality to women. For that service to her sex, her "young ladies" were willing to endure their somewhat milder chastisement.

Following the untimely death of her husband in 1890, Crowe stayed on for one more year as principal before departing to pursue a distinguished career as professor of English literature at the University of Chicago and later Northwestern. In her letter of resignation from Iowa College she issued one final blast at the trustees for their pretending they believed in the principle of coeducation. She once again forcibly emphasized the progress the women of Iowa College had made in obtaining equality in education in spite of the trustees' attitude. She concluded the letter with a defiant challenge to male domination. "It is the woman's era, and the young women will enter every door that is left ajar."

The only person Martha Crowe felt was her true ally was George Gates. She returned only once to Grinnell, in 1912, to give a eulogy at the memorial service for Gates in which she praised the former president's support of women's rights.[12]

•   •   •

Another brilliant woman gave the main address at President Gates's memorial service—Clara Millerd, who graduated from Iowa College in 1893. She was appointed by Gates first as preceptress of the Academy, and then, after graduate work at the University of Chicago, as a member of the Department of Greek and Philosophy. In her memorial address Miss Millerd spoke of President Gates as "a living presence, because all who really know and love Grinnell College, know and love some things that are due to his influence." She named the three passions in his life: "his fearless devotion to truth; his enthusiasm for social righteousness; and his confident faith in the presence of God in all of life." Miss Millerd believed that "The College to his last day was a part of his life ... on this campus he did his constructive work. He injected the spirit of service into every brick and foundation stone."[13] During his presidency Gates brought other faculty members to the college who loved and admired him as Clara Millerd did. When he left the college there were heartfelt expressions of their love and respect for him.

He appointed almost an entirely new staff of distinguished faculty, a number of whom stayed for many years. His concern for preserving tradition through the study of language and literature resulted in the strengthening of modern languages in the curriculum and soon finding John Scholte Nollen to teach them. Nollen and John Hanson Thomas Main, appointed earlier to the Greek department by Gates, both became presidents of the college. Main was one of Gates's closest associates. He would have been the immediate successor to the presidency after Gates if the trustees had not wanted a minister as president of the college.[14]

Literature also became more important in the curriculum. The Rev. Charles Noble, the last clergyman in the department, was joined by Selden L. Whitcomb, an 1886 graduate of Iowa College. Whitcomb had studied at Columbia University, Cornell University, Harvard College and Colorado. He expanded the offerings of the department adding literary criticism and, in cooperation with colleagues in other languages, comparative literature. Whitcomb was a poet as well as a teacher. His wife willed his estate to Grinnell for the Whitcomb poetry prizes.

President Gates was determined that the study of science should have an important place in the college. Frank Herriot of the class of 1890, quotes Gates as saying: "Science and its devotees are the Lord's torch bearers and evangels."[15] He believed cultivating the scientific spirit and practicing the inductive method were essential for a disciplined mind.

Professor Joseph Torrey, Jr., esteemed by both faculty and students (partly because of his enthusiasm for sports), taught science from 1885–1890. His replacement, Walter Scott Hendrixson, stayed on to develop the chemistry de-

248

partment and work with Harry Waldo Norris (known among students as "Bug") in biology to make the college an effective center for both scientific research and teaching. Another legendary scientist was Frank F. Almy, who came in 1893 to occupy the first chair in physics and stayed for thirty-nine years. Physics became a department separate from mathematics and has had a distinguished record. Philosophy, another newly organized department, was developed under John Simmons, Jr., from the Department of Mental and Moral Philosophy after Magoun's death in 1890, and included the study of pedagogy and elementary psychology.[16]

With more and stronger departments, the faculty took a larger degree of responsibility in their work. Gates has been given credit for establishing the principle of faculty control of the educational concerns of the college and with it "the independent sovereignty of each department."[17]

The sovereignty was exceptional for the new department founded during Gates's presidency. Applied Christianity had an endowment of its own and came with its own professor— George D. Herron. The generous funding for the department and its chair eventually caused feelings of inequity among the faculty of other departments and at least some concern about overlapping in subject matter. In the trustees minutes in 1894 it was noted that Jesse Macy and Herron would meet with Gates to arrange as to the provinces of their departments. They were both interested in the same problems—the harmful effects that industrialism, carried out in ways contrary to the teachings of Christ, was having on the lives of the people. Both Macy and Herron identified economics as an important part of the problem. In 1895 Herron would offer a teacher of political economy for his own department which the trustees gratefully accepted.[18] The funding for this new position came no doubt from the same source a the original endowment for the department—Mrs. Elbridge Dexter Rand.

Mrs. Rand, a wealthy widow in Burlington, Iowa, had been impressed with a speech, "The Message of Jesus to Men of Wealth," given at a Congregational meeting in Minnesota by a young minister from Wisconsin, George D. Herron. She persuaded her Congregational pastor in Burlington, William Salter, of the Iowa Band, to accept Herron as his assistant pastor. Soon Mrs. Rand wanted her protégé to have a wider audience and offered Iowa College an endowment for a Department of Applied Christianity, to be headed by Herron.

The idea of a Department of Applied Christianity was eminently appealing to President Gates. He had a deep interest in working for the Kingdom of God on earth which had grown out of his study with Herman Lotze at the University of Göttingen. From Lotze he learned of the personalist philosophy which sees the ultimate reality of God as personal, each person having a share in it, and each person concerned for and respectful of every other person.[19] On his return from Europe, Gates studied at Andover Seminary under William Jewett Tucker, who stressed the social implications of personalism. This philosophy was at the heart of the Social Gospel Movement, to which an Applied Christianity department would give expression.

Gates had already known Herron, having invited him to a retreat of a few socially-minded clergymen at Iowa College in June 1892. Professor Charles Noble remembers that "we met in the little tower room in Goodnow Hall." Out of this small retreat came the Kingdom Movement which was "one of the chief factors in stimulating interest in social Christianity in the 1890's." Gates and Herron were leading figures in this movement, centered on the campus of Iowa College. The purpose was "to awaken the churches to the seriousness of social issues." Its influence was felt in all denominations, although the Congregational Church was most affected. The Kingdom Movement retreats at Iowa College met in June for four years, 1892 to 1896, searching for ways to widen the influence of the movement. Though Herron became the most conspicuous prophet in the Kingdom Movement, much of its success was because of the "administrative skill" of Gates and the "constant encouragement" he gave to Herron. Herron's classes and lectures in Grinnell attracted crowds of students and visitors who came many miles to hear him. Gates said of Herron: "No man of this generation has uttered the prophetic voice ... of this age in so nearly adequate terms as Herron has done." The word of the Kingdom Movement was spread not only through Herron's lectures. A weekly journal, *The Kingdom*, was issued with President Gates as editor-in-chief and Professor Macy as one of the associate editors. Another educational project was "Schools of the Kingdom," intended for earnest and interested people who wished to study about the Kingdom of God and discover ways and forces for its realization on earth. The schools were held in Grinnell in 1894 and 1895 for eight days after commencement. In 1894 the school was sponsored by the Department of Applied Christianity and the American Institute of Christian Sociology. Four hundred ministers and laymen from fourteen states gathered in Grinnell to hear speakers of "great prominence." Of course Gates and Herron were leaders in these Kingdom schools.

The following description of Herron gives an idea of how effective he must have been as a teacher and lecturer.

> He was of arresting appearance; slender, medium in height, dark, bearded, brown-eyed. He had unusual platform abilities, though he spoke in a solemn, slow, impressive manner and used rather awkward gestures. His deep sincerity and perfect self-assurance gave him a tremendous hold over his audiences, upon which he exerted almost hypnotic power.[20]

President Gates was glad to have George Herron as a co-worker in the Kingdom Movement and as head of the Department of Applied Christianity, to help communicate the ideas of the Social Gospel movement.

Unfortunately the presence of Herron at the college lit the spark of a controversy between the old and the new which had been presaged by some of the reactions to Gates's inaugural address. Herron arrived in 1893 and by 1894 there was concern among the Congregational churches in Iowa, some of the trustees and even a few of the faculty because his religious and political views differed from theirs and from those of people they hoped would support the college financially.

Within the college things were going well for Herron and his department. In 1894 a graduate program in Applied Christianity was established and half a dozen of the strongest students planning to go into Christian work returned for an added year's study.[21] Among these students was Harlan Paul Douglass, graduate of 1891, who became a distinguished educator in the American Mission Association.

The Applied Christianity department reached out to the community by organizing a neighborhood settlement house, following the example of William Jewett Tucker's work in Boston. It brought the outside world to Grinnell through the Rand lectures, a gift from Mrs. Rand and her daughter, Carrie, who had moved to Grinnell, continuing their close friendship with George Herron. The Rand lectures were presented by leaders of the Christian Reform movement, the most notable being Jane Addams. Perhaps the most colorful of the Rand lecturers was W. T. Stead, an English investigative journalist, and author of *If Christ Came to Chicago!*, a survey of social conditions in Chicago. Stead's name had been suggested by alumni trustee, Albert Shaw, editor of the *Review of Reviews*. Each lecturer spent several days in Grinnell, giving a series of lectures open to the public. This pattern for lecture series has continued in succeeding epochs of Grinnell history.

The Rand lectures were in addition to lectures by distinguished advocates of social reform which were already a part of the college life. Some of the lecturers were active in the effort to improve race relations which was centered in the American Mission Association until the Federal Council of Churches was founded in 1907. Albion Tourget, strong advocate for African-American civil rights, received a positive response from students for his biracial National Civil Rights

Association. Harlan Douglass, alumnus of Iowa College, supervised the seventy-five schools of the American Mission Association in the South, bringing about more participation and cooperation between the races.[22] He was undoubtedly influential in bringing four Congregational ministers from Iowa to be presidents of American Mission Association colleges in the South. President Gates, a member of the Board of the American Mission Associates, was another important Iowa connection. He believed the Association had "the most glorious opportunity God ever gave to any people ... to preach the gospel of solidarity of the human race."[23] The spirit of the abolition movement, strong in earlier Grinnell history, had come forward in a new context.

In spite of all the positive developments in Grinnell, already in 1894 the trustees had received a letter of complaint against Herron from the venerable Leonard F. Parker, recently returned from the University of Iowa to the Iowa College faculty, to occupy a chair carrying his own name. Although he had been a forward-moving force in his early days at the college, he was critical of the new era. The trustees responded to his letter by appointing a committee of trustees to report on the Applied Christianity department at the June meeting. The report was supportive of the goal of the department and favorable to its effect on campus. It admitted that the college had become more widely known by the "more public utterances" of Professor Herron, as well as President Gates, on the vital questions of the day. Unfortunately these utterances, although "in their true meaning and main intent ... seem worthy and true," have affected "the confidence and esteem of the natural constituency" of the college. A warning followed of the possibility of a resulting "loss of students, cessation of gifts ... to be avoided if it can be done consistently with truth and right." The report ended with strong support for the work of both Professor Herron and President Gates, almost pleading with the Board to be patient, and not to interfere with the liberty of anyone connected with the college "to speak as the spirit may move." The trustees accepted the report expressing "faith and hope that the skies will clear" allowing "more and more" progress toward "fulfilling the desires of the founders." Ephraim Adams, one of those founders, was on the Board committee and undoubtedly made his voice heard in the report.[24] He would be steadfast in his support of President Gates and Professor Herron. The students were earnestly pro-Herron in editorials in *The Unit* in May 1894.

Herron's 1894 Commencement address at the University of Nebraska brought forth amazed and alarmed responses from both the audience and the press. Herron came out strongly against the "anarchy" he saw resulting from "the open violations of the interstate commerce law [and] the use of our legislative institutions for corporate private interests." He observed that at this time when "all nations are full of a dread of anarchy, our nation is in a state of anarchy." After the address the outraged Governor of Nebraska rose angrily to denounce Herron as an anarchist! Herron had also brought forth his heartfelt goals of "a political system that shall associate them [the people] in justice; association [rather than competition] is the law of preservation and progress; the land and its resources are to be held by the State in sacred trust for the people." He observed that "the theory of private ownership has practically absolved private ownership for the vast majority of people." The Governor's response to this assertion was, perhaps more rationally, a cry of "Communist!" Herron, however, called what he was advocating, "industrial democracy [which] would be the actualization of Christianity."[25] Christianity of course was what held all the constituencies of Iowa College together for awhile in support of Herron and of Gates, who was setting forth the same central idea of social justice in all his baccalaureate sermons and other speeches and writings. The telling difference, though, was that Herron made an outright attack on the churches which he said, "stand for religion but not for the practice of Christ's kind of righteousness."

The trustees sent the 1894 report of its committee to

Herron and awaited a response. In 1895 in addition to offering to the trustees a professor in political economy for his department, Herron came forth with funds for an assistant in his own area of teaching.[26] Assistance was needed partly because of the attraction of these new courses, but perhaps more because of Herron's extremely busy nationwide lecture schedule. Garrett Polhemus Wyckoff, a teacher in the Academy, was appointed to the new post and went off to Columbia for study in preparation.

Wyckoff had graduated from Iowa College in the early 1890s. He returned after teaching in South Dakota to study with Jesse Macy having found more interest in populism than in the classics among his students. In his undergraduate days Wyckoff had known Macy as "a mighty man who came whooping down the field in the great community mass football game held every evening in the Fall on the Campus open field North of Goodnow Hall."[27] Wyckoff spent many more years at the college until his retirement in 1941. He contributed with distinction to American Red Cross work in Europe where he served with his wife after the First World War.

The 1895 faculty report to the trustees proposed to set forth the facts in regard to assertions about the effects of Herron and his department. Rather than barely holding its own in enrollment, the college had one of its largest freshman classes in spite of increased tuition and admission requirements in foreign languages; there was no decrease in total enrollment reported, although a new method of counting the students showed a smaller number than the old one would have. In the matter of fund-raising the faculty recommended appealing to men of large resources. The great depression of 1893 meant that the $200,000 endowment never was realized. Yet in the fearful concern over the possible effect of Herron's radicalism on the finances of the college, the effect of the depression seems to have been overlooked.

By 1896 Herron had been rejected by the churches and had influence only in radical social circles. That year his health failed and he had to go abroad for a year. The Grinnell-based Kingdom Movement declined and virtually disappeared, although leaving a lasting influence.[28] At their annual meeting in July 1896 the trustees felt that attempts to come to an understanding with Herron, to persuade him to temper his rhetoric, had been disregarded. They had waited in vain for a reply to the very reasonable and courteous report from their 1894 meeting. Now they readopted the report, this time having it "spread upon the records." A committee of J. M. Chamberlain and R. M. Haines were to present the paper to Gates, Herron, and Miss Rand.

By 1897 the annual report to the trustees by President Gates was discouraging. No work had been done on the endowment. It was considered unwise and impossible to pursue it. As for the Herron affair, the committee appointed in 1896 had had a pleasant conversation with Gates but Herron was out of the country. At this point the Board sent a letter directly to Herron stating that his interpretation of the Scripture was exaggerated and distorted; generalizations were presented as doctrines; enemies had been made of those the college needed as friends; other departments had been encroached upon; invitations to him to lecture had not come from churches; there had been a decline in interest in his department among the students. After all this the trustees concluded optimistically: "Nevertheless we do not despair nor do we believe that it is impossible for a better condition to be brought about through you."[29]

Herron's letter in reply dated May 25, 1897, was conciliatory, first thanking the trustees for their kind and considerate candor and courtesy. He followed with truly admirable expressions of his own candor and courtesy and respect. He told them that even before their letter, he realized he had shown "too much condemnation" in his lectures and "too little real consideration of the opinions and feelings of those who saw things differently" and had not "taken the time and patience to make myself understood." He said that with a different approach antagonism could perhaps be changed to "friendliness of attitude" and he would try to accomplish this.

To the claims against him made by the trustees, Herron asserted that: The controversial ideas he had espoused had brought an advance—in the consideration of the teachings of Jesus in a sociological rather than a theological context; never having given interviews or seen reporters in Chicago, Lincoln, or California, he could not have said things the press reported; he was shocked at the credence given these reports; he had received invitations from churches all over the country (a long, impressive list). He added that he had been disappointed not to have the opportunity to speak to more diverse groups.

Herron felt that the trustees had taken an "extremely local point of view. ... I do feel that through the words I have so awkwardly and unworthily spoken there has come a name to Iowa College that you do not yet appreciate and that rises up even in far distant lands." Herron said his work had been poor and unworthy and credit should go to the "noble work and brave and patient administration of our beloved President." His letter ended with sympathy for the problems he had caused the trustees in carrying out their sacred responsibilities, and gave them "utmost freedom to do their duty" without fear that he would pose as a martyr.[30]

In this 1898 baccalaureate sermon, Gates spoke eloquently to the problems resulting from Herron's teachings, observing that when the "setting forth of human right collides with current opinions ... trouble falls upon his head who interferes with either the comforts or profits from those established injustices. ... Progress means interference with a great many people [who are] only conscious of resisting annoyance and personal loss." Referring to the fifty-year anniversary of the College that year, he spoke of how the "early Missionaries of Iowa (who founded and nursed its tender years) flung away the preferments of earthly success and gave their lives to this new naked land." Referring to the war with Spain in the Philippines in which "some of our best and beloved students are enlisted," he said that to the young, war sometimes "seems less terrible than it is, but to die daily for one's country is infinitely harder. ..." College experience has cost much "but the use of education in Christian service will cost more."[31]

The early summer meetings of the Iowa Congregational Association and the June meetings of the trustees of the college year by year would bounce off against each other with the faculty in between. In this year of 1898 the Rev. Clinton Douglass gave a very critical supplemental report on Herron to the Congregational Association. The faculty refuted some of the points made, saying that Herron's Applied Christianity classes were smaller but only because the subject was no longer required, and there were now two teachers in the department and four courses offered. The faculty finance committee did agree that the controversy over Herron made it more difficult to raise money, and stated that the faculty was not happy with the "abnormal relationship" of the department to the college, that is, the special endowment for one department which also had its own board of trustees. Nevertheless it was maintained that the work of the Applied Christianity department was never more important. The faculty defended academic freedom, stating that it would deem it one of the greatest misfortunes ... "if retirement of any instructor were insisted upon because of opinions expressed regarding questions regarding the work of his department."

The trustees, however, were sympathetic to Clinton Douglass's complaint about the exceptional status of the Department of Applied Christianity. They asked for and believed they had won the consent of Mrs. Rand to place the department, along with the other departments, under the aegis of the Iowa College Board of Trustees. This step gave encouragement to the anti-Herron faction, who hoped it would pave the way for his departure.[32]

By 1899 the attacks on Herron had intensified. Col. John Meyer, a trustee from Newton, set forth instances of teachers who were graduates of Iowa College not being hired because of Herronism, and high school graduates not coming to Iowa

College to study. In northwest Iowa they were going to Northfield, Minnesota, where Carleton College was not "infected" with Herronism.[33] Students attending Iowa College had a different viewpoint. An editorial in the *Scarlet and Black* expressed enthusiastic support for Herron and his effect on the college.

The Marshalltown *Times-Republican* of February 5, 1899, reported Herron's lecture at the Chicago meeting of the Political Equality League in which he said marriage was (or should be) doomed because no true comradeship is possible when one partner is dependent on the other. Suffrage would not be enough if there were political, economic and religious dependency within the marriage.

In June H. H. Robbins, secretary of the Board of Trustees, wrote that something must be done to change the relationship of Herron to the college as it was impossible to raise money. The trustees took no action at their annual meeting. Mrs. Rand was not ready after all to agree to the change in the control of the Applied Christianity endowment. And President Gates asked for time to work things out.

In August Herron lectured at the Populist Convention in Des Moines where he found his most sympathetic audience and made some of his most provocative pronouncements: "McKinley has committed treason," (this in relation to war in the Philippines), "the system cannot be mended—only ended, anti-trust legislation not enough," "great individual wealth is never earned or produced—always stolen," "We are on the earth only on terms of those who own the land."[34]

On October 13, 1899, Herron submitted his letter of resignation making clear it was voluntary. He defended the success of the Applied Christianity department and noted that it had not hindered the steady growth in number of students, that the faculty was "harmonious—cooperative," and the "college spirit unequaled in moral tone and intellectual seriousness." He stated that the needs of the college perhaps could not be met if he remained, declaring "I am myself unwilling to retain a position ... and so be chargeable with possible impoverishment of the College." He used conciliatory and courteous words to the trustees: "You have met your trying position with sincere purpose to your whole duty to all. ... You have sought to take patiently the official consequences of my remaining as a teacher." He repeated his disclaimer of martyrdom to the cause of free teaching expressed in his earlier letter, saying, "I shall defend the constituency and trustees ... in their right to choose what they shall have taught."[35]

The trustees' reply was equally conciliatory, praising Herron for his kindness and consideration and his excellent spirit and commending his department for its excellent work. They did express the underlying disagreement as to how social reform should be accomplished: "To us it seems clear that the most promising course for promoting the ultimate right is at present to impress upon men their present duty rightly to use what wealth shall come properly to them under the present organization of society."[36] Both Herron and the trustees have been praised for having "emerged from the controversy their statures enhanced by their balanced and generous statements."[37]

In the November 4, 1899, *Scarlet and Black,* Herron's resignation is reported as a surprise to the students. An editorial praises his teachings which "have been such as to invite deeper and more earnest thought ... the college will lose ... one of the most valuable and inspiring teachers which it has ever had." The January 20, 1900, *Scarlet and Black* reported a testimonial to Herron signed by forty-five of the forty-six members of his classes citing his "inspiration to noble and unselfish living." The faculty also commended Herron for the work of his department and told him his influence and presence would always be welcome on campus.

Herron did not return to the campus. A year and a half after his resignation, his wife was granted a divorce. Two months later, in an untraditional ceremony, George Herron married Carrie Rand in New York. Divorce and remarriage caused shock in Grinnell and brought severe criticism from the American press which never ceased its attacks on Herron and Carrie, eventually driving them from the country to live in Italy. The Congregational Church deposed Herron from the ministry, directing his and Carrie's work for social reform even more into politics. They were active in the Socialist Party of America, and, through the rest of his life, Herron was closely associated with famous progressive leaders such as Eugene Debs, Upton Sinclair, and Woodrow Wilson. He felt deep sorrow and regret, however, that he had not achieved success in bringing about ethical and humanitarian reform.[38] George Herron could not know the far reaching effect he and his Department of Applied Christianity would have on Grinnell College. By stressing service and concern for the public welfare, he and President Gates set the path which the college has continued to follow. Grinnell students in every era since have been active in protests, education on issues, support for policies, and action on causes they believe in. Grinnell Alumni have played important roles in the history of the country, and in their own communities. George McJimsey, 1958 alumnus and biographer of Harry Hopkins, 1912 alumnus, believes that "the objectives of the New Deal were fully in line with Grinnell's Social Gospel. Indeed the pluralist insistence on a larger synthesis carried forward Grinnell's Social Gospel emphasis on the Unity of all persons."[39]

George Gates, the president who brought George Herron to the campus and defended him to the end, was even more responsible than Herron for influencing the college in its service-oriented direction. Six years before Herron's appointment to the faculty, Gates in his inaugural address had stressed "the conception of life as an opportunity for service." In his second baccalaureate sermon in 1889, President Gates set forth his personalist philosophy which had led him to the Social Gospel. He developed his theme that "personality is the ultimate fact of all our philosophy," that "the person shares God's own nature, is made in the image of God." Refuting the idea of labor as a commodity, he stated that "there is no such thing as human labor. Human labor is a person laboring." Coming to the essence of Social Gospel, he asserted it is just as important to inquire how a man treats his fellow man as to ask what he thinks or believes.[40]

Gates never wavered in his support for the Social Gospel, expressing it many times as in his baccalaureate sermon in 1894 when he spoke of "enthusiasm and passion for service."[41] The advocacy of Gates, if not as inflammatory as that of Herron, was often as outspoken and as politically concerned. In his baccalaureate sermon of 1892, the year before Herron's arrival in Grinnell, Gates optimistically expressed his belief that "the world is moving along lines of brotherhood. ... This may not be socialism, but it is the great truth after which the various forms of socialism are feeling."[42] It was not the last time socialism would be viewed with favor at the college. Norman Thomas, the Socialist party candidate for president in 1940, spoke at Grinnell before the election, inspiring many students to wear Norman Thomas political buttons. Again in 1948, when neither Dewey nor Truman had strong backing, Norman Thomas was a candidate with considerable appeal, at least among some of the faculty.

In 1895 Gates moved farther away from speaking of religion as it had been thought of in the early years of the college. In his baccalaureate sermon, he asserted: "Morality carried to its summit is religion. The men who have done the most for the world have been men of religious nature, not all of them Christianly religious, but men of reverence and devotion to the highest and best they know. ... The law of sacrificial service must pervade all."[43]

By 1897 Gates increasingly felt the need to support Herron. In his baccalaureate sermon he declared that "Genuine progress is ever fundamentally evolutionary, however sometimes necessarily revolutionary in its methods." He decried the "moral atrophy" and "ethical callousness" of the way our country had regarded the three-fold rise in unemployment in the last year. In further support of Herron, Gates cited famous examples of great men such as Martin Luther, John

Calvin, Patrick Henry, and Samuel Adams ("son of Harvard"), who came from "great schools" that through their faculty and alumni have made "large contributions to the spirit of progress."[44]

In his 1898 baccalaureate address, Gates explained the adverse reaction to Herron's message for change by pointing out that change always brings criticism and that the status quo is difficult to dislodge. Shortly before Herron's resignation in 1899, Gates warned against narrowness, saying different viewpoints should be listened to, giving as an example town and gown relations. He urged that the best cure for narrowness is "to be lavish without limit in our service to our fellow man."[45]

President Gates resigned in March 1900, five months after Herron's resignation. In his letter of resignation, Gates stated that his wife's health prevented her from living in Iowa and he could not be separated longer from his family. Perhaps he felt tarred by the same brush that had brought about Herron's resignation and, like Herron, did not want to feel responsible for the financial downfall of the college. He certainly had intended to join his family in Colorado but possibly not this soon.

In his letter of resignation to the trustees Gates expressed his appreciation for their support and listed the accomplishments they and he had "on yonder campus ... wrought together": an increase in the annual income of college from $19,000 to about $50,000; increase in annual graduates from twenty to over sixty; the best in academic quality; the maintenance of the most worthy traditions in American college education. He urged the trustees to continue the cooperation with the faculty in filling instructor vacancies and to use the same practice even in choosing the president of the college. Gates stated the duty of the president is to support faculty members especially those who have been appointed with the unanimous vote of the trustees. He declared that in spite of all the controversy, the college had made immeasurably larger gains than losses. He had "one chief anxiety for the college—that it go forward and not backward," adding: "Let there be only a fearless courage, unconditioned loyalty to truth, and the forward look ... [of] those who believe in a Kingdom of God on earth and in great reforms [necessary for] the realization of that Kingdom."

George Gates continued to look forward in his work to bring Heaven on Earth for everyone. He served a brief pastorate in Wyoming before becoming a distinguished president of Pomona College. He ended his career as president of Fisk University where he was able, for the last three years of his life, to have a more direct effect on race relations.

Life for the whole college during the Herron years continued apace under the administration of President Gates. Herron was carrying forward both on and off campus the spirit of Christian service that Gates held as the foremost value in education. The nature of Herron's message as well as the increasing criticism of the messenger assured the involvement of Gates's attention. Nevertheless the more mundane matters of the college were not neglected. All aspects of a liberal arts education moved forward. The college was started on its modern course during the presidency of George Gates.

To a president who considered a sound body the first essential element of a complete education, the burgeoning of interest and activity in athletics must have been gratifying. Sports had gradually become more important in college life in the West but it had not been formally organized at Iowa College before Gates's arrival. G. W. Cowden, an 1888 graduate, in his contribution to the *Blue Book,* a student publication to celebrate the semicentennial of the college, gave science Professor Torrey credit for the early instigation of sports on campus. Cowden remembered the spirited games in the fall of 1885 between the teams of two gentlemen literary societies. He described the first field meet in the fall of 1886 held in a cow pasture, with contestants running "sans shoes," "sans hose."[46]

Under the liberal spirit of President Gates, formal athletic programs and an athletic administration were developed. The famous football victory, 24-0, of Iowa College over the State University of Iowa in 1889 gave impetus to the enthusiasm for athletics throughout the years, waxing and waning with the success of the Iowa College (later Grinnell College) teams. In a picture of the acclaimed 1889 football eleven taken by the well-known Grinnell photographer, Child, we can still admire the victorious team.[47]

Already in 1890 associations were formed within the college and with other schools to make rules and regulations for athletic activities. The faculty committee for athletics created the Athletic Union and then the college joined the Iowa-Inter-Collegiate Athletic Association.[48] The same year in June the first Iowa Field Day was held in Grinnell. There were tennis matches for men and women followed by the half-mile run, pole vault, hurdle race, 50-yard dash, 100-yard dash. The State University of Iowa won over the closest competitor, Iowa College, by only a few points, and Iowa College kept its promise of serving ice cream and strawberries to all who came to the meet.[49]

The biggest problem to be dealt with by the various athletic associations was professionalism, always discouraged at Iowa College. In 1893 the trustees had insisted that only bona fide students of this college could be involved in the athletic teams. President Gates in his 1894 report to the trustees assured them that the "spirit of professionalism is practically dead. ... The rule concerning the standing of a student in his classroom as a condition upon which he can become a member of any of the athletic teams has been strictly enforced." There was little occasion for the college to have to deal with professionalism, as among the qualified students there were sufficient numbers and talent to form competitive teams. Indeed a student publication in 1891 indicated that among the athletic team members, one can find "a large number of the best students of the college."[50]

Another concern of the trustees was betting, gambling, and riotous behavior at athletic contests. Gates reported to the trustees in 1891 that "it is impossible to prevent some betting though I have every reason to believe that a good deal less of that is done by Iowa College students than by others." In the same report Gates gave testimony to the belief expressed in his inaugural address that excess student energy can be spent in sport, rather than destructive activities; "During the year there has been no destruction of property, carrying off or burning up of signs of fences or sidewalks, ... nocturnal bonfires and general hullabaloos. A great part of this good order I know to have been due to athletics."

An editorial in the *Scarlet and Black* in 1894 corroborates Gates's opinion in praising physical activity as a healthy vent for superfluous energy and also seems to echo Gates's inauguration emphasis on a sound body by describing sports as a means of keeping the physical condition necessary for the best school work and fostering purity and right living.[51]

In contrast to Magoun and in spite of a trustee pronouncement in 1893 against "extended tours," President Gates encouraged participation by Iowa College teams in out-of-town, even out-of-state, athletic events. His attitude may be seen in his remarks about the Minneapolis football trip in 1891. "The students from Iowa College did themselves credit the whole time they were there ... went to church in a body on Sunday ... there was not a single objectionable feature of the game ... many exceedingly pleasant episodes. In my opinion it was a wholly good thing."[52] To be sure, the Minneapolis football trip and a six-day sortie by the baseball team came before the objection to such trips from the trustees, but the tours did not stop after the expression of disapproval.

A cooperative connection between athletics and various other parts of college life was encouraged by Gates. He found it "highly commendable that the Christian Association and Athletic Association work together as they do."[53] The literary societies played a very important part in college life at this time, and in the early days of sports competition, teams from the men's societies, the Chrestomathian (meaning "useful learning" in Greek) and the Grinnell Institute, were the competitors. In 1891 a joint committee from the men's and women's literary societies were urged to meet and decide upon new college colors, to be presented at a mass meeting where a change in the college yell also could be agreed upon. Scarlet and black were the colors adopted almost unanimously, "strong, virile colors" to replace the "weak, neutral, fading pink." It was hoped that the new colors would strengthen spirited support of the games. That the deciding mass meeting was attended by only 100 instead of 400 was a cause of regret. The report in *The Unit* went on to say that college meetings in general were not well attended.[54]

Oratorical contests, once on center stage in student life, were being overshadowed by athletics. These two competitive groups could not be supportive of each other. 1893 had been a devastating one for oratory at Iowa College. No contest was held to choose a delegate to the State Oratorical Contest. An election by the local group provided a delegate—a freshman. No junior or senior was ready to do the work of preparation for the contest.[55] There was criticism in the *Grinnell Herald* that decline in oratory was the result of the ascendancy of athletics over academics. *The Unit* replied that "never in the history of Iowa College has the standard of scholarship been so high and it is constantly being raised."[56] An 1896 editorial defended the college against a description of it as an athletic college rather than a literary one. "Grinnell's literary department is the strongest in the state, having two full professors in English literature."[57] At about this time a way was suggested to increase interest in the literary societies, athletics, and oratory all at one time. The literary societies should celebrate Washington's birthday by inviting an indoor track exhibition in the morning (to tide athletics over the winter season) and a debating contest in the evening.[58]

A decisive blow to the position of oratory in student life was a unanimous faculty vote in 1893 to replace class ora-

tions at Commencement with an address by a guest
speaker.[59] The students had been advocating this change and
in 1889 had won the small victory of having the number of
orations limited to nine.[60] Shortly before his death in 1891,
the old orator J. B. Grinnell came forth with strong support
for Commencement orations: "One who has felt the emotion
of natural pride and has seen countenances lighted up with
paternal glow on a son's or daughter's graduation, respects
the old college custom."[61] Now the pattern was set for a continuing list of distinguished Commencement speakers. The
first one in 1894 was Henry Demarest Lloyd, prominent for
his work in social reform. His topic was the rights and duties
of the "Scholar in Contemporary life" and his message was a
hopeful one: "There is a great inspiring doctrine marching
just ahead of us, its name is social sympathy."[62] This address
coming in the year of Herron's arrival in Grinnell must have
been eminently satisfactory to both Herron and Gates.

As student interest in oratory was waning, enthusiasm
for athletics grew steadily. Participation in sports increased
as intercollegiate associations were joined, making more incentive to train. Good publicity for the college followed as
Iowa College teams continued to be strong. The number of
students on athletic teams doubled between 1889 and 1899.
Thirty-five percent to 45 percent of male students played on
one of the three teams, usually concentrating on one sport.
Three coaching positions were created: football coach in
1893, baseball in 1894, track in 1895. In 1897 Iowa College's
first director of athletics was finally appointed, and at the
same time the approval of the faculty in appointing the
coaches was established and permanent athletic rules were
adopted.[63]

As athletic fervor grew Gates must have sometimes won-
dered about what he had inspired in advocating the development of the sound body. In a letter to the *Chicago Chronicle*
because of a discussion of football by the Chicago Board of Aldermen, Gates wrote "[football] is dangerous to life and limb
... too dangerous to endure. Human life and unbroken bodies

are worth too much. ... I never quite breathe freely till an important game with students is over."[64]

Tennis was sometimes put forward as perhaps an ideal sport. In the 1890 report to the trustees the faculty asserted that tennis is "a peculiarly healthful amusement—adapted to both sexes—free from the muscular injury and over-exertion incident to baseball and football" and were gratified by the rising popularity of this sport. Six years later a great interest in tennis was reported, with forty players being listed.[65]

In 1891 a ladies tennis association was urged with a ladies' tournament each spring to select Field Day representatives. "A well conducted association will do wonders for nerveless wrists, strengthless arms, and weak lungs." It was felt that tennis was the best sport for women, "manifestly adapted to their needs."[66]

The physical training of women at Iowa College was soon to be given primary attention. Carrie Rand who came to Grinnell with her mother, Mrs. E. D. Rand, sponsor of George D. Herron, was prominent in women's life on campus. She was appointed principal for the young women of the college in 1893, and was concerned with "the whole social, physical and spiritual development" of the women under her influence. The need for a gymnasium in taking care of these concerns prompted her to present to the college Rand Gymnasium in memory of her father, Elbridge Dexter Rand, and her brother E. Dwight Rand. The architect was H. K. Holsman, an 1891 graduate. In the *Blue Book* George Herron wrote of both Carrie Rand and the new gymnasium in glowing terms. "It is one of the finest and completest gymnasiums in America."[67]

In June 1894 all women students were required to take physical training.[68] As principal for the young women, Miss Rand with President Gates drew up general rules, or suggestions as they preferred to call them, for the guidance of women students and the householders where they lived. The biggest difference between these rules and similar ones through the years until the last half of the 1960s was the restrictive pattern for Sunday social life. President Gates and Miss Rand stated at the end of written rules: "Hearty and generous co-operation with our desires will make [possible] ... the continuance of the large liberties now enjoyed."[69]

Faculty members Helen B. Morris and Emmeline B. Bartlett in an article in the *Midland Monthly* of May 1898 wrote of "The Social Life of a Girl in Iowa College." They told of seemingly an ideal society "that opens legitimate avenue for its students to gain from mutual intercourse the benefits which can never be reaped from book lore alone." They believed that in every community the social life depends largely upon the influence of the women. So it was, they reported, at Iowa College. The women took the lead in social matters even though they were outnumbered by the men. The women did the planning for the parties and the men carried out their plans. The authors believed this cooperative arrangement explained why there were more marriages among coeducational graduates. Morris and Bartlett wrote of the importance of the other side of college life, just among the women students in their boarding houses or in Mears Cottage, the first college dormitory building. Morris and Bartlett considered living in Mears Cottage preferable because meals were served there and parties and receptions held. They believed that "one of the greatest needs of Iowa College is to have enough such houses for all the girls."[70] Until that time came, there were a number of rooming houses in town, and, in 1890, seven dining clubs, some for men, some for women, and, most popular, some for both.[71]

Morris and Bartlett were enthusiastic about the new gymnasium, a common meeting ground for all women. They appreciated the literary societies, the Ellis named for the second lady principal, Mary Ellis, and the Calocagathia (meaning "the beautiful and true" in Greek), as a "broadening influence." Regular meetings were held Friday afternoons from 4:00 to 6:00. "Their aim is to supplement the college course along less scholastic but yet very important lines. ... Dramatics are not wholly lost sight of though one who believes in them as an educational factor might wish they played a more important part." "The Young Women's Christian Association ... fills quite a different need." It helps the new girls "feel at home and get a right start in their college course."[72] The YWCA was connected with the YMCA but each seemed to function separately. The YMCA continued to be an important element in the college history at least into the 1920s when it was very important in the "Grinnell in China" project.

The men got their gymnasium eventually. During Commencement in 1899 the cornerstone was laid for the Men's Gymnasium (known as the Women's Gym after Darby Gymnasium was built in the mid-1940s). The dedication organized by the senior class was held on the newly completed gym floor with the sky overhead. There were speeches, singing by the Glee Club and a prayer. The stone contained pictures of the athletic teams of that year, copies of the first and last issues of the college publications and the president's last report to the trustees.[73]

It was to be the last report of Gates to the trustees before his letter of resignation in March 1899. President Gates had seen the need for better physical education facilities since his inauguration, and had with strong encouragement from the students attempted to improve the basement gym, at one time hoping the YMCA would help at least to clean it up. It was only in September 1898 when a subscription of $14,372.33 from students, alumni and old students, and Grinnell merchants was reported that the trustees voted to erect a men's gymnasium building and to begin at once.[74]

It is not surprising that alumni and old students made the most substantial contribution to the men's gymnasium. Following the fortunes of the athletic teams from year to year made a strong tie between former students and the college. After the semicentennial banquet in 1898 the alumni committed themselves to "the vigorous athletic policy of the institution."[75] Another alumni event during the celebration was the baseball game played by the opposing teams made up of the alumni on one side and the varsity team on the other. Several games were played, the alumni winning them all. J. Fred Darby, later to be donor of the next men's gymnasium was mentioned as a star alumni player.[76]

Sports did not provide the only highlight of the fiftieth-year celebration. Henry Bullen, who taught mathematics and the natural sciences at the College in Davenport and the Reverend Ephraim Adams, of the Iowa Band and the only surviving member of the original Board of Trustees, spoke of the early history of the college. Professor and Mrs. L. F. Parker then recalled the development of the college in Grinnell. Professor J. Irving Manatt of Brown University, graduate of 1870, along with a number of other alumni, gave "sentence toasts" to the college.[77]

The quinquennial catalogue of 1897 published a list of the fields of life work into which the six hundred graduates of previous years had entered.[78] There were thirty-six professors besides Manatt. Henry C. Adams, class of 1874, son of Ephraim Adams, was professor of Political Economy and Finance at the University of Michigan. Jesse Macy, probably Grinnell's most famous professor, graduated from Iowa College in 1870. Several of the distinguished faculty appointed by President Gates were Iowa College graduates. Albert Shaw, one of the twenty-seven alumni listed as journalists, continued an active connection with the college. He was elected as alumni trustee in 1887, and was on the Board roster for the centennial year of 1946. Shaw was the first, in 1894, to suggest the change of name from Iowa College to Grinnell College.[79] (Gates also was in favor of the new name but the change did not come until 1907.) Shaw's greatest contribution was influencing Andrew Carnegie to contribute funds for a college library.

The largest number, 213, of these early alumni had become teachers; another sixteen were music teachers. The next largest category, along with business, was superintendents and principals, each numbering ninety-five. The number of ministers was fifty-three, and attorneys fifty-one. The rest of the six hundred were scattered among thirteen categories, from architects to surveyors. All of these graduates, though especially those in the teaching profession, were important in bringing students to the college.

Ten years earlier *The News Letter* had published brief accounts of the lives of all the alumni through the class of 1878. Some of the careers recounted would be in the category of missionaries, numbering 23 alumni. Ella B. Marsh, an 1868 graduate, taught among Freedmen in Greenville, South Carolina, from 1868 to 1870 and again in 1874 in Mobile, Alabama. She was part of the early Social Gospel work in the South and could have been classified as a missionary or a teacher. George D. Marsh, an 1867 graduate and perhaps a brother of Ella, did missionary work in European Turkey, the Philippines and Bulgaria. Hester Hillis, a graduate of 1865, was a missionary in Ceylon and in Central India where she died in 1887. Some of the graduates of the 1880s who entered into missionary service were Alice Heald in Turkey and Grace Brewer in Honolulu.[80]

During the semicentennial year the students had put together a hard-cover book, the *Blue Book*, dedicated "To the Alumni of Iowa College." It gave the account of the current college year with wonderful photographs pasted in, and many cartoons with faces taken from life. It featured the history of Iowa College with a section of "Reminiscences" by alumni, beginning in the year when William Windsor came to Davenport to enter college, 1848, the founding year celebrated by the semicentennial, and continuing with memories, year by year through 1897.

Among the most famous of Iowa College alumni is Katayama Sen. He came to Grinnell from Japan in 1889 at the invitation of Professor L. F. Parker. After graduating from Iowa College and studying at Andover Seminary and Yale, he returned to Japan to do social work. Eventually he helped organize Japan's Social Democratic Party and later the Communist Party in Japan.[81] Katayama wrote his impressions of college during his first year in Grinnell. He said he had come to gain "true knowledge of higher civilization." Three courses of study were offered at that time: philosophy, natural sciences, and literature. He chose literature because he especially liked Greek and Latin.

A new curriculum was adopted in 1894 soon after Katayama's graduation. The three Parallel Courses were replaced by the Group System, planned to provide "ladders leading up to special callings, as preliminary to modern professions and technical pursuits." The six groups were: English, Modern Language, Social Science (History or Political Science), Philosophy (Psychology and Ethics), Laboratory Sciences, Mathematics. Common requirements from each group assured a liberal arts education with the core of the curriculum "a fundamental group of studies necessary to every student's education." The big changes brought about by the Group System were the drastic reduction in foreign language requirements and the removal of the religious science requirement. The Christian purpose of the college, however, was not abandoned.[82] Applied Christianity was not a required course but attracted a strong following on campus and beyond.

Music and art also were not required courses but both gained greater recognition on campus in the last decade of the nineteenth century. In 1893 the trustees accepted the terms of transfer of the conservatory valued at $8,400, making it an integral part of the college.[83] In 1894 the trustees minutes reported a need for additional instructors for the conservatory.

Extracurricular music flourished. The Glee Club (men's) was finally founded in 1894, with Professor R. G. Cole, from Ann Arbor, as director. There had been several "spasmodic and futile" efforts to organize an Iowa College Glee Club before 1891. At that time some students felt that there was no reason such an organization should not be formed—plenty of musical and managerial talent were available. Motivation for practice would be concerts given in the "large cities of the state." Of benefit to the rest of the college would be "the large amounts of the expenses of the athletic teams" that could be raised. Of course the primary purpose would be for the "honor of the college ... nothing could be a better advertisement."[84] The first home concert by the Amphion Orchestra and the Glee Club in March 1895 featured songs written especially for the singers by Professor Cole who also trained the players of the twenty-three instruments.[85] In 1896 the first spring Glee Club tour was organized. The club had six dates mostly in the north on the Iowa Central (Railroad). In 1897 eleven dates were arranged for the spring tour. This time large cities—Davenport and Burlington—were included.[86] The Promenade Concert given by the Glee Club standing on Blair Hall steps was a regular Commencement event by 1899[87] and remained so halfway through the twentieth century, as long as Blair was still standing.

Art was a marginal part of college life, having no place in the curriculum or even on campus when George Gates became president. Painting instruction was available in town, as it had been from the earliest days. Soon, however, an art school was founded in 1890 by E. H. Barbour, Professor of Natural Sciences. He had done art work for the college annual as an undergraduate at Yale, and since that time had done illustrations a well as articles for *Scribners, St. Nicholas,* and several scientific journals. The College welcomed the idea of an art school and gave it a large room in Blair Hall.[88] The next year it had become a regular department in the college, and five years later art was made an elective study in all groups.[89]

An article about the new art school in the 1893 *Cyclone* noted "the growing taste for Art which year by year is becoming stronger in our country." An indication of this trend was the fact that the Rand Lectures in 1896, given by Miss Ellen G. Starr of Hull House, Chicago, were about "Art and Social Revolution." She did not approve of art for art's sake but believed that "all good art is constructive, ... [and that] to be saved art must be socialized ... must be of the people." She maintained that the artist must be free and independent. "The life of the poor is too painful, the life of the rich too vulgar to create an art at the present day. A new and happy life must be ere an American art is possible."[90]

Drama at Iowa College in this era was totally extracurricular. It was the literary societies who, in their self-proclaimed role of enriching the culture of the campus, produced the drama. The two men's and women's societies paired up for these productions. The Chrestomathian and Ellis presented "The Rivals" in 1893.[91] Just the year before they had produced Sophocles' "Electra." *The Unit* was impressed with this undertaking and gave it a good send-off mentioning the strong cast and "the considerable money spent for costumes." College instructors in classics and elocution helped, and Professor Jacobsen of the music department composed choral odes for the Attic Maidens.[92] Production date was June 10. When permission was given by the trustees it was specified that the play not interfere with preparations for Commencement.[93] Calocagathia Women's Society and the men's Grinnell Institute were the other pair who cooperated in presenting plays or "similar entertainment." In 1896 their production, "The Lady of Lyons," was "greeted by a very good house and received most flattering favor."[94] Drama would come into its own at the college in the twentieth century, fortunately no longer needing the literary societies to produce it.

The last part of the nineteenth century when George A. Gates was president of Iowa College was a very important time in its history. The era was one of change. The modern world was emerging in all areas—from industry and business to religion and education. It was a period of political activism against conventional ideas in Christianity, capitalism, education, women's status, and African Americans' place in society. Iowa College, soon to be called Grinnell College, was able to move forward in positive ways in great part because President Gates was ready to lead in that direction. The Social Gospel was a great modern movement for social justice the effect of which is still with the world, sometimes stronger, sometimes weaker, but always alive.

The fact that Grinnell was one of the great centers of Social Gospel not only brought national attention and stature for the college, it brought the outside world to Grinnell. The serious problems caused by the rough disregard of social justice were brought sharply into the consciousness of the students through the Applied Christianity classes and all the great lecturers who came to the college. The college was aware of what lay beyond Grinnell. Iowa College sent a series of fifteen large historical photographs to be in the Iowa Building at the 1893 Chicago World's Fair.[95] The faculty collected contributions to help the suffering caused by the Johnstown flood;[96] endorsed petitions for repealing the tariff on imported books and for the establishment of international copyright laws.

Both students and faculty took interest in the presidential campaign of 1896. The *Scarlet and Black* felt called upon to refute "an untrue statement in a nearby town" that many faculty members were avowed free silverites. "Only two, possibly three, faculty members would vote for Bryan," the *Scarlet and Black* maintained.[97] The college publications included news items from other campuses; the proposal of the University of Southern California to establish an observatory on Mt. Wilson, and the establishment of Barnard College for women by Columbia College.

Reports in the college publications showed that the students were alert to the social justice issues which they heard about from visiting lecturers, from President Gates, from Professor Herron. In September 1894 *The Unit* rejoiced in the vindication of Dr. Frederick Ely, director of the School of Economics at the University of Wisconsin. He had been charged with approving the use of violence by the labor unions in the conduct of strikes and boycotts, but the University accepted testimony of his nonviolent attitude.[98] President Gates, in a chapel talk April 18, 1896, told of the garment makers strike in Chicago. He explained that the strike was amply justified by the destitute condition of the strikers. Sixty dollars was contributed by the students to help the strikers and to encourage people in Chicago to be generous.[99]

The debates in the literary societies in this time were on

more interesting topics than those which Jesse Macy recalled from his first college days in 1865, such as whether country life or town life was the more desirable. Macy wrote in the *Blue Book* of 1899: "It is difficult for a youth of today to imagine the poverty of debating material in that early day." Two questions debated by the Chrestomathian in 1900 were "the construction of the Nicaragua Canal independently by our government" and "the popular election of Senators."

As the new era came along the old era passed. The memorials to notable leaders in Grinnell's history marked the end of the college's early pioneer history. When J. B. Grinnell died in 1891, the faculty minutes instructed that his funeral be attended by the faculty and students in a body. A long statement of admiration included in the faculty minutes marked the death of George Magoun in 1896. Sarah Candace Parker (wife of L. F. Parker) first lady principal and preceptress of the Academy was appropriately memorialized. In 1897 J. M. Chamberlain, trustee, treasurer, librarian and friend of the students died. He had donated the land on which Mears Cottage was built. President Gates said of him: "No man during the ten years of my connection with the college has stood so near to me as this one."

George Gates was not as interested in the passing of the old era as the progress of the new. Even after he left Grinnell he was thinking of the future of Iowa College. He corresponded with Acting-President John H. T. Main, to whom he felt very close. After sharing with Main his complete shock at the dénouement of the Herron story, he expressed his concern for the future of the college, for the choosing of a new president, although when referring to one candidate he wrote "Of course nothing must come from me." Gates expressed his fear of a "dark horse" who would give the trustees "entire contentment with ... [his] vision and spirit. ... That is what I fear. But we must all be nevertheless brave and hopeful. God can overrule even inadequacy. The sweep of the stars is in the line of light and progress and sure hope. Only this large and long view requires much patience."[100]

278

N O T E S

FOREWORD

1. Martha Foote Crowe, former principal of the Ladies Department, who had left the college in 1891 to be professor of English at the University of Chicago and then Northwestern University.

2. George McJimsey '58, chair of the Department of History at Iowa State University and the biographer of Harry Hopkins '12. Quoted from the *Grinnell Magazine,* Winter, 1996.

CHAPTER 1: *Mission to the Prairie Land*

1. Much has been written about the Iowa Band. The most useful secondary sources are Ephraim Adams, *The Iowa Band,* (Boston: The Pilgrim Press, 2nd ed., 1902); Truman O. Douglass, *Pilgrims of Iowa,* Boston, The Pilgrim Press, 1911; Truman O. Douglass, *Builders of the Commonwealth,* vols. 1 and 2, an unpublished manuscript in the Grinnell College Archives (hereafter referred to as GCA); John S. Nollen, *Grinnell College,* (Iowa City: The State Historical Society of Iowa, 1953); and Ruth Beitz, "The Iowa Band," *The Iowan,* Spring, 1963, pp. 9–13. I am indebted to all of these accounts for the material in this chapter.

2. Nollen, *op. cit.,* p. 41.

3. Douglass, *Pilgrims,* pp. 55–56.

4. D. Mitchell, Andover, to William Salter, 3 October 1843, William Salter Letter File in GCA (hereafter referred to as WSL).

5. Adams, *The Iowa Band,* p. 17.

6. Ibid., p. 29.

7. Ibid., pp. 25–26.

8. Letters from Asa Turner to American Home Missionway Society (hereafter referred to as AHMS) quoted in Douglass, *Builders,* vol. 1, pp. 42–43.

9. Adams, "Pioneering in Iowa," an address given in 1897. GCA.

10. Douglass, *Builders,* vol. 1, p. 277.

11. Adams, *Iowa Band,* p. 30.

12. Adams, "Pioneering in Iowa," GCA.

13. Asa Turner as quoted by Julius Reed in Douglass, *Builders,* vol. 1, p. 125.

14. Mary M. Gaylord to Professor Leonard Parker, 1 Jan. 1896, in Leonard F. Parker Papers (hereafter referred to as LFP), in GCA.

15. Promotional pamphlet of Harvard College, "New England's First

Fruits," first published in London in 1643. These words now appear on stone tablets at the entrance to Harvard Yard.

16. Nollen, *op. cit.*, p. 38.

17. Douglass, *Pilgrim*, p. 58

18. Adams, *Iowa Band*, pp. 30–31.

CHAPTER 2: *Churches and a College for Iowa*

1. Quoted in Nollen, *op. cit.*, p. 33.

2. E. Adams, "Pioneering in Iowa," *loc. cit.*, GCA.

3. E. Adams, *The Iowa Band*, pp. 34–35.

4. William Salter to Mary Ann Mackintire, 28 Nov. 1845, in "William Salter's letters to Mary Ann Mackintire 1845–46," Philip D. Jordan, ed., *The Annals of Iowa*, 3rd Series, vol. 24, Jan. 1943.

5. Salter to Mary Ann Mackintire, 6 Sept. 1845; ibid., pp. 119–120.

6. Ephraim Adams's report to the Home Missionary, March 1846 on the death of Hutchinson, quoted in Douglass, *Builders*, vol. 2, pp. 386–87.

7. Asa Turner to E. Adams, undated, in "A Collection of Letters of Ephraim and Elisabeth Douglass Adams," unpublished manuscript, ed. by James Douglass Adams, 1973, GCA. (Hereafter referred to as AFL.)

8. E. B. Turner to William Salter, 10 Dec. 1860, WSL.

9. Quoted in Douglass, *Builders*, vol. 2, p. 47.

10. Annual reports on Benjamin Spaulding to the AHMS, quoted in Douglass, *Builders*, vol. 2, pp. 279, 289–90.

11. *The Investigator*, 30 Dec. 1833, quoted in Mary R. Whitcomb, "Abner Kneeland: His Relations to Early Iowa History," *Annals of Iowa*, 3rd Series, vol. 6 (1904), p. 346.

12. Quoted by Ephraim Adams in Douglass, *Builders*, vol. 2, p. 483.

13. Quoted by Harvey Adams, ibid., p. 22.

14. Ibid., p. 48.

15. See letters from Julius Reed to Allen Hitchcock, 20 Feb. 1844 and William Salter, 2 March 1844, Early College Papers in GCA, (hereafter referred to as ECP).

16. See Clarence Aurner, "The Founding of Iowa College," *The Palimpsest*, vol. 24, March 1944, p. 76.

17. Daniel Lane to Salter, 18 March 1844, WSL.

18. Nollen, *op. cit.*, p. 42.

19. The complete minutes of the meeting of 28–29 May 1844 in Boston appear as Appendix II in E. Adams, *The Iowa Band*, pp. 231–33.

20. George F. Magoun, "A History of Iowa College," 19 July 1865, reprinted in its entirety in the *Grinnell Herald Register*, Nov. 1927.

21. E. Adams to Salter, 3 Sept. 1844, AFL.

22. Ebenezer Alden to "My dear Parents," 30 Sept. 1844, ECP.

23. Quoted in Nollen, *op. cit.*, p. 43.

24. Theron Baldwin to J. A. Reed, 16 May 1846, ECP.

25. Quoted in Douglass, *Builders*, vol. 2, p. 240.

26. Salter to Mary Ann Mackintire, 10 June 1846, in Jordan, ed., "William Salter's Letters", *loc. cit.*

27. Stephen Peet to J. C. Holbrook, 26 June 1846, ECP.

28. Holbrook to Reed, 2 July 1846, ECP.

29. E. Alden, Jr. to Rev. Ebenezer Alden, Sr., 1 July and 29 Aug. 1846, ECP.

30. Alden, Jr. to Alden, Sr., 24 Nov. 1846, ECP.

31. Holbrook to Reed, 15 Dec. 1846, ECP.

32. Charles Burnham to Reed, 21 Dec. 1846, ECP.

33. Alden, Jr. to Alden, Sr., 30 Jan. 1847, ECP.

34. The original charter is reprinted in Nollen, *op. cit.,* p. 44.

35. See Reed's letter to Salter, 20 Feb. 1847, detailing the assets and liabilities of Iowa College, WSL.

36. William Deminoff, "Where Grinnell College Was Born," *Grinnell Herald Register,* 11 October 1984.

37. See Erastus Ripley's letter to the Trustees of Iowa College, 14 April 1848, ECP.

38. Ripley to Salter, 26 Nov. 1849, ECP.

39. Iowa College Catalogue for the year 1849–1850, GCA.

40. Daniel Lane to E. Adams, 27 Aug. 1850, informing him that he has turned down the offer to be principal of Iowa Academy, ECP. Also see the College Catalogue for 1850–1851, GCA.

41. E. Adams's annual report of 1850 to AHMS, quoted in Douglass, *Builders,* vol. 2, p. 406.

42. Dartmouth v. Woodward, 4 Wheaton (1819), 518. U.S. Supreme Court.

CHAPTER 3:   *The College in Davenport*

1. Daniel Lane to William Salter, 4 Aug. 1851, WSL. The italics are Lane's.

2. Iowa College Catalogue, 1850–51; See also Shelton L. Beatty, "A History of Grinnell College and Its Curriculum to 1931," Claremont, CA, unpublished manuscript, 1955, copy in GCA.

3. Ibid.

4. Lane to E. Adams, 15 Jan. 1851, AFL, Sec. 2, GCA.

5. E. Adams to Jabez Douglass, 3 May 1850, AFL, 2, GCA.

6. H. Adams to Reed, 13 Sept. 1851, ECP.

7. See Reed's letter to E. Adams, 12 Aug. 1851, AFL, Sec. 2.

8. Application from the Exec. Comm. of the Trustees, Iowa College to the Society for the Promotion of Collegiate and Theological Education at the West, 3 July 1851, ECP.

9. E. P. Mackintire to Reed, 20 July 1851, ECP.

10. Reed to E. Adams, 12 Aug. 1851, AFL, Sec. 2, ECP.

11. See Theron Baldwin's letter to E. Adams, 16 July 1851, requesting additional information regarding the College's cooperation with the N.S. Presbyterians and the reasons for locating the College in Davenport. Reed's reply to this request, 12 August 1851. Both in ECP.

12. Baldwin to Reed, 17 Dec. 1851, ECP.

13. E. Adams to Salter, 15 Nov. 1852, WSL, ECP.

14. E. Adams, *Iowa Band,* p. 110.

15. E. Adams to his wife, E. D. Adams, 18 July 1851, AFL, Sec. 2.

16. See E. Adams letter to Salter, 4 Feb. 1851, WSL.

17. Nollen, *op. cit.,* p. 47.

18. Baldwin to E. Adams, 13 Aug. 1852, ECP.

19. See John Holbrook's letter to Salter, 12 July 1852, reporting on his plan to collect funds in Chicago, WSL; also letters from James Mershon to Reed reporting on his activities in the East, 23 and 30 June 1854, ECP.

20. Holbrook to Salter, 19 Feb. 1853; E. Adams, Clerk of the Board of Trustees, to Salter, 26 June 1853, informing Salter of his election to the Board, both in WSL.

21. Lane at Andover Seminary to E. Adams, 4 June 1853, AFL, Sec. 2.

22. Nollen, *op. cit.,* pp. 47–8; Beatty, *op. cit.,* p. 94.

23. See Elizabeth D. Adams letter to her mother, 9 March 1854, reporting on her husband's fundraising efforts, AFL, Sec. 2.

24. E. Adams to his wife, 19 Jan. 1857; see also the several letters to his wife, and letters to and from W. Barrows and W. L. Coleman in the winter and spring of 1855–56 regarding the establishment of a colony and Adams's trip to northwest Iowa to look for a site, all in AFL, Sec. 2.

25. See Douglass, *Builders,* vol. 2, p. 410 for his tribute to Adams.

26. Mrs. Mary M. Gaylord to L. F. Parker, 1 Jan. 1890, GCA.

27. Elizabeth Adams to her sister Esther Douglass, 18 Jan. 1853, AFL, Sec. 2.

28. E. Adams to Salter, 2 March, 1854, WSL.

29. Lane to Salter, 19 June 1854, WSL.

30. Reed to Salter, 19 June 1854, WSL.

31. See Asa Turner's letter to E. Adams, undated [1854] AFL, 2 and Baldwin to Reed, 2 March 1854, ECP.

32. E. Adams to Salter, 19 June and 22 June 1854, WSL.

33. Deminoff, *op. cit.;* Franc B. Wilkie, *Davenport: Past and Present* (Davenport: Luce, Lane & Co., 1858), p. 301.

34. "Report of the Faculty of Iowa College for the Year Ending July 13, 1853." ECP.

35. E. Ripley to Baldwin, 6 Oct. 1856, ECP.

36. A. B. Robbins to Salter, 24 June 1856, WSL.

37. Asa Turner, A. B. Robbins and George F. Magoun to Ray Palmer, D.D., 15 Aug. 1856, ECP.

38. Palmer to Comm. of Trustees of Iowa College, 5 Nov. 1856, ECP.

39. J. M. Post to George F. Magoun, 22 Dec. 1856, GCA.

40. See article on "Jonathan Blanchard" by Albert Britt in the *Dictionary of American Biography* (hereafter referred to as the DAB), vol. 2, pp, 350–51.

41. Robbins to Salter, 9 Sept. 1857, WSL.

42. E. Adams's diary entries for 23 and 26 June 1858, AFL, Sec. 2.

43. E. Adams to Deacon Whitcomb, undated [1856], GCA.

44. Lane to E. Adams, 26 Nov. 1846, AFL, Sec. 2.

45. Asa Turner to E. Adams, 26 Aug. 1850, AFL, Sec. 2.

46. Asa Turner, quoted in William Salter, *The Life of James W. Grimes* (N.Y.: D. Appleton, 1876), pp. 115–6. Grimes quoted in ibid., p. 238. See also

Leland L. Sage, *A History of Iowa* (Ames: Iowa State University Press, 1974), pp. 127–8 for an account of the fusion of the Free Soil and Whig parties in 1854.

47. The alumni reminiscences, which provide information on student life in Davenport in the 1850s, can be found in the letters of William and John Windsor to the Class of 1889, and in the article by H. H. Belfield, "Iowa College in Its Infancy," written for the Class of 1898, all in GCA.

48. Faculty Minutes, vol. 1, 1852–58, 24 Sept., 4 Oct., 13 Oct., 20 Oct., 3 Nov. 1852, and 11 May 1853, GCA.

49. John Windsor and Belfield, *loc. cit.*

CHAPTER 4: *The Big Move*

1. James Harlan to Reed, 28 June 1853, ECP.

2. Committee of the Trustees to Ray Palmer, 15 Aug. 1856, ECP.

3. J. B. Grinnell, *Men and Events of Forty Years* (Boston: D. Lothrop, 1891), p. 36. See also Charles E. Payne, *Josiah Bushnell Grinnell* (Iowa City: State Historical Society of Iowa, 1938).

4. Payne, *op. cit.*, p. 17.

5. Ibid., p. 21.

6. For an account of the true source of "Go West, young man" and Greeley's disavowal of being the author of the phrase, see Berger Evans, *Dictionary of Quotations,* (New York: Delacorte Press, 1968), p. 745:2. John L. Selch, Newspaper Librarian of the Indiana State Library, in a letter to William Deminoff, 12 Dec. 1983, confirms that Soule was the source for the statement.

7. Payne, *op. cit.*, pp. 28–29; Nollen in his history of the college gives a slightly different version of Grinnell's meeting Farnam as having taken place in Missouri. See Nollen, *op. cit.*, p. 54. Payne's account, which is taken from Grinnell's autobiography, seems the most likely, however, and is the source I have used.

8. Theodore Bacon's letter to Grinnell, quoted in Grinnell, *op. cit.*, pp. 88, 92.

9. Payne, *op. cit.*, pp. 31–32.

10. Amos Bixby to Marcellus Bixby, 22 June 1854. I am much indebted to Stephen B. Dudley of Wilsonville, Oregon, the great-grandson of Lewellyn Bixby, Amos's brother, for making a selection of Bixby family letters available to me.

11. For the initial funding of the proposed institution, see the following sources: Nollen, *op. cit.*, p. 54; Beatty, *op. cit.*, pp. 38–39; letter from Amos Bixby to Lewellyn Bixby, 20 Nov. 1859 in which he informs his brother that he has given $400 to the College; the records of the Trustees of the Literary Fund of Grinnell University, covering the period from its organization on 9 Jan. 1855 until the funds were transferred to the Trustees of Iowa College on 11 Jan. 1861, GCA.

12. See the list of the first settlers prepared by Julia Chapin Grinnell for L. F. Parker in 1904, LFP.

13. See Grinnell's letter to Reed, 20 Jan. 1854, ECP, thanking him for

the information Reed had sent. Grinnell informed Reed that he planned to bring a few families to Iowa in the spring, but he carefully avoided mentioning where he planned to settle. For Magoun's meeting with Grinnell in Wisconsin, see Payne, *op. cit.,* pp. 18–19.

14. Harvey Adams to Salter, 20 June 1854, WSL.

15. E. Adams to Salter, 18 Dec. 1854, WSL.

16. E. Adams diary entry, 22 May 1855, AFL, Sec. 2.

17. Circular, dated 1 Jan. 1856, GCA.

18. Report of the Executive Committee to the Iowa College Board of Trustees, George F. Magoun, Clerk of the Committee, undated but sometime in the early spring of 1858, ECP.

19. See Daniel Lane's letter to E. Adams, 13 April 1858, stating "The street will go through the grounds without a doubt." He once again expresses his opinion "the college must be moved," AFL, 2. See also Salter's letter to E. Adams, 21 April 1858, stating his opposition to a move, and "I shall advise against it, but I shall not interfere." AFL, 2.

20. Letter to "The Board of Trustees of Iowa College" from Hiram Price et al., undated, and the response of Magoun for the Board of Trustees, 14 July 1858, both in ECP.

21. Letter of Magoun, Salter, and Charles Atkinson on behalf of the Board of Trustees to "His Honor the Mayor and the Aldermen of the City of Davenport," giving the city the opportunity to bid for keeping the college, published in the Davenport *Daily Morning News,* undated clipping in GCA. Report of the city's offer in same paper's editorial of 15 July 1858, GCA.

22. See Bullen's letter to Salter 1 Dec. 1857, outlining the plans for a Scientific School for Salter to present to Hendrie, WSL; also Magoun's report to the Board of Trustees, undated, sometime in the early spring of 1858, ECP. The president's reports are to be found in the Trustees' Minutes.

23. Faculty Minutes, vol. 1, 8 and 10 July 1858. Ripley's report on the faculty's resignation. Both in ECP.

24. Letter to the editor, signed "x," in Davenport *Gazette,* 28 July 1858.

25. Davenport *Daily Morning News,* 2 October 1858.

26. Nollen, *op. cit.,* p. 60.

27. Salter's and Baldwin's hostility to the move, see John C. Holbrook's letter to Salter of 30 May 1863 in which Holbrook urges Salter not to resign from the Board and also expresses his belief that Baldwin has finally accepted the move as being a wise decision. See also J. B. Grinnell to Salter 31 May 1885, still urging Salter to return to the Board twenty-two years after he left it. Both in WSL.

28. J. B. Grinnell to editors of the *New York Independent,* undated, rough copy of the letter in ECP.

29. There are passing references to the Lambrite scandal in Nollen, *op. cit.,* p. 60, and in George F. Magoun, "The Past of Our College," an address to the Alumni Association of Iowa College, 11 June 1895, copy in GCA, which attributes the loss to Lambrite's dishonesty. See also Jacob Butler's letter to "Dear Bro." [unidentified, but probably another trustee] 5 Nov. 1858, urging the college to have its lawyer investigate the loss, ECP.

30. Letter of Reed to Loyal C. Phelps in Grinnell, 22 Nov. 1858, telling of the shipment of lumber, ECP. The quote describing what Reed personally

brought to Grinnell is that of Magoun in *The Past of Our College.* p. 20. See also Nollen, *op. cit.,* p. 60.

31. Beatty, *op. cit.,* p. 78, provides the information on the occupations of the first ten graduates of the college.

32. Beatty, *op. cit.,* p. 27.

33. Nollen, *op. cit.,* pp. 45–46.

34. Asa Turner to Magoun, 26 Dec. 1856, ECP.

35. A.B. Robbins to Magoun, 24 Dec. 1856, GCA.

36. Faculty report to Trustees 1858 for year 1857-58.

CHAPTER 5: *The College at War*

1. See Beatty, *op. cit.,* Appendix B, pp. 475–76 for a description of Iowa College's scientific apparatus which was transported to Grinnell.

2. Estimates of the number of students in the Grinnell Preparatory Department in 1858–59 range from J. B. Grinnell's exaggerated figure of nearly 100 to what is probably the more accurate figure of 36 as given by Magoun.

3. Julius Reed to Theron Baldwin, 13 Nov. 1860, ECP.

4. Joanna Harris Haines, "Seventy Years in Iowa," an interview given by her to her son-in-law, Frank I. Herriott in January 1928, published in the *Annals of Iowa,* 3rd Series, vol. 27, Oct. 1945, p. 114.

5. Ibid., pp. 113–14.

6. The letter of John Brown to an acquaintance in Tabor detailing the aid given to him by the people of Grinnell is quoted in Payne, *op. cit.,* pp. 111–12.

7. Nollen, *op. cit.,* pp. 70–71.

8. Henry Adams, *The Education of Henry Adams* (Boston: Houghton Mifflin, Sentry Edition, 1961), p. 53.

9. Beatty, *op. cit.,* pp. 105–15.

10. For an account of this incident see Thomas A. Lucas, "Men Were Too Fiery for Much Talk: The Grinnell Anti-Abolitionist Riot of 1860," *The Palimpsest,* vol. 68, Spring 1987. Although Parker and Bixby prevented a physical attack on the blacks, the youths were persuaded to withdraw from the public school, and Bixby's aunt, Sarah Bixby, taught them in her home until they left town via the Underground Railroad some weeks later.

11. Nollen, *op. cit.,* p. 62.

12. Turner, quoted in Douglass, *Builders,* vol. 5, p. 50.

13. See Haines, *op. cit.,* p. 112, in which she states that it was common knowledge in Grinnell that Parker had been considered for the presidency, but was not chosen by the trustees because he was infected with "Oberlinism."

14. Douglass, *op. cit.,* p. 50 ff.

15. William T. Sherman spoke these words at a GAR convention in Columbus, Ohio, 11 Aug. 1880. The full statement was, "There is many a boy here today who looks on war as all glory, but, boys, it is all hell"—a more meaningful statement than the shortened version known to the public as "War is Hell."

16. Rev. William Salter, "Our National Sins and Impending Calamities—A Sermon Preached in the Congregational Church, Burlington, Iowa." A printed copy in GCA.

17. See Iowa College catalogues for the years 1861–62; 1862–63; 1863–64; 1865–66.

18. Haines, *op. cit.*, pp. 116–18.

19. James L. Hill, "Iowa College in the War," a paper read at the Commencement Exercises at Iowa College, June 1898, reprinted in *The Grinnell Review*, Jan. 1907, p. 48.

20. See Faculty Minutes, vol. 2, 30 Oct. 1863.

21. The trustee responses to Leonard Parker quoted are: (a) Daniel Lane, 16 Nov. 1863; (b) A. B. Robbins, 11 Nov. 1863; (c) George Magoun, 19 Nov. 1863; (d) John C. Holbrook, 30 Jan. 1864; (e) General George B. Sargent, 12 Nov. 1863; and (f) J. M. Chamberlain, 16 Nov. 1863. All of these responses, as well as others are in LFP.

22. L. F. Parker to the Iowa College *The News Letter*, 19 July 1864, quoted in Douglass, *Builders*, vol. 5, pp. 401–03; see also Faculty Minutes, vol. 2, 11 May 1864, in which the faculty voted approval for Parker to "accompany the young men to the field." The trustees took no formal action, but did discuss his leaving and there was a consensus that he should be allowed to go. For the earlier request for Parker to go as a chaplain for a company of college students, see the student petition to the Board of Trustees and Parker's accompanying letter, dated October 1861 in ECP.

23. See Iowa College's list of fatalities in the Civil War on the stone plaque in Herrick Chapel, Grinnell College.

24. Holbrook to Salter, 19 May 1863, WSL.

25. Ephraim Adams to his wife Elisabeth, 10 Aug. 1864, AFL.

26. Nollen. *op. cit.*, p. 63.

27. Samuel J. Buck, "Forty-one Years in Iowa College," an address given on June 1905, at the time of Buck's retirement, printed in *The Grinnell Review*, Oct. 1905.

28. Minutes of the Executive Committee of the Board of Trustees (hereafter referred to as ECBT), 17 July 1868.

29. Jesse Guernsey to J. M. Chamberlain, 27 July 1870, ECP.

30. Ephraim Adams Diary entry, 4 July 1863, AFL, Sec. 2.

31. Esther Douglass to Elisabeth Adams, 10 July 1863, AFL, Sec. 2.

32. Ephraim Adams Diary entries, 11 April, 16 April and 17 April 1865, AFL, Sec. 2.

33. Quoted in Joseph Frazier Wall, *Iowa: A History* (New York: W. W. Norton, 1978), pp. 114–15.

CHAPTER 6: *Through Fire and Storm*

1. Leonard Parker, "Notes on Iowa College in the Civil War," written for James Hill, 5 April 1898, GCA. In these notes, Parker gives the names of all the college students who served in the war and the unit to which they were attached.

2. Ibid.

3. Quoted in Nollen, *op. cit.*, p. 63.

4. Magoun to Leonard Parker, 20 Aug. 1862, GCA.

5. Magoun to the trustees of Iowa College, 8 July 1864, GCA.

6. Quoted in Nollen, *op. cit.*, p. 63.

7. See Jesse Guernsey's letter to J. M. Chamberlain, 24 Aug. 1870, in which he states that "while I regard his resignation at the very opening of the year without preliminary notice or hint as not all together courteous and fair, I think a greater calamity might befall this college than his removal from it. He was too long at the head of affairs at Grinnell ... [and] so jealous of personal interests ... to work in pleasantly under this President or any other man fit for the President's position."

8. Macy's evaluation of Henry Parker, quoted in Douglass, *Builders*, vol. X, pp. 47–8.

9. Nollen, *op. cit.*, p. 65.

10. Ibid.

11. Letter from Helen Parker to her sister, quoted in ibid., pp. 65–66.

12. Jesse Macy regarding the Parkers, quoted in Douglass, *Builders*, vol. X, p. 47.

13. George Magoun to Mrs. Samuel Williston, 26 Oct. 1870, GCA. The italics are Magoun's.

14. Truman Douglass's description of Elizabeth Magoun, as quoted by Nollen, *op. cit.*, p. 73.

15. J. Irving Manatt, "A Tribute to Dr. Magoun," an article originally published in the *New York Independent,* at the time of Magoun's death in Jan. 1896. A reprint of this article is in pamphlet form in GCA.

16. J. P. Lyman to "Dear Friend," 26 Dec. 1871, GCA. The recipient of this letter had sent money for the college immediately following the burning of East College in 1871 and had asked Lyman to send it on to J. M. Chamberlain, the college treasurer. Apparently the donor did not wish to communicate directly with the college. Very possibly "Dear Friend" was Leonard Parker inasmuch as Lyman writes, "I feel perfectly satisfied that your motive in giving will be misconstrued, and *I know that you are not under any obligation to Iowa College.* The italics are Lyman's.

17. Charles C. Starbuck, former minister at Wittenberg, Ohio to Leonard Parker, 25 May 1894, GCA.

18. Stow Persons, *American Minds: A History of Ideas* (New York: Henry Holt & Co., 1958), p. 241.

19. George F. Magoun, "Evolutionism at Bay Among Scientists," *The College News Letter,* October 1873.

20. "From the Code of College Laws, Passed July 1871, Chap V. Deportment of Students," printed in the College Catalogue, 1871–72, p. 35.

21. Faculty Minutes, III, 25 June 1880.

22. D. W. Norris, class of 1872, in the Special College Annual, *Blue Book,* published to commemorate the 50th Anniversary of the college in 1898, p. 55.

23. Faculty Minutes, III, 18 Dec. 1879.

24. Faculty Minutes, II, 2 October 1865.

25. Address of George Magoun at the Inauguration of President Gates, published as a pamphlet in 1887, GCA.

26. Kyle Schaub, "Housing Options Vary Through History," *Scarlet and Black,* (hereafter referred to as *S&B*), 13 April 1973.

27. D. W. Norris, *loc. cit.,* p. 55.

28. Henry Carter Adams to Ephraim Adams, 4 May 1872, AFP, 4.

29. *The News Letter,* Nov. 1880.

30. Faculty Minutes, III, 29 Nov. 1880.

31. Ibid., 20 Jan. 1881.

32. Ibid., 28 Jan. and 21 June 1881.

33. Report of the Special Committee of the Board of Trustees on the News Letter Association, including supporting documents, 14 Sept. 1881, GCA.

34. Faculty Minutes, III, 15 Sept. 1881.

35. Ibid., 31 Oct. and 5 Nov. 1881.

36. See Louise R. Noun, *Strong Minded Women* (Ames: Iowa State University Press, 1969) for a full account of the struggle for woman suffrage in Iowa; also Wall, *op. cit.,* pp. 116–17.

37. Jesse Macy, class of 1870, in *Blue Book,* p. 49.

38. Professor of Greek, William McKibben, states that Calocagathia may be loosely translated as "genteel culture." This virtue is clearly what the society sought to promote.

39. Nollen, *op. cit.,* p. 173.

40. Ibid.

41. Jesse Macy, quoted in Nollen, *op. cit.,* p. 173.

42. There are many complaining letters written by Magoun in 1869 and the early 1870s to J. B. Grinnell and others, telling of his efforts at fundraising and the hardships he had to endure on the road. GCA.

43. Benjamin St. John, "The Burning of East College," *Blue Book,* pp. 61–2. For other accounts of the fire see J. P. Lyman to "Dear Friend," (probably L. F. Parker) 24 Dec. 1871, GCA, and the report in *The News Letter,* 27 Dec. 1871.

44. See Iowa College catalogues for the years 1870–71; 1871–72 and 1872–73. Van Noorden's name appears only in the 1871–72 catalogue and lists his home as Brussels, Belgium.

45. See Trustees Executive Committee Minutes of 5 Feb. and 19 March 1867, GCA.

46. Ibid., 6 July 1870.

47. See the lead editorial, "Our College Campus," in *The News Letter,* Dec. 1883.

48. First said by Prof. Edwards Park of Andover Seminary, quoted in Nollen, *op. cit.,* p. 79, and repeated many times by others.

49. S. H. Herrick, "The Grinnell Cyclone of 17 June 1882," *Annals of Iowa,* 3rd series, July 1897, pp. 81–96.

50. Quoted in ibid., p. 96.

51. Katherine A. Jones, "Cyclone Reminiscences," a newspaper clipping, source and date not given, in GCA.

52. This writer, while a student at the college in 1940, met an elderly alumnus of the class of 1882, who had been a member of that baseball team. He gave a moving account of the shock he and his teammates experienced

upon returning to Grinnell after the storm to find that their college no longer existed.

53. For Mear's graphic account of the storm, see Nollen, *op. cit.,* p. 79.

54. David W. Jordan's article, "And God Was in the Whirlwind: The Cyclone of 1882," *Grinnell Magazine,* April–May 1982, pp. 9–12.

55. The two pamphlets, "The Losses of Iowa College," and "An Appeal for Aid," can be found in GCA.

56. This anonymous reporter's account was later printed as a pamphlet, "Chicago, Iowa and Grinnell—a Study of Great Disasters" (no publisher or date given) in which the author tells of the aid given by the people of Iowa to Chicago after the Great Chicago Fire of 1871, and Chicago's reciprocal aid to Grinnell in 1882. Copy in GCA.

57. S. H. Herrick, *op. cit.,* pp. 91–93, gives figures as to amounts received from outside Grinnell.

58. To whom J. B. Grinnell first made this remark is not known, but it has been repeated many times by Nollen, Payne and other Grinnellians.

CHAPTER 7: *Secularizing the Mission*

1. The Annie Savery gift for scholarships is listed in the 1868–69 Iowa College Catalogue. Louise Noun provided the citation in the 15 April 1891, *Des Moines Register* obituary for Annie which tells of her gift to Iowa College to be used for scholarhips for women.

2. Catalogues of Iowa College: 1849–50; 1862–63; 1880–81; 1890–91; 1900–01. In contrast to the college's first Board of Trustees, which had one token businessman among its members, a century later there were two token ministers—the superintendent of the Congregational churches of Iowa and the Episcopal bishop of Iowa on the Board.

3. This story was told to me by Dean Earl Strong, who in turn had heard it firsthand from Professor Norris.

4. For an account of Almy's X-ray experiment, see *The Unit,* 29 Feb. 1896.

5. For an excellent account of the founding and development of the Alumni Association, see Margaret Matlack Kiesel, "The Alumni and the College," an unpublished manuscript, GCA.

6. Nollen, *op. cit.,* pp. 152–53.

7. Reconstructed minutes of the Board of Trustees for June 1881, vol. 1, GCA. This book of minutes on page 1 contains the notation "By the cyclone of 17 June 1882, the book in which the record of Iowa College had been kept from the beginning, both in Davenport and Grinnell, was entirely destroyed. Any records of the past of this Institution, aside from the memory of men, are as follows: ... " There then follows reconstructed minutes of the annual meetings of the Board of Trustees only for the years 1880 and 1881. Fortunately for later historians not "all records of the past" were entirely destroyed. Those records which had not been deposited in the college's administrative office, including faculty minutes, minutes of the Executive Committee of the Board, and some exceedingly valuable personal letters of the

trustees and other members of the college community were discovered many years later by the former Dean of Men, Shelton L. Beatty, who was engaged in research on the curriculum of the college in the late 1940s. They are now available in GCA.

8. Trustee minutes, 23 June 1883, GCA.

9. Trustee minutes, 21 and 23 June 1884, GCA.

10. For curricular changes approved by the trustees for both the Academy and the college, see Trustee minutes, 7 July 1884, GCA.

11. For the trustees' consideration of college governance, see Trustee minutes of 7 July 1884, GCA.

12. "Suggestions to the Faculty by the Trustees for the Government of Students," a trustee report incorporated in the Trustee minutes of 7 July 1884, GCA.

13. Trustee minutes, 21 Aug. 1884, GCA.

14. Information on the initial consideration of David O. Mears for the presidency, including an account of the letters of Robbins and Adams to Mears is contained in Mears's letter to J. M. Chamberlain, 4 Sept. 1884, in the Chamberlain papers (hereafter referred to as JMC papers), GCA.

15. Executive Committee minutes, 11 Aug. 1884, GCA.

16. Mears to Chamberlain, 4 Sept. 1884, JMC papers, GCA.

17. Ibid.

18. Minutes of a special meeting of the trustees, 9 Dec. 1884, GCA.

19. Executive Committee minutes, 31 March 1885, GCA.

20. Faculty minutes, 6 Feb. 1885, GCA.

21. Mears to Chamberlain, 9 March 1885, JMC papers, GCA.

22. Trustee minutes, 23 June 1885, GCA.

23. Mears to Chamberlain, 7 July 1885, JMC papers, GCA.

24. See E. Adams's letter to Chamberlain, 29 Aug. 1885, JMC papers, GCA.

25. Ibid.

26. Mears to Trustees of Iowa College, 16 Nov. 1885, GCA.

27. Executive Committee minutes, 16 Dec. 1885, GCA.

28. Goodnow quoted in Mears's letter to Chamberlain, 16 Nov. 1885, JMC papers, GCA.

29. Trustees report to Messrs. Goodnow and Mears, in the Trustee minutes of 19 June 1886, GCA.

30. Mary G. Mears to Chamberlain, 3 July 1886, JMC papers, GCA.

31. Mears to the Trustees of Iowa College, 13 July 1886, GCA.

32. Executive Committee minutes, 21 Sept. 1886, GCA.

33. Mears to Chamberlain, 9 March 1885, JMC papers, GCA.

34. Mears to Chamberlain, 2 March 1886, JMC papers, GCA.

35. Mears to the Trustees of Iowa College, 13 July 1886, GCA.

36. Executive Committee minutes, 31 Dec. 1886, GCA.

37. Nollen, *op. cit.*, p. 84.

38. Minutes of a special meeting of the trustees, 22 Feb. 1887, GCA. Mention is made in this entry of Ephraim Adams having received a letter from Gates, expressing willingness to accept an invitation to the presidency of Iowa College, GCA.

39. Letters of George A. Gates in accepting the presidency: To The

Trustees of Iowa College, 3 March 1887; and to Professor S. J. Buck and Others of the Faculty of Iowa College, 8 March 1887, GCA.

CHAPTER 8: *The Social Gospel Era*

1. The quotations given below are from "Inaugural Address" by George A. Gates, published as a pamphlet in 1887, GCA.

2. Martha Foote Crowe, "Welcome to the Work of Co-Education," an address given at the inauguration of President Gates, published in *The News Letter*, Sept. 1887.

3. Gates does not identify the source of the quotation, but so closely does it reflect his own ideals that he might well claim it as his own.

4. The italics throughout this address are those of Gates.

5. *The News Letter*, Sept. 1884.

6. Trustee minutes, 16 June 1887, announcing the Steele Chair in Mathematics; notice of the Annie Savery scholarship fund appears in the 1867-68 College Catalogue; Louise R. Noun informed this writer of Mrs. Savery's later gift to the college of $10,000.

7. See the Iowa College Catalogue of 1890-91 for a list of contributions to the "Two Hundred Thousand Dollar Endowment Fund," GCA.

8. See passing references to the Reickoff case in the Executive Committee minutes throughout the decade of the 1880s, GCA. The Iowa College Catalogue of 1894-95 notes under the section Gifts to the College, "By will of William Reickoff, Orange City, Iowa—$35,000."

9. Faculty report to the Trustees, 1888, GCA.

10. President Gates's Report to the Trustees, 1894, GCA. Italics are those of Gates. The president's reports are to be found in the Trustees minutes.

11. Nollen, *op. cit.*, p. 87.

12. Letter of resignation, Martha Foote Crowe to the Board of Trustees, reprinted in part in *The Unit*, vol. 2, No. 1, 1891, p. 15.

13. *The Grinnell Review*, VIII, #3, pp. 35-37. Clara Millerd, beginning in 1915, also offered courses in Greek and Roman sculpture and the Italian Renaissance as art history and theory developed in the curriculum. (Nollen, *op. cit.*)

Alumna (1900) Fanny Phelps Johnston loved and admired both Clara Millerd and Carrie Rand. She wrote of Clara's death in the late 1930s when "the dreadful word flashed across the Pacific." A drowning was implied in the context of Johnston's typescript. (CGA)

14. Nollen, *op. cit.*, p. 104.

15. Frank I. Herriot, "My Years at Grinnell," transcript, p. 24 CGA.

16. Nollen, *op. cit.*, pp. 88-91.

17. Ibid., p. 99.

18. Trustee minutes, 1895. Fanny Phelps Johnston, graduate of 1900, in her memoir of Carrie Rand and Clara Millerd, gives credit for the endowment of the Applied Christianity Department to Carrie Rand, then only nineteen years old, although it is generally accepted that her mother was the donor.

19. Ralph E. Luker, *The Social Gospel in Black and White: American Racial Reform, 1885–1912.* Chapel Hill: Univ. of North Carolina Press,1991. p. 249; also lecture (unprinted) at Grinnell College, "Defining Moments: Harlan Paul Douglass and Martin Luther King, Jr.," 11 Sept. 1995.

20. Robert T. Handy, "George D. Herron and the Kingdom Movement," *Church History,* vol. 9, June 1950, pp. 103, 109.

21. Trustee minutes, 1894.

22. Luker, *op. cit.,* pp. 301–310.

23. Ibid., p. 14.

24. Trustee minutes, 1895.

25. News clippings, CGA.

26. Trustees minutes, 1895.

27. G. T. Wyckoff, letter to Letitia Moon Conard, Aug. 1944, GCA.

28. Handy, *op. cit.,* p. 112.

29. Trustees minutes, 1897.

30. Letter of Herron to Trustees, 25 May 1897.

31. George A. Gates, Baccalaureate sermon, reprinted in *Scarlet and Black* (hereafter referred to as S&B), June, 1898.

32. Trustee minutes, 16 June 1898.

33. "Herronism Exposed," in *Des Moines Register,* 6 Jan. 1899. Reprint of article by friends of Iowa College, 9 Feb. 1899.

34. Reported in Marshalltown *Times Republican,* 9 Sept. 1899.

35. Printed in *S&B,* 4 Nov. 1899.

36. Trustee minutes, 2 Nov. 1899.

37. H. R. Dietrich, "Radical on the Campus," *Annals of Iowa,* vol. 37, No. 6, 3rd Series, Fall 1964, pp. 411–412.

38. Linda A. Rabben, "The Utopian Vision of George D. Herron," *Grinnell Magazine,* April–May, 1981.

39. George McJimsey, "The Social Gospel and the New Deal," Lecture at Grinnell College, 2 Nov. 1995.

40. Printed in *The News Letter* XV-10, 26 June 1889.

41. Printed in *The Unit,* XIII-17, 13 June 1894.

42. Printed in *The Unit,* IV-9, 22 June 1892.

43. Printed in *The Unit,* X-17, 12 June 1985.

44. Printed in *S&B,* vol. 2, #36, 16 June 1897.

45. Printed in *S&B* in June 1898 and June 1899.

46. *Blue Book,* p. 77.

47. GCA. Child's signature was on many of the college photographs of this era and into the twentieth century. He built the brown shingle "honeymoon cottage" (with a heart-shaped little balcony below the gable in front) and had a large studio upstairs on Broad Street downtown in the Child building, torn down when the addition to the Louis Sullivan Bank was built. Gary Cooper was a friend of Mr. and Mrs. Child when he attended college in the 1920s.

48. Raymond E. Britt, "A Sound Mind and a Sound Body, The Development of Athletics at Grinnell College Between 1889 and 1919, p. 5, typescript, 20 May 1982, GCA.

49. Bruce E. Mahan, "The First Iowa Field Day," *The Palimpsest,* vol. IV, no. 5, May 1923.

50. *The Unit.* vol. III, #2, 3 Oct. 1891.

51. *S&B,* Dec. 1874.

52. Gates's report to the trustees, 1891, typescript, GCA.

53. *The Unit,* vol. II, #2, 1 Nov. 1890.

54. *The Unit,* vol. III, #2, 5 Oct. and 14 Oct. 1891.

55. *The Unit,* vol. V, #16, 4 Feb. 1893.

56. *The Unit,* vol. VII, 30 Sept. 1893.

57. *S&B,* 8 Oct. 1896.

58. *The Unit,* vol. V, #3, 1 Jan. 1893.

59. Faculty minutes, 15 Sept. 1893.

60. *The Pulse,* vol. II, #5, 11 Jan. 1889, GCA.

61. Ibid., vol. II, #5, 9 Nov. 1889.

62. *The Unit,* o.s., vol. 10, 12 June 1895. (o.s. after *The Unit* means old series numbering.)

63. Britt, *op. cit.,* pp. 6–12.

64. *S&B,* vol. 3, #18, 1897, p. 4.

65. *S&B,* vol. 5, #13, 8 Oct. 1896.

66. *The Unit,* III, #2, 31 Oct. 1891.

67. *Blue Book,* p. 195. Rand Gymnasium was dedicated in 1897 and was well used until it burned in 1939.

68. Faculty minutes, 26 Jan. 1894.

69. Printed and handwritten copies, GCA.

70. Copy of article cited in text, in GCA, pp. 450–452. Emmeline Barston Bartlett (A. B. Vassarr 1894), as acting preceptress in the mid-1890s, introduced to the campus basketball which like tennis was originally a women's sport at the college. She married John S. Nollen in 1906. After her death in 1910, Nollen married her sister, Louise Stevens Bartlett. (Nollen, *op. cit.)*

71. *Cyclone,* 1890, p. 115.

72. Helen Morris and Emmeline B. Bartlett, "The Social Life of a Girl in Iowa College," *Midland Monthly,* pp. 450–452.

73. *S&B,* 14 June 1899. The architect for the men's gymnasium was the same as for Rand gymnasium: H. K. Holsman, class of 1891.

74. Trustee minutes, Sept. 1898.

75. News clipping 1898, dateline Grinnell, 21 June, GCA.

76. Ibid., 20 June.

77. Ibid., 21 June.

78. Also published in Annual Report of President, 1898.

79. Albert Shaw, Letter to Trustees, June 1894.

80. "Lives of the Alumni," *The News Letter,* vol. XVI, #11, May 1889. Hester Hillis at the time of her death was eulogized in *The News Letter* of November 1887 as the first foreign missionary from Iowa college. She was an early recipient of a loan from the Ladies Education Society. In 1890 an alcove was established in her honor for missionary materials in the library in Goodnow, with a crayon drawing of her over the entrance. (CGA)

81. Charles G. Cleaver, "Our second most famous alum: Katayama Sen," *S&B,* 7 April 1978.

82. Shelton L. Beatty, "History of Grinnell College and Its Curriculum to 1931," GCA, p. 454.

83. Trustee Executive Committee minutes, 31 May 1893.

84. *The Unit,* o.s., vol. 3, 28 Nov. 1891.

85. *S&B,* IV, #4, 22 Feb. 1895.

86. *Blue Book,* p. 104.

87. *S&B,* 14 June 1899.

88. *The Unit,* vol. III, #2, 3 Oct. 1891.

89. Trustee Executive Committee minutes, 26 June 1895. Alfred Vance Churchill was professor of art from 1891 to 1893. After leaving Grinnell he taught in St. Louis and at Columbia University's Horace Mann School before going to Smith College where he was instrumental in the development of the art museum collecting admirable impressionist paintings in Europe.

90. *S&B,* vol. IV, #4, 19 Feb. 1892.

91. *The Unit,* vol. IV, #11, 20 May 1893.

92. *The Unit,* o.s., vol. 4, 2 May 1892.

93. Trustee minutes, 11 May 1992.

94. *The Unit,* vol. XII, #15, 30 May 1896.

95. Trustee Executive Committee minutes, 4 March 1893.

96. Faculty minutes, 1 Feb. 1893.

97. *S&B,* 8 Oct. 1896.

98. *The Unit,* vol. IX, #2, 29 Sept. 1894.

99. *The Unit,* vol. XII, #9, 18 April 1896.

100. Undated letters of George Gates to John H. T. Main.

SELECTED BIBLIOGRAPHY

Adams, Ephraim. *The Iowa Band*. 2nd ed. Boston: Pilgrim Press, 1902.

――――. "Pioneering in Iowa." Address given in 1897, Grinnell College Archives.

Adams, Henry. *The Education of Henry Adams*. Boston: Houghton Mifflin, Sentry Edition, 1961.

Adams, James Douglass, ed. "A Collection of Letters of Ephraim and Elizabeth Douglass Adams." Unpublished manuscript, Grinnell College Archives, 1973.

Aurner, Clarence. "The Founding of Iowa College." *The Palimpsest* 24 (March 1944).

Beatty, Shelton L. "A History of Grinnell College and Its Curriculum to 1931." Unpublished manuscript, Grinnell College Archives, 1953.

Beitz, Ruth. "The Iowa Band." *The Iowan,* Spring 1963.

Belfield, H. H. "Iowa College in Its Infancy." Unpublished paper written for class of 1898, Grinnell College Archives.

Bixby family letters. In possession of Stephen B. Dudley, Wilsonville, Oregon.

Britt, Raymond E. "A Sound Mind and a Sound Body: The Development of Athletics at Grinnell College between 1889 and 1919." Unpublished manuscript, Grinnell College Archives, 1982.

Buck, Samuel J. "Forty-one Years in Iowa College." Address given June 1905. Printed in *The Grinnell Review,* October 1905.

Cleaver, Charles G. "Our second most famous alum: Katayama Sen." *Scarlet and Black,* April 7, 1978.

Crowe, Martha Foote. "Welcome to the Work of Co-Education." Address given at inauguration of President George Gates. Printed in *The News Letter,* September 1887.

Deminoff, William. "Where Grinnell College Was Born." *Grinnell Herald Register,* October 11, 1984.

Dietrich, H. R. "Radical on the Campus." *Annals of Iowa* 37, no. 6 (Fall 1964).

Douglass, Truman O. "Builders of the Commonwealth." 2 vol. Unpublished manuscript, Grinnell College Archives, circa 1915–17.

Douglass, Truman O. *Pilgrims of Iowa.* Boston: Pilgrim Press, 1911.

Gates, George A. "Baccalaureate Sermon." *Scarlet and Black,* June 1898.

————. "Inaugural Address." Pamphlet, Grinnell College Archives, 1887.

Grinnell, J. B. *Men and Events of Forty Years.* Boston: D. Lothrop, 1891.

Haines, Joanna Harris. "Seventy Years in Iowa." Interview by Frank I. Herriot, January 1928. *Annals of Iowa,* 3rd ser., 27 (October 1945).

Handy, Robert T. "George D. Herron and the Kingdom Movement." *Church History* 9 (June 1950).

Herrick, S. H. "The Grinnell Cyclone of 17 June 1882." *Annals of Iowa,* 3rd ser. (July 1897).

Herriot, Frank I. "My Years at Grinnell." Typescript. n.d. [no date]

Hill, James L. "Iowa College in the War." Paper read at Iowa College Commencement Exercise, June 1898. Printed in *The Grinnell Review,* January 1907.

Jones, Katherine A. "Cyclone Reminiscences." Newspaper clipping, source and date unknown, Grinnell College Archives.

Jordan, David W. "And God Was in the Whirlwind: The Cyclone of 1882." *The Grinnell Magazine,* April–May 1982.

Jordan, Philip D., ed. "William Salter's Letters to Mary Ann Mackintire." *Annals of Iowa,* 3rd ser., 24 (January 1943).

Kiesel, Margaret Matlack. "The Alumni and the College." Unpublished manuscript, 1986 Grinnell College Archives.

"Lives of the Alumni." *The News Letter* 16, no. 11 (May 1889).

Lucas, Thomas A. "Men Were Too Fiery for Much Talk: The Grinnell Anti-Abolitionist Riot of 1860." *The Palimpsest* 68 (Spring 1987).

Luker, Ralph E. "Defining Moments: Harlan Paul Douglass and Martin Luther King, Jr." Lecture given at Grinnell College, Nov. 9, 1995.

————. *The Social Gospel in Black and White: American Racial Reform 1885–1912.* Chapel Hill, University of North Carolina Press, 1991.

Magoun, George. "The Past of Our College." Address given to Alumni Association of Iowa College, June 11, 1895, Grinnell College Archives.

————. Address given at inauguration of President George A. Gates, 1887. Pamphlet, Grinnell College Archives.

————. "Evolutionism at Bay Among Scientists." *The News Letter,* October 1873.

————. "A History of Iowa College," July 19, 1865. Printed in *Grin-*

nell Herald Register, November 1927.

Mahan, Bruce E. "The First Iowa Field Day." *The Palimpsest* 4, no. 5 (May 1923).

Manatt, J. Irving. "A Tribute to Dr. Magoun." *New York Independent,* January 1896. Reprinted as pamphlet, Grinnell College Archives.

McJimsey, George. "The Social Gospel and the New Deal." Lecture given at Grinnell College, November 2, 1995.

Meyers, John (Col.) "Herronism Exposed." *Des Moines Register,* January 6, 1899. Reprinted Feb. 2, 1899, in revised form by friends of Iowa College, Grinnell College Archives.

Morris, Helen, and Emmeline B. Bartlett. "The Social Life of a Girl in Iowa College." *Midland Monthly,* May 1898.

"New England's First Fruits." Promotional pamphlet of Harvard College, first published in London, 1643.

Nollen, John S. *Grinnell College.* Iowa City: State Historical Society of Iowa, 1953.

Noun, Louise R. *Strong Minded Women.* Ames: Iowa State University Press, 1969.

"Our College Campus." *The News Letter,* December 1883.

Parker, Leonard. "Notes on Iowa College in the Civil War." Written for James Hill, April 5, 1898, Grinnell College Archives.

Payne, Charles E. *Josiah Bushnell Grinnell.* Iowa City: State Historical Society of Iowa, 1938.

Persons, Stow. *American Minds: A History of Ideas.* New York: Henry Holt, 1958.

Rabben, Linda A. "The Utopian Vision of George D. Herron." *The Grinnell Magazine,* April–May 1981.

Sage, Leland L. *A History of Iowa.* Ames: Iowa State University Press, 1974.

Salter, William. "Our National Sins and Impending Calamities—A Sermon Preached in the Congregational Church, Burlington, Iowa." Grinnell College Archives.

———. *The Life of James W. Grimes.* New York: D. Appleton, 1876.

Schaub, Kyle. "Housing Options Vary Through History." *Scarlet and Black,* April 13, 1973.

St. John, Benjamin. "The Burning of East College." *Blue Book,* 1898, Grinnell College Archives.

Wall, Joseph Frazier. *Iowa: A History.* New York: W. W. Norton, 1978.

Whitcomb, Mary R. "Abner Kneeland: His Relations to Early Iowa History." *Annals of Iowa,* 3rd ser., 6 (1904).

Wilkie, Franc B. *Davenport: Past and Present.* Davenport: Luce, Lane, 1858.

GRINNELL COLLEGE ARCHIVES

Blue Book, 1898 (Special publication commemorating the fiftieth anniversary of Grinnell College)

Board of Trustees Minutes including Faculty and President's Reports to Trustees.

J. M. Chamberlain Papers, 1884–86

Early College Papers, 1844–70

Executive Committee of the Board of Trustees Minutes, 1867–99

Faculty Minutes, 1852–94

The Grinnell Review, 1905–07

Iowa College Catalogue, 1849–95

The News Letter, 1871–89

Leonard F. Parker Papers, 1862–1904

The Pulse, 1889–1890

William Salter Letter File, 1843–85

Scarlet and Black, 1874–99

The Unit, 1885–96

NEWSPAPERS

Davenport Daily Morning News
Davenport *Gazette*
Des Moines Register
Grinnell Herald Register
Marshalltown *Times Republican*
New York Independent

INDEX